JOSEPH HAYDN

1732–1809

To pure and efficacious religion we owe the moral qualities that adorned this respectable man: his modesty, his kindness, his total lack of envy for his rivals, his love for parents, country, patrons, his moral purity, preserved in company with a fiery imagination and a tender heart, his charity towards the poor; in sum, the fact that Haydn was both a great genius and a great gentleman in the eighteenth century.

CARPANI, *Le Haydine*

JOSEPH HAYDN

From the Ihrwach Medallion

Photograph by courtesy of the Library of Congress

Haydn

TWO CONTEMPORARY PORTRAITS

A TRANSLATION WITH INTRODUCTION AND NOTES BY

VERNON GOTWALS

OF THE

Biographische Notizen über Joseph Haydn
by G. A. Griesinger, d. 1828.

AND THE

Biographische Nachrichten von Joseph Haydn
by A. C. Dies

THE UNIVERSITY OF WISCONSIN PRESS

MADISON, MILWAUKEE, AND LONDON, 1968

Published by
The University of Wisconsin Press
Box 1379, Madison, Wisconsin 53701
The University of Wisconsin Press, Ltd.
27–29 Whitfield Street, London, W. 1

Second printing, 1968

Printed in the United States of America
Standard Book Number 299-02791-0 Clothbound Edition
Standard Book Number 299-02794-5 Paperbound Edition
Library of Congress Catalog Card Number 62-17399

TO Doris Silbert
Haydn Scholar and Friend

PREFACE

HESE TRANSLATIONS need no other apologia than that of Griesinger himself: "The man whom they concern is of interest to many persons." The suggestion that they would be useful came originally from Oliver Strunk, and the encouragement to complete them from Philip Keppler.

The translation is rather a literal rendering than a literary recreation. Names of persons and places have been standardized in most instances: thus Griesinger's *Haimburg* and Dies's *Haymburg* are both rendered *Hainburg;* but where it seemed worth while to preserve the original spelling, as in the lists of Haydn's operas or in Dies's faulty transcriptions of French and English, this has been done. Everything bracketed is editorial comment; there are no brackets in the original texts.

All notes at the bottom of a page are part of the original text. All of the translator's annotations have been placed at the back of the book. They are necessarily numerous and would disfigure the text in a more convenient location. The modern German editions of the texts by Grasberger and by Seeger are not always accurate, and their notes are in each case inadequate, leaving many errors and misconceptions unnoted and uncorrected.

The present annotations rely as much on the recent researches of H. C. Robbins Landon as on the classic work of C. F. Pohl. The translator has had much help from Marie Schnieders and Philip Keppler, of the Departments of German and Music at Smith College, and has been assisted at the Music Department of the Boston Public Library, and by the Music Library and its librarian, Mary Ankudowich, at Smith College.

Thanks are due the *Musical Quarterly* for permission to use material originally published in its pages, and Smith College for grants of time and money to complete the manuscript.

"Thus, aided by professors of acknowledged skill and ability, the Translator dismisses his volume, with *little fear* as to its accuracy and fidelity; but, for the general execution of his work, he cannot but be conscious that he requires all the indulgence and candour of his readers." So wrote John Belfour of his translation of Yriarte's poem *Music* (London, 1807). If "less fear" be substituted for "little fear," his envoy will serve here. ❧

V. G.

Northampton, Massachusetts
June, 1962

CONTENTS

ILLUSTRATIONS

INTRODUCTION

N<small>O BOOK</small> on Haydn goes very far without naming Griesinger and Dies. Both men lived in Vienna during the last decade of Haydn's life, were acquainted with Haydn, and made notes of their conversations with him in order to publish some account of his life. Though Haydn was an old man who loved to spin variations on his favorite tales, and suffered from a weakening memory, he nevertheless helped his two younger friends produce the "as-told-to" autobiography that makes their two little books still indispensable for anyone interested in the composer.

Georg August Griesinger (d. 1828) first went to Vienna as tutor in the household of the Electoral Saxon Ambassador. Eventually he became Royal Councilor to the Saxon Legation. He was sent to Haydn in 1799 by Gottfried Härtel. This meeting ultimately brought about that happy relationship between Haydn and Härtel's firm detailed in Hermann von Hase's *Joseph Haydn und Breitkopf & Härtel* (Leipzig, 1909). In a brief preface to his book, Griesinger explains that his "biographical notes concerning Joseph Haydn, originally intended for the *Allgemeine Musikalische Zeitung* . . . 1809, are here separately printed because the man they concern is of interest to many persons who perhaps do not read the above musical journal. Various additions will be found." This widely circulated book was known to Beethoven, who addressed Griesinger in a letter as a "meritorious man (in general—and in particular in Haydn's biography)"; but it was not republished until 1954, when Franz Grasberger edited it for Paul Kaltschmid in Vienna.

Griesinger's book is hardly more important than his success in obtaining from Haydn, during the latter's somewhat captious old age, many important works for Breitkopf and Härtel, the firm that brought out in the last decade of Haydn's life a so-called *Oeuvres complettes* more or less under the composer's personal supervision. From his ten years as go-between, Griesinger left letters to the firm that provide many particulars concerning Haydn. These letters, which H. C. Robbins Landon "hopes to publish separately" (*Collected Correspondence,* p. xxiii), and what remains of Haydn's letters to the firm, show that without Griesinger a series of business arrangements extremely profitable both to Haydn and to Breitkopf and Härtel might never have been concluded at all.

Griesinger's book at the same time is not to be undervalued. The stories that originate with him or with Dies (frequently with both) are often more attractive and more revealing of Haydn as a person in their original form than when they have been summarized by Pohl or by later biographers. But perhaps the author's own apologia is the best evaluation of this compact little volume. Since he had the fortune to be uninterruptedly associated with Haydn in the last ten years of his life and to be honored with his confidence, he says, "My story may lay some claim to truth and accuracy, and I hold it my duty often to intersperse Haydn's own words, just as I wrote them down on returning home from him."

Albert Christoph Dies, born at Hanover in 1755, was a painter and engraver. His apprentice years were spent in Hanover, Düsseldorf, and briefly, Mannheim and Basel on the way to Rome. By his twenty-first birthday he was established as a professional water-colorist and a student of landscape painting in Rome, where his son Johannes (Giovanni) was born in 1776. There he remained for twenty years in the practice of various forms of painting. On July 22, 1787, Goethe wrote from Rome, in the *Zweiter römischer Aufenthalt,* "At the moment I am engaged in something from which I learn a great deal; I have found and sketched a landscape that a clever artist, Dies, colored in my presence; thus eyes and mind grow ever more accustomed to color and harmony." In May, 1796, Dies apparently eloped with a young girl to Salzburg. The next year he settled down in Vienna, his health undermined by lead poisoning. He was a teacher of landscape painting at the Imperial and Royal Academy and occupied himself with literary and musical matters. His last post was as gallery director to Prince Esterházy. Whether this appointment preceded or followed his acquaintance with Haydn is not clear. He died in Vienna on December 28, 1822. Examples of his painting are—or were—to be found in the Esterházy Gallery at Eisenstadt and in the Archbishop's Residence at Salzburg. Friedrich Noack in his article in the Thieme and Becker *Allgemeines Lexikon der Bildenden Künstler,* describes Dies's work as clumsy, mediocre, and prosaic. His literary style is hardly better, but his biography of Haydn is saved by its subject from the oblivion the author's paintings have suffered. His book was not republished until 1959, when Horst Seeger edited it for Henschelverlag in Berlin.

Dies was introduced to Haydn by Anton Grassi, the Viennese sculptor who made several busts of Haydn, expressly to collect the materials for a biography. Haydn's reaction was typical: his biography could interest nobody. Nevertheless, in the course of three years (1805–8) Dies paid Haydn thirty separate visits and noted down whatever took place. He was not unenterprising about the matter. As the visits progressed, he learned to assess Haydn's moods, and he frequently introduced topics for conversation that would lead naturally to the information he wished to obtain. The task required patience and tact, and cost Dies much time and compassion.

An interesting forecast of Dies's book appeared in Carl Bertuch's *Bemerkungen auf einer Reise aus Thüringen nach Wien im Winter 1805 bis 1806* (Weimar, 1808–10). This book, in the form of letters, reported a visit to Haydn on October 13, 1805, arranged by Griesinger, who had already supplied the sketches of Haydn's early days that Bertuch first printed anonymously in the July, 1805, issue of the

Journal des Luxus und der Moden, pp. 449–52. Bertuch took over this material practically verbatim in his book (twelfth letter), as did Gerber in the *Neues Lexikon.* In his fifteenth letter, dated December, 1805, Bertuch said that he had visited Dies in his Vienna studio, described three current oil paintings that Dies had shown him, and added that Dies, one of the few people besides Griesinger whom Haydn would still see, was at work on a biography that already went as far as Haydn's stay in England. In a footnote added later, he reported that nothing had yet appeared from Dies, but that he could now identify the source of his own Haydn material as Griesinger, who had just published his sketch of Haydn's life in the *Musikalische Zeitung.*

Dies wrote a longer book than Griesinger (220 compared to 121 pages). It is doubtful whether he provides much more factual information, since his (and Haydn's) garrulity probably accounts for most of the additional pages. He does, however, tell a story better than Griesinger. His organization, by visits, reveals Haydn more clearly as a person and makes much more entertaining reading than the seriatim method of Griesinger. His genial portrait of Haydn is more detailed and more lifelike.

The first of Dies's thirty visits took place on April 15, 1805, the last on August 8, 1808. Dies attempted to hold Haydn to some chronological order but took what he could get, occasionally postponing the use of the day's gleanings until a more appropriate time. The sense of immediacy he sought to give his relationship with Haydn is not altogether convincing. It is sometimes impossible to be certain when he quotes Haydn whether these are the master's own words to Dies personally, or only remarks gathered at second hand. But the book is not without touching evidence of authenticity.

If Dies and Griesinger were paying regular visits to Haydn at the same time, it seems inevitable that they should have met. It is therefore not surprising that Dies speaks at length of the circumstances of his acquaintance with Griesinger. Dies had pressed Haydn repeatedly to let a third person judge his accumulating manuscript. Haydn replied that he had never doubted Dies's sincerity and never would.

But Dies persisted, and finally Haydn named Griesinger. "When I afterwards became acquainted with this worthy man, it was soon revealed that he quite quietly and without Haydn's knowing it had for several years been collecting materials for Haydn's biography, which is one day to appear in shortened form in the *Leipzig Musikalische Zeitung.*"

If we agree with Carpani that "all is important when referring to one of those rare geniuses who in the course of their intellectual development bring only solace and pleasures to the world" (*Le Haydine,* p. 3), then we have much for which to thank these two persistent Germans who would not be put off by Haydn's assertions that his biography could interest nobody, who rather plagued the poor old man into remembering as much as possible, however inaccurately at times, and who diligently wrote it all down in order as best they could.

A literary appraisal of our two books as well as an assessment of the position of Giuseppe Carpani as a Haydn biographer will be found in "The Earliest Biographies of Haydn," *Musical Quarterly,* October, 1959. A description of the money Haydn used will be found in "Joseph Haydn's Last Will and Testament," *Musical Quarterly,* July, 1961. A monetary table, based upon this article, will be found on page 213.

Biographische Notizen

über

Joseph Haydn

—◆—

Von

Georg August Griesinger

Königl. Sächsischem Legations-Rath.

———————

Leipzig,

bey Breitkopf und Härtel.

1810.

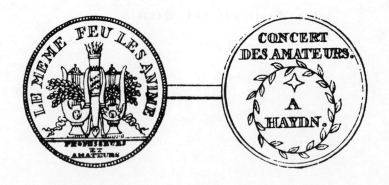

Biographical Notes

Concerning

JOSEPH HAYDN

BY

Georg August Griesinger

ROYAL COUNCILOR TO THE SAXON LEGATION

Leipzig

BREITKOPF AND HÄRTEL

1810

Preface

THE BIOGRAPHICAL notes concerning Joseph Haydn, originally intended for the *Allgemeine Musikalische Zeitung,* where they were included in numbers 41 to 49 from July 12, to September 6, 1809, are here separately printed because the man whom they concern is of interest to many persons who perhaps do not read the above musical journal. Various additions will be found, and the engravings [of several medals] also are new. It remained the chief aim of the author to sketch Haydn as faithfully as possible as he lived and was, and he thus deemed it necessary to resist every temptation to include controversy and artistic notions that people often like to hear themselves talk about.

The *Notice sur J. Haydn par Mr. Framery* that appeared in Paris in 1810 the author could not obtain, despite all efforts. Judging alone by the excerpts that the French journals supplied, Mr. Framery's accounts are sometimes distorted, and sometimes drawn from unreliable sources. In Paris also a minuet by Haydn was printed with the name of Ox Minuet and a note that Haydn had once composed this minuet for the wedding of a butcher who paid him for it with an ox. This anecdote, unimportant in itself, is mythical; at least Haydn's oldest and most intimate friends do not remember ever hearing it from him, and he surely would not have forgotten it.[1]

Vienna, July, 1810.

5

JOSEPH HAYDN has ended his glorious career. By his death Germany again suffers a national loss; for Haydn was founder of an epoch in musical culture, and the sound of his harmonies, universally understood, did more than all written matter together to promote the honor of German artistic talent in the remotest lands. Haydn's quartets and symphonies, his oratorios and church pieces, please alike on the Danube and on the Thames, on the Seine and on the Neva, and they are treasured and admired across the sea as in our own part of the world. Original and abundant ideas, deep feeling, fantasy wisely controlled by penetrating study of the art, skill in the development of an idea basically simple, calculation of effect by a clever distribution of light and of shadow, pouring forth of the slyest humor, an easy flow and free movement—these are the qualities that distinguish Haydn's earlier and latest works alike.

Haydn has labored for more than half a century as a writer of music, and all his works together constitute a not inconsiderable library. He set down in the year 1805 the *incipits* of those compositions he could casually recall writing between his eighteenth and his seventy-third years.[2] In this still incomplete catalogue are 118 symphonies, 83 quartets, 24 trios, 19 operas, 5 oratorios, 163 compositions for the baryton, 24 concertos for various instruments, 15 masses, 10 smaller church pieces, 44 clavier sonatas with and without accompanying instruments, 42 German and Italian songs, 39 canons, 13

7

three- and four-part choruses, harmonization and accompaniment
for 365 old Scotch songs, and many more divertimenti, fantasias, ca-
priccios, five-, six-, seven-, eight-, and nine-part compositions for sun-
dry instruments.

A productiveness so unusual is astonishing. Even Haydn used to
wonder about it, and to say that he knew no epitaph more suited to
him than the three words *Vixi, scripsi, dixi!* [I lived, I wrote, I
spoke!] Nevertheless, he who had already accomplished so much
said on his seventy-fourth birthday that his field was limitless; what
could still happen in music was far greater than that which had already happened. Ideas oftentimes came to him whereby his art
might still be carried much further, but his physical powers no
longer permitted him to put them into execution.

Haydn has not outlived his fame; close to two generations have
done homage to his works, and from this alone his worth as an artist
must be judged. But may one not also be curious to learn of his in-
dividuality, the story of his development, his character, his manner
of living, and the views of a man so widely celebrated, to whose muse
every lover of music owes so many happy hours?

Since I had the fortune to be uninterruptedly associated with Joseph Haydn in the last ten years of his life and to be honored with
his confidence, my story may lay some claim to truth and accuracy,
and I hold it my duty often to intersperse Haydn's own words, just
as I wrote them down on returning home from him.

Haydn's life is marked by no great event; but it is the story of a
man who had to struggle under manifold pressures from without,
and who solely by the strength of his talent and by tireless exertion
happily worked up to the rank of the most important men in his
field. In this regard also seemingly petty circumstances are not uninteresting to the psychologist, and perhaps many an artist striving under similar conditions will thereby be buoyed up, and encouraged to
a more zealous perseverance in the future.

Joseph Haydn was born on March 31, 1732, at Rohrau, a village
in Lower Austria, in the district Unter Wiener Wald near the Hungarian border, not far from the town of Bruck an der Leitha. Of the

twenty children from two marriages of his father Mathias, a cart-wright by profession, Joseph was the eldest. The father had seen a bit of the world, as was customary in his trade, and during his stay in Frankfurt am Main had learned to strum the harp. As a master craftsman in Rohrau he continued to practice this instrument for pleasure after work. Nature, moreover, had endowed him with a good tenor voice, and his wife, Anne Marie,[3] used to sing to the harp. The melodies of these songs were so deeply stamped in Joseph Haydn's memory that he could still recall them in advanced old age.

One day the headmaster from the neighboring town of Hainburg, a distant relative of the Haydn family, came to Rohrau.[4] Meister Mathias and his wife gave their usual little concert, and five-year-old Joseph sat near his parents and sawed at his left arm with a stick, as if he were accompanying on the violin. It astonished the schoolteacher that the boy observed the time so correctly. He inferred from this a natural talent for music and advised the parents to send their Sepperl (an Austrian diminutive for Joseph) to Hainburg so that he might be set to the acquisition of an art that in time would unfailingly open to him the prospect "of becoming a clergyman." The parents, ardent admirers of the clergy, joyfully seized this proposal, and in his sixth year Joseph Haydn went to the headmaster in Hainburg. Here he received instruction in reading and writing, in catechism, in singing, and in almost all wind and string instruments, even in the timpani. "I shall owe it to this man even in my grave," Haydn oftentimes said, "that he set me to so many different things, although I received in the process more thrashings than food."

Haydn, who even then wore a wig for the sake of cleanliness, had been some three years in Hainburg when the Court Kapellmeister Reutter, of Vienna, director of music at St. Stephen's Cathedral, visited his friend the dean in Hainburg. Reutter told the dean that his older choirboys, whose voices were beginning to break, would be useless to him, and that he had to replace them with younger sub-jects. The dean proposed the eight-year-old Haydn, and he and the schoolmaster were called at once. The poorly nourished Sepperl cast longing glances at the cherries that were sitting on the dean's table.

Reutter tossed a few handfuls into his hat, and seemed well pleased
with the Latin and Italian strophes that Haydn had to sing. "Can you
also make a trill?" asked Reutter. "No," said Haydn, "for not even
my cousin can do that." This answer greatly embarrassed the schoolteacher, and Reutter laughed uproariously. He demonstrated the mechanical principles of trilling, Haydn imitated him, and at the
third attempt succeeded. "You shall stay with me," said Reutter. The
departure from Hainburg soon followed, and Haydn came as a
pupil to the Choir School at St. Stephen's Cathedral in Vienna,
where he stayed until his sixteenth year.[5]

Besides the scant instruction usual at the time in Latin, in religion,
in arithmetic and writing, Haydn had in the Choir School very
capable instructors on several instruments, and especially in singing.
Among the latter were Gegenbauer, a functionary of the Court
Chorus, and an elegant tenor, Finsterbusch.[6] No instruction in music
theory was undertaken in the Choir School, and Haydn remembered
receiving only two lessons in this from the excellent Reutter. But
Reutter did encourage him to make whatever variations he liked on
the motets and *Salves* that he had to sing through in the church, and
this practice early led him to ideas of his own which Reutter corrected. He also came to know Mattheson's *Der vollkommene Kapellmeister* [1739], and Fux's *Gradus ad Parnassum* [1725] in German
and Latin—a book he still in his old age praised as a classic and of
which he had kept a hard-used copy. With tireless exertion Haydn
sought to comprehend Fux's theory. He worked his way through the
whole method, did the exercises, put them by for several weeks, then
looked them over again and polished them until he thought he had
got them right. "I did, of course, have talent. With that and with
great diligence I progressed." Stimulated by his imagination, he
even ventured into composition for eight and sixteen parts. "I
used to think then that it was all right if only the paper were pretty
full. Reutter laughed at my immature output, at measures that no
throat and no instrument could have executed, and he scolded me
for composing for sixteen parts before I even understood two-part
setting."

At that time there were still many *castrati* employed at the court and in the churches in Vienna, and the director of the Choir School doubtless supposed he was making young Haydn's fortune when he came up with a plan to turn him into a soprano, and actually asked the father for his permission. The father, whom this proposal utterly displeased, set off at once on the road for Vienna; and thinking that the operation might perhaps already have been undertaken, he entered the room where his son was with the question, "Sepperl, does anything hurt you? Can you still walk?" Delighted to find his son unharmed, he protested against all further unreasonable demands of this sort, and a *castrato* who was present even strengthened him in his resolve.

The truth of this anecdote was vouched for by persons to whom Haydn had oftentimes told it.[7]

Soon after his departure from the Choir School Haydn made a pilgrimage to Mariazell.[8] He had in his pocket several motets of his own composition and asked the *Regens chori* there for permission to take them into the church and sing them. This request was denied him; but to achieve his purpose of gaining himself a hearing, he had recourse to trickery on the following day. He placed himself in the choir behind the boy who had the alto part to sing, and offered him a coin [*Siebzehner*] to give up his place to him. The boy did not dare to make the bargain, for fear of the director, so then Haydn reached quickly over the boy's head, seized the music on the desk, and sang to everybody's satisfaction. The *Regens chori* got together a collection of sixteen gulden and sent the hopeful youth back to Vienna with it.

Haydn was dismissed from the Choir Shool in his sixteenth year [9] because his voice had broken. He could not expect the least support from his poor parents and so had to try to make his own way by his talent alone. In Vienna he moved into a wretched little attic room without a stove (in the house at No. 1220 in the Michaelerplatz) [10] in which he was scarcely sheltered from the rain. Innocent of the comforts of life, he divided his whole time among the giving of lessons, the study of his art, and performing. He played for money in serenades and in the orchestras, and he was industrious in the practice of composition, for "when I was sitting at my old worm-eaten clavier, I envied no king his lot." About this time Haydn came upon the first six sonatas of Emanuel Bach. "I did not come away from my clavier till I had played through them, and whoever knows me thoroughly must discover that I owe a great deal to Emanuel Bach, that I understood him and have studied him diligently. Emanuel Bach once made me a compliment on this score himself." [11]

In the same house in which Joseph Haydn was quartered dwelt also the celebrated poet Metastasio. The latter was educating a Fräulein Martinez. Haydn gave her lessons in singing and clavier playing and received in return free board for three years. [12] Through Metastasio Haydn also learned to know the now aged Kapellmeister Porpora. Porpora gave the mistress of Correr, the Venetian ambassador, lessons in singing, and because Porpora was too grand and too fond of his ease to accompany on the pianoforte himself, he entrusted this business to our Giuseppe. "There was no lack of *Asino, Coglione, Birbante* [ass, cullion, rascal], and pokes in the ribs, but I put up with it all, for I profited greatly with Porpora in singing, in composition, and in the Italian language." Correr traveled in summer with the lady to the then much frequented baths at Mannersdorf, not far from Bruck. Porpora went there too in order to continue the lessons, and he took Haydn with him. For three months here Haydn acted as Porpora's servant, eating at Correr's servants' table and receiving six ducats a month. Here he sometimes had to accompany on the clavier for Porpora at a Prince von Hildburghausen's, in the presence of Gluck, Wagenseil, and other celebrated masters, and the approval of such connoisseurs served as a special encouragement to him.

The author was told by a very reliable source [13] that the violinist Mysliveczek, a Bohemian by birth, had heard some quartets performed during his stay in Milan, and when Giovanni Battista Sammartini, then seventy years old, was named to him as their composer, he had exclaimed in utter astonishment, "At last I know the forerunner of Haydn, and the model on whom he patterned himself!" It seemed to me worth the trouble to hunt a further basis for this statement, since I had never heard Haydn's originality doubted, especially in his quartets. So I made inquiry of Haydn whether he had known Sammartini's works in his youth, and what he thought of this composer. Haydn answered me that he had heard Sammartini's music before that time, but had never valued it "because Sammartini was a scribbler [*Schmierer*]." He laughed heartily when I came out with Mysliveczek's supposed discovery, and said that he recognized only Emanuel Bach as his prototype, and the following purely chance circumstance had led him to try his luck at the composition of quartets. A Baron Fürnberg had a place in Weinzierl, several stages [about fifty miles] from Vienna, and he invited from time to time his pastor, his manager, Haydn, and Albrechtsberger (a brother of the celebrated contrapuntist,[14] who played the violoncello) in order to have a little music. Fürnberg requested Haydn to compose something that could be performed by these four amateurs. Haydn, then eighteen years old, took up this proposal, and so originated his first

quartet which, immediately it appeared, received such general approval that Haydn took courage to work further in this form.

Strict theoreticians meanwhile found much to take exception to in Haydn's compositions, and they cried out especially over the debasement of music to comic fooling. He was not put out by this, for he had soon convinced himself that a narrow adherence to the rules oftentimes yields works devoid of taste and feeling, that many things had arbitrarily taken on the stamp of rules, and that in music only what offends a discriminating ear is absolutely forbidden.

In the beginning Haydn received only two gulden a month for lessons, but the price gradually rose to five gulden, and then he could look around for more suitable quarters. While he was living in the Seilerstadt, all his few possessions were stolen. Haydn wrote to his parents to see if they might send him some linen for a few shirts; his father came to Vienna, brought his son a seventeen-kreutzer piece and the advice, "Fear God, and love thy neighbor!" By the generosity of good friends, Haydn soon saw his loss restored. One had a dark suit made for him, another presented him with underclothing, and so on, and Haydn recovered himself through a two-month stay with Baron Fürnberg that cost him nothing. Haydn also in this period was first violinist [*Vorspieler*] for the Brothers of Mercy in the Leopoldstadt, at sixty gulden a year. Here he had to be in the church at eight o'clock in the morning on Sundays and feast days. At ten o'clock he played the organ in the chapel of Count Haugwitz, and at eleven o'clock he sang at St. Stephen's. He was paid seventeen kreutzers for each service. In the evenings, Haydn oftentimes went out serenading with his musical comrades, when one of his compositions was usually played, and he recalled having composed a quintet to that end in the year 1753.[15]

Once he went to serenade the wife of [Johann Joseph Felix] Kurz, a comic actor very popular at the time and usually called Bernardon. Kurz came into the street and asked for the composer of the music just played. Hardly had Haydn, who was about nineteen years old, identified himself when Kurz urged him strongly to compose an opera for him. Haydn pleaded his youth in vain; Kurz encouraged him, and Haydn actually composed the opera, *Der krumme Teufel* [The Crooked Devil], a satire on the lame theater director Affligio, on whose account it was forbidden after the third performance.

Haydn liked to linger over the story of composing his first opera, because it reminded him of Bernardon's many comic traits. Harlequin ran away from the waves in *Der krumme Teufel*. To illustrate this, Bernardon lay down at full length over several chairs and imitated all the movements of a swimmer. "See how I swim! See how I swim!" Kurz called out to Haydn who was sitting at the clavier, and who at once, to the poet's great satisfaction, fell into six-eight time.

When Haydn was ready with his opera, he brought it to Kurz. The maid wanted to send him away because her master was busy studying. But how astonished Haydn was when he saw Bernardon through a window in the door standing before a large mirror making faces and producing the most laughable contortions with hands and feet! Such were the studies of Herr Bernardon.

Haydn received for his opera twenty-four ducats, a sum which at that time he thought made him a very rich man.[16]

Besides performing and teaching, Haydn was untiring in his composing. Many of his easy clavier sonatas, trios, and so forth belong to this period, and he mostly took into account the need and the capacity of his pupils. Only a few of the originals remain in his possession. He gave them away and felt honored when they were accepted. Unaware that the music dealers were doing a good business in them, he lingered with pleasure before the shops where one or another of his works in print had been placed on display.

In the year 1759 Haydn was appointed in Vienna to be music director to Count Morzin with a salary of two hundred gulden, free room, and board at the staff table. Here he enjoyed at last the good fortune of a care-free existence; it suited him thoroughly. The winter was spent in Vienna and the summer in Bohemia, in the vicinity of Pilsen. He liked to tell in his later years how, when he was sitting once at the clavier and the beautiful Countess Morzin was bending over him to see the notes, her neckerchief came undone. "It was the first time I had such a sight; it embarrassed me, my playing faltered, my fingers stopped on the keys. 'What is it, Haydn, what are you doing?' cried the Countess. Full of respect, I answered, 'But, your grace, who would not be upset here?'" [17]

Haydn had oftentimes received help in the house of a hairdresser in Vienna (in the Landstrasse) named Keller; he also gave music lessons to the eldest daughter, and his preference for her grew with closer acquaintance. But she went into a convent, and Haydn then decided, since his future was somewhat secured by a fixed salary and the hairdresser, to whom he felt grateful, kept urging it, that he would marry the second daughter.[18]

Haydn had no children by this marriage. "My wife was unable to bear children, and I was therefore less indifferent to the charms of other ladies." His choice did not turn out very well in general, for his wife was of a domineering, unfriendly character. He had to be careful to conceal his income from her, because she loved to spend, was bigoted on the subject, was continually inviting the clergy to dinner, had many masses said, and was freer with charitable contributions than her situation warranted. Once when I was obliged to inquire of Haydn how a favor he had shown, and for which he would take nothing, could be repaid to his wife, he answered me: "She does not deserve anything, and it is all the same to her if her husband is a shoemaker or an artist." She died in the summer of 1800 at Baden near Vienna.[19]

As music director in the service of Count Morzin, Haydn composed his first symphony. The Count in a short time squandered his

considerable fortune. He had consequently to disband his orchestra, and Joseph Haydn went on March 19, 1760, as Kapellmeister to Prince Nikolaus Esterházy,[20] whom the aforesaid symphony had pleased, with a salary of four hundred gulden and other emoluments. Haydn's father thus had the pleasure of seeing his son in the uniform of that family, blue, trimmed with gold, and of hearing from the Prince many eulogies of the talent of his son. A short time after this visit, a wood pile fell on Meister Mathias while he was at work. He suffered broken ribs and died soon thereafter [September 12, 1763].

Prince Nikolaus Esterházy had a connoisseur's taste and was a passionate lover of music, as well as a good violinist. He had his own opera, comedy theater, marionette theater, church music, and chamber music. Haydn had his hands full. He composed, he had to direct all music, help to rehearse everything, give lessons, even tune his own clavier in the orchestra. He oftentimes wondered how it had been possible for him to write so much when he was obliged to lose so many hours in mechanical tasks. Haydn's compositions belonging to the period from 1761 until 1790, when Prince Nikolaus Esterházy died, include 163 pieces for the baryton, the favorite instrument of that prince, the oratorio *Il Ritorno di Tobia,* many masses and church pieces, the operas *Acide e Galatea, La Canterina, L'incontro improviso, Lo Speziale, La Pescatrice, Il mundo della luna, L'Isola disabitata, L'infedeltà fedele, La fedeltà premiata, La vera costanza, Orlando Palatino, Armida, L'infedeltà delusa, Genovefens vierter Theil, Philemon und Baucis, Dido, die bestrafte Rachgier oder das abgebrannte Haus,*[21] likewise many trios, quartets, songs, concerti, and symphonies. Haydn spent these thirty years for the most part at Eisenstadt in Hungary with his Prince, and only in winter came for two or three months to Vienna.[22] He did not know himself how celebrated he was abroad, and he heard of it only occasionally from traveling foreigners who visited him. Many of these, even Gluck, advised him to travel to Italy and France, but his timidity and his limited circumstances held him back; and if he spoke a word about it in the hearing of his Prince, the latter pressed a dozen ducats into his hand, and so he abandoned all such projects again. Haydn himself believed that because of his good foundation in singing and in instrumental accompaniment, he would have become an excellent opera composer if he had had the fortune to go to Italy. The accident twice befell him of having his house in Eisenstadt burn down, and each time the Prince had it rebuilt. Several of Haydn's operas and other compositions were thus a prey to flames, and there exists hardly a copy of them.[23]

Although, moreover, Haydn's outward circumstance was anything but brilliant, it nevertheless provided him the best opportunity for the development of his many-sided talent. "My Prince was content with all my works, I received approval, I could, as head of an orchestra, make experiments, observe what enhanced an effect, and what weakened it, thus improving, adding to, cutting away, and running risks. I was set apart from the world, there was nobody in my vicinity to confuse and annoy me in my course, and so I had to be original." [24]

Haydn had on the whole a good opinion of his operas, which were little known to the greater public, although he probably realized that they could hardly be successfully performed in a newer era in their original shape.

The oratorio *Il Ritorno di Tobia* Haydn wrote in 1774 in order to be received into the Society for Musicians' Widows and Orphans in Vienna. His application was accepted upon payment of the prescribed amount; how great then was his surprise on being further informed the following day by the directors that he must also engage himself whenever requested to write cantatas, oratorios, symphonies, and the like for the Society. Prince Esterházy was so angry over this unreasonable demand that he ordered Haydn to reclaim his deposit forthwith. In 1792, after his first stay in England, Haydn without asking was elected a free member of the Society.[25]

In December, 1808, the oratorio *Il Ritorno di Tobia,* revised by Herr Neukomm, the instrumentation enriched according to current taste, was performed again in Vienna for the benefit of the Widows and Orphans Society. The choruses in it are full of strength and vigor, and they received the greatest applause; but the plan of the oratorio as a whole is unsuccessful and much too monotonous. From beginning to end the not very interesting dialogue is followed always by an aria, without any alteration with duos and trios. The poet (Giovanni Gastone Boccherini from Lucca) treats the return of Tobias and the healing of his father's blindness merely historically, and it is regrettable that the poet and the musician did not spend their effort on more promising material.[26]

Perhaps I may here insert several among many anecdotes that Haydn recalled from his earlier years.

He had once an urgent composition to get ready, and so ordered his servant to admit no one. Shortly thereafter, chance brought several strangers there. The servant informed them of his master's order, but they explained that they had traveled to Hungary solely to make Haydn's acquaintance and would be very sorry not to have obtained their purpose. The servant bade them sit down in the antechamber and stationed himself to listen at the door of the room where Haydn was improvising at the clavier. When in the course of his ideas he thundered around in the bass, the servant suddenly called out to the strangers, "You will soon be able to see my master, because he has now worked down to the bottom."

About the year 1770 Haydn succumbed to a heavy fever, and the doctor strictly forbade him, during his gradual recovery, to occupy himself with music. Soon afterward, Haydn's wife went out to church, having first sternly impressed upon the maid that she must see her master did not go to the clavier. Haydn, in bed, pretended he had heard nothing of this order, and hardly was his wife gone when he sent the maid out of the house on an errand. Then he leaped in a hurry to his clavier. At the first touch the idea for a whole sonata came to him, and the first part was finished while his wife was at church. When he heard her coming back, he promptly pitched himself back into bed, and there he composed the rest of the sonata, which he could not identify for me more specifically than that it had five sharps.[27]

In Prince Esterházy's orchestra were several vigorous young married men who in summer, when the Prince stayed at Esterháza castle, had to leave their wives behind in Eisenstadt. Contrary to his custom, the Prince once wished to extend his stay in Esterháza by several weeks. The fond husbands, especially dismayed at this news, turned to Haydn and pleaded with him to do something.

Haydn had the notion of writing a symphony (known as the Farewell Symphony) in which one instrument after the other is silent. This symphony was performed at the first opportunity in the presence of the Prince, and each of the musicians was directed, as soon as his part was finished, to put out his candle, pack up his music and, with his instrument under his arm, to go away. The Prince and the audience understood the meaning of this pantomime at once, and the next day came the order to depart from Esterháza.

Thus Haydn told me the origin of the Farewell Symphony; and the variant, that Haydn thereby dissuaded his Prince from the intention of disbanding his whole orchestra and thus reassured many men of their livelihood, is to be sure poetically more attractive, but not historically correct.

The baryton was, as reported above, the favorite instrument of Prince Nikolaus Esterházy. Haydn, wishing to give his Prince a pleasant surprise, practiced the baryton, without letting it be observed, for several months and gave a concert on it one evening entirely unexpectedly. The Prince expressed some feeling to the effect that Haydn wished to usurp his position with this instrument, and from that hour on Haydn never again touched his baryton.

Hunting and fishing were Haydn's favorite pastimes during his stay in Hungary, and he never forgot that he once brought down with one shot three hazel-hens, which appeared on the table of the Empress Maria Theresa. Another time he aimed at a hare, only shot off his tail, but at the same time killed a pheasant that chanced to be close by; and his dog, pursuing the hare, strangled itself in a snare.[28] In riding Haydn developed no skill, because after he had fallen from a horse on the Morzin estates, he never again trusted himself to mount. Even Mozart, who liked riding horseback for exercise, was always made fearfully anxious by it.

Once when Haydn was going through the streets in Vienna with Dittersdorf, they heard some Haydn minuets being very badly played in a tavern. "We ought to have some fun with these bunglers," said one to the other. They went into the tavern, ordered a glass, and listened a while. "Who wrote these minuets anyway?" Haydn finally asked. They gave him his own name. "Ach, that's pretty miserable stuff!" he exclaimed.[29] At this the musicians flew into such a rage that one of them would have broken his violin on Haydn's head if he had not speedily taken flight.

About the year 1780 an officer's daughter wrote to Haydn from Coburg that she had gone for a walk with her sweetheart (a captain), his dog, and a friend; the captain had been praising the talents of his poodle, and wagered that the dog would recover a taler that he would put under a bush. The wager was taken up. They were home again when the captain called to his poodle, "Lost! Go find it!" At once the dog went back to the place where its master had been walking. By chance an itinerant tailor had sat down in the shade of the bush in question. As he rested, he spied the taler and stuck it in his pocket. Soon the poodle came along. It smelled the taler and nuzzled the tailor. The latter, overjoyed to have found in one hour a taler and a poodle who thus made up to him, took it along to the inn in the town. The poodle watched over the tailor's clothes all night; but when the door of the room was opened early in the morning, it stole out with the tailor's trousers and brought them together with the taler to its master.

This little adventure was made into verse with the title "The Sly and Ever-helpful Poodle," and Haydn was to set the poem to music for the officer's daughter. She wrote to him that she was poor, that she had heard tell of his kind heart, and hoped he would be satisfied with the enclosed ducats. Haydn set about composing the verses at once. He sent back the ducats and wrote to the beauty that she should, as punishment for her poor opinion (as though he would not as a favor to a worthy person employ his talent for nothing!) knit him a pair of garters. The garters, of red and white silk with a painted garland of forget-me-nots, actually arrived, and Haydn kept them carefully with his jewelry. In 1806 the song was newly published by Breitkopf and Härtel.[30]

A canon in Cadiz requested Haydn, about the year 1785, to make an instrumental composition on the Seven Words of Jesus on the Cross which was to be suited to a solemn ceremony that took place annually during Lent in the cathedral at Cadiz.[31] On the appointed day the walls, windows, and piers of the church were draped with black, and only a single lamp of good size, hanging in the middle, illuminated the sacred darkness. At an appointed hour all doors were locked, and the music began. After a suitable prelude the bishop mounted to the pulpit, pronounced one of the Seven Words, and delivered a meditation upon it. As soon as it was ended, he descended from the pulpit and knelt down before the altar. The music filled in this pause. The bishop entered the pulpit a second, a third time, and so on, and each time the orchestra came in again at the end of the talk.

It was indeed one of the most difficult tasks to make out of thin air, with no text, seven adagios following one another that would not weary the listener but would stir in him all the feelings inherent in each of the Words uttered by the dying Saviour. Haydn oftentimes declared this work to be one of his most successful. It was only many

years later that a canon in Passau [Joseph Friberth] fitted a German
text to Haydn's music, and so Swieten's contention that an analogous
poem could be written to go with each of Haydn's compositions was
literally confirmed. Breitkopf and Härtel in Leipzig printed this
work in 1801.

One of the main epochs in Haydn's life is his stay in England, and
we must therefore dwell on this somewhat longer.

Salomon, a native of Cologne and formerly engaged as violinist by
Prince Henry of Prussia, had oftentimes written to Haydn from
London to urge on him a journey to England. Haydn always answered that so long as his Prince was alive, he could not leave him.
Prince Nikolaus Esterházy died on September 28, 1790, at a time
when Gallini had gone to Italy for singers and to recruit among
others the celebrated Davide for his London Professional Concerts
in Hanover Square. Salomon himself was in Cologne on his way
back to London after he had engaged several German musicians for
Gallini.[32] As soon as he heard of the death of Prince Esterházy, he
hurried to Vienna. Toward evening someone knocked at Haydn's
room; Salomon walked in, and his first words were, "Get ready to
travel. In a fortnight we go together to London." Haydn began by
resisting the proposal. He pointed to his ignorance of the English
language and to his inexperience in travel. These objections, however, were soon put aside. It was agreed that Haydn should receive
three thousand gulden for an opera and a hundred gulden for each
new composition he conducted in twenty concerts. Haydn was thus
already covered up to five thousand gulden, and this sum was to be
deposited by Gallini in the Fries and Company Bank in Vienna as
soon as Haydn should tread upon English ground. This foresight
was not superfluous, for without it Haydn would have been exposed
to many a piece of chicanery and he would not have been paid for his
opera, *Orfeo ed Euridice,* because its performance was not allowed
in the hall that Gallini intended to open without prior permission of
the authorities.

Mozart said to Haydn, at a happy meal with Salomon, "You will
not bear it very long and will probably soon come back again, be-

cause you are no longer young." "But I am still vigorous and in good health," answered Haydn. He was at that time almost fifty-nine years old, but he did not find it necessary to conceal the fact. Had Mozart not hastened to an early death on December 5, 1791, he would have taken Haydn's place in Salomon's concerts in 1794.

Shortly before his departure, Haydn took to King Ferdinand of Naples, who was in Vienna at that time, several works that he had commissioned. "The day after tomorrow we will perform them," said the King. "I am eternally sorry," Haydn replied, "that I cannot be present, because the day after tomorrow I leave for England." "What? and you have promised me to come to Naples?" The King left the room rather indignantly and only came back an hour later. Haydn had to promise him again to make a journey to Naples after his return from England. He received a letter of introduction to the King's envoy in London, Prince Castelcicala, and the King sent after him a valuable snuffbox.[33]

Haydn counted the days he spent in England among the happiest of his life. He was universally respected there, a new world was opened up to him, and he was enabled by generous profits at last to pull out of the limited circumstances in which he had grown old and gray; for in 1790 he had hardly two thousand gulden capital of his own.

Haydn set out on his journey with Salomon on December 15, 1790. They made the acquaintance of Cannabich in Munich; and in Bonn the Elector Maximilian, after divine service, presented to them his entire musical company, whom he had had perform a Haydn mass.

During his stay in England, Haydn had noted down in thoroughly rhapsodic fashion various things that happened to him and that struck him in the manner of living and in the customs of the British. Very little of this would interest my readers, and I accordingly confine myself to quoting from these notebooks that which has special bearing on music.[34]

On November 5, 1791, he attended a celebration occasioned by the appointment of the Lord Mayor. After the banquet there was a ball in three salons. In the one, where were the highest nobility, only minuets were danced. Haydn, however, could hardly bear it there a quarter of an hour, partly on account of the heat in the crowded room, partly on account of the wretched dance music, "for the entire orchestra consisted of only two violins and one violoncello, and the minuets were rather of the Polish than the German or Italian sort." In another room, "which was more like an underground cave, there was English dancing. The music there was better, because a drum played with it and covered up the wretched fiddlers." In the large room the orchestra was bigger and somewhat more bearable. "But here the men had camped around the tables drinking. It is most remarkable that one group here dances without hearing a note of the music because now at this table, now at that, either songs are roared forth or healths are drunk amidst the wildest screaming and waving of glasses: Hurrey, Hurrey, Hurrey [*sic*]!"

On June 15, 1791, Haydn visited Dr. Herschel, and inspected his great telescope. "Herschel in his younger years served in the Prussian army as an oboist. He deserted, with his brother, came to England, supported himself for many years with music, became organist at Bath and at the same time applied himself unceasingly to astronomy." I cannot guarantee that this statement is correct.*

Concerning the opera *The Woodman*,[35] which was given in London on December 10, 1791, Haydn makes the following observation: "It was the same day on which the controversial memoir of Mad. Billington had been announced. She sang this evening somewhat timidly, but very well. (On another occasion Haydn said of her that she was a great genius.) The first tenor has a good voice, and pretty good manner, except that he uses the falsetto too much. He made a trill on high C and went up as far as G. The second tenor tries to do the same, but he cannot join his natural voice and his falsetto, and is besides very unmusical. He makes his own tempo, now three, now two quarters, and makes cuts wherever it occurs to him, but the orchestra is very used to this. The conductor is Herr Baumgärtner, a

* A completer and more reliable account of Herschel's youth, by his boyhood friend D. Miller, will be found in the 8th volume of the *Allgemeine Musikalische Zeitung*, No. 47, pp. 735 ff. The Publisher.

German who, however, has almost forgot his mother tongue. The mob in the galleries is very impertinent in all theaters everywhere and sets a violent fashion. The parterre and the loges often have to clap a great deal before something good can be repeated. This was just the case this evening with the pretty duet in the third act. Almost a quarter-hour went by with pro and contra until finally the parterre and the loges won out and the duet was repeated. The two actors stood very anxiously on the stage. The orchestra is asleep."

"On May 21, 1791,[36] was Giardini's concert in Ranelagh; he played like a pig."

February 8, 1792, was the first Ancient Concert; on February 13 the Professional Concert began, and on February 17 Salomon opened his own in Hanover Square. "The week before Whitsuntide I heard in St. Paul's Church four thousand charity children sing the following song; a leader gave the beat. No music moved me so greatly in my whole life as this, full of devotion and innocent.

All the children were in new clothes, and marched in procession; the organist played the melody very simply and well, and then they all began to sing at the same time." [37]

The music in Vauxhall on June 4, 1792, Haydn found pretty good, and he saw Handel's statue in stone set up there.

At the time Haydn was in London there was no lack of musicians either theoretical or practical, and he made the following catalogue of them:

Singers, male and female: Mara, Storace, Billington, Cassentini, Lops, Negri, Celestini, Corri, Benda, Mrss. Barthelemon and her daughter, Schinotti, Maffei (*bella, ma poco musica*), Capelletti, Daevis (*detta Inglesina,* she sang in Naples when she was 13 years old; now she is somewhat old, but she has a good school). Mad. Seconda (*passabile*), Poet

Badini, Mad. de Sisley, Bacchierotti, Kelly, Davide, Albertarelli, Dorelli, Lazarini (in the Pantheon), Mazzanti, Morelli, Calcagni (first soprano of the King of Sweden), Crouch, Harrison, Simoni, Miss Poole, Miss Bark, Mrss. Bland, Miss Nield.

Composers: Baumgarten, Clementi, Dussek, Gyrowetz, Choris, Dr. Burney, Hüllmandel, Graff, Diettenhofer, Storace, Arnold, Barthelemon, Schield, Carter, Cramer, Tomish, Frike, Callcot (Scholar), la Trobe (dedicated his clavier sonatas to me), Mazingi (at the clavier in the Pantheon), Friderici.

Clavier players: Clementi, Dussek, Gyrowetz, Diettenhofer, Burney, Mstrss. Burney, Hüllmandel, Graf (likewise flautist), Miss Barthelemon, Cramer, Hummel from Vienna, Mrss. Jansen, Lenz (still very young), Hässler.

Violin players: Salomon, Giornovich, Cramer, Clement (*petit*), Schield, Hindmarsch (English), Scheener (German), Raimondi (Italian), Marquis von Serra, Durazzo, Borghi, Felix Janiewicz, Jarowez, Giardini.

Violoncellists: Grosdill, Menel, Mara, Sperati, Schram.

Oboists: Fischer, Harrington, Lolli and his son (come from Stockholm).

Flautist: Mr. Ashe.

Doctors: Burney, Hess in Oxford, Arnold, Dupuis (a great organist).[38]

On November 24, 1791, Haydn was invited to the Duke of York at his castle at Eatland [Oatlands], eighteen miles from London. The Prince [i.e. the Duke], his consort, a German princess, and the Prince of Wales overwhelmed him with the marks of their esteem. The latter asked him for his portrait. For two days there was music in the evening from ten o'clock until two hours past midnight.

On December 14 [1791] Haydn dined with a Mr. Shaw. "He received me at the street door, and took me to his wife, who was with her two daughters and several ladies. When I made my compliments all around, I was aware that all the ladies were wearing pearl-colored head bands on which the name Haydn was very nicely embroidered in gold. Mr. Shaw had the same name embroidered in very fine steel beads on both ends of his coat-collar. Mistriss Shaw is the handsomest woman I ever saw. Her husband desired a souvenir from me. I gave him a snuffbox that I had bought shortly before for a guinea; he gave me his in return. When I visited him several days later, he had had a silver case made for my snuffbox on the lid of which a lyre was very prettily engraved, and all around were the words: *ex dono celeberrimi Iosephi Haydn.* The mistriss gave me a pin as a souvenir." Haydn also kept the band which she wore that day with his most precious treasures.

"In the first concert the Adagio of the new symphony in D was repeated. In the second concert the chorus and the first Allegro and the Adagio of the above symphony were repeated. In the third concert the new symphony in B flat was given, and the first and last Allegro done again." [39] "Hardy, Otto, Guttenbrunn, Hoppener painted my portrait. Desoie made a wax model."

"On November 23 [1791] I was invited to the *Theatre of varietés amusantes* in Saville-Row. It is a marionette show, the puppets were well handled, the singers were bad, but the orchestra was pretty good."

"Mara before her departure to Italy sang the English opera *Artaxerxes,* [40] by Dr. Arnd [Arne], four times in the Haymarket Theater. She received each time a hundred pounds and the roundest applause. In Oxford she was hissed because she did not rise from her seat for Handel's *Alleluja* chorus."

"On March 26, 1792, at Mr. Barthelemon's concert, there was an English preacher who, when he heard my Andante, sank into deep-

est melancholy because he had dreamed the night before that such an Andante foreshadowed his death. He immediately left the company, went to bed, and today, April 25, I learned through Herr Barthelemon that this Protestant minister was dead." [41]

On May 18, 1792, was the last of Salomon's concerts in Hanover Square. "A band of wild (stunted) fellows sang this song so noisily

and shouted so that you could hear it a thousand feet from the street in the remotest corner."

Near the end of the diary of the first London journey is the following verse, which Haydn had probably left behind as a memento with some friend or other:

Clippings from English newspapers of the year 1792, which Haydn had kept in his diary, are full of the highest praise for the originality, versatility, and productiveness of his talent. His first attempt to set English words to music (*The Storm*, also published by Breitkopf and Härtel in Leipzig) was crowned with the greatest success. The original text is attributed to the poet [John Wolcot] known as Peter Pindar and goes:

> Hark! the wild uproar of the winds, and hark,
> Hell's Genius roams the regions of the dark;
>   And thund'ring swells the horrors of the main.
> From cloud to cloud the Moon affrighted flies,
> Now darken'd, and now flashing through her skies—
>   Alas! bless'd calm, return, return again.

Haydn set out on his second journey to England on January 19, 1794, and his stay there lasted again one year and a half.

When he was going through Schärding on the Austrian border, the customs officials inquired about his character. Haydn answered that he was a *Tonkünstler* [musician]. "What is that?" asked the one. "A potter!" [*Ton*, clay; *Künstler*, artist] answered the other.

"Exactly," Haydn agreed, "and this man sitting next me in the carriage (his servant) is my journeyman."

The following passages are to be found in Haydn's diary during his stay in England in 1794 and 1795.

"Dr. Arnold composed an opera for Drury Lane Theater. Because the entrepreneur was afraid it would meet with no success, Dr. Arnold agreed to give it three times at his own expense. He spent over seven hundred pounds on it, but the entrepreneur each time paid a lot of men to hiss the opera. Finally Arnold turned over to the entrepreneur the opera together with the costumes for two hundred pounds. He gave it with several changes, better costumes and sets, and in one year earned from it twenty thousand pounds; the publisher alone made about five thousand, and the poor composer lost five hundred. O swindlers!" [42]

"On December 15, 1794, I visited Mr. Baze, who conducts the Ancient Concert from the organ, and plays pretty well. His wife has a very pleasant, flexible voice, good intonation, her pronunciation is clear, she sings like Bachierotti, but trills somewhat too fast." [43]

"If a singing, clavier, or dancing master charges half a guinea a lesson, he requires an entrance fee of six guineas at the first lesson. This is because many Scotch and Irish in the winter proudly wish their children given lessons by the best masters and then at the end cannot pay. The entrance fee is waived if the master charges a guinea, but the guinea must be paid at each lesson."

"On January 21, 1795, I dined at Dr. Parsons', where a quarrel arose as to which of the three doctors, Parsons, Dupuis, or Arnold, should direct in the orchestra the Handel anthem at the marriage of the Prince of Wales. Dr. Parsons is Kapellmeister of the Royal Chapel, the other two are Court Organists. But in England it is the organist who is chief director in all churches, and the singers are under him. Each of the three wished to conduct. As I was pressed to give my opinion, I said, 'Let the junior organist play the organ, the other direct his choir, and Dr. Parsons the *Instrumental Performers;* and because the singer always takes precedence over the instrumentalist, let him stand with his choir on the right, the other on the left.'

But this they would not have. I left the fools ([*die Gispeln*] an Austrian provincialism for *Thoren*) and went home." [44]

"On April 8, 1795, was the marriage of the Prince of Wales to the Princess of Brunswick. On the tenth I was invited to a musical evening at the Prince of Wales' in Carlton House. An old symphony was given, which I accompanied at the clavier, afterwards a quartet; then I had to sing German and English songs. The Princess also sang with me; she played a concerto on the pianoforte pretty well."

"On February 1, 1795, I was invited by the Prince of Wales to a musical evening at the Duke of York's, at which the King, the Queen, her entire family, the Duke of Orange, and so on, were present. Nothing but compositions of mine was played. I sat at the clavier; at the end I had to sing. The King, who up to then could or would listen only to Handel's music, was attentive. He conversed with me, and took me to the Queen, who said many flattering things to me. I sang my German song, *Ich bin der verliebteste*.[45] On February 3 I was invited to the Prince of Wales; the fifteenth, seventeenth, and nineteenth of April, 1795, I was also there; the twenty-first, at the Queen's in Buckingham Palace."

"On November 14, 1794, I went with Lord Avingdon to Preston, twenty-six miles from London, to Baron von Aston; he and his wife love music."

"On March 24, 1795, Mara gave a benefit musicale in the Hanover Square Rooms, but she had not more than sixty persons. They said that she never sang better than then. Janiewicz directed, Clementi sat at the clavier. She gave after that [June 8, 1795] a second concert in the name of the flute-player, Ash. The house was pretty full; I sat at the clavier."

"On March 30, 1795, I was invited to a great concert by Dr. Arnold and his supporters. A great symphony was to have been played under my direction, but since they had not been willing to have a rehearsal, I refused and did not show up."

"On March 28, 1795, I saw the opera *Acis e Galathea* by Bianchi. The music is very rich in wind instruments, and it seemed to me that if it were less so, one might hear the main melody better. The opera is too long, especially since Banti has to sustain it alone, for Brida, a good youngster with a beautiful voice, but not very musical, Rovedino, and the good Braghetti and wretched second lady deserved and got not the least applause. The orchestra this year has more personnel, but even so is mechanical and badly placed as it was before, and indiscreet in accompaniment. In short, it was the third time that this opera was presented, and everything was unsatisfactory."

"Spectas et tu spectabere [See and be seen], an inscription over the curtain in the Little Haymarket Theater. I was there on July 29, 1794,[46] at a national opera. It is the same wretched stuff there as in Sadler's Wells. A fellow screams an aria so frightfully and with such extreme grimacing that I began to sweat all over. N.B. He had to repeat the aria. *O che bestie!"*

"On April 10, 1795, I was at the Covent Garden Theater to see the great spectacle piece, *Windsor Castle.* The music by Salomon quite passable. The sets, costumes, changes, crowd scenes are overdone. All the gods of Heaven and of Hell and everything that lives on the earth turns up in it."

"On May 4, 1795, I gave my Benefit Concert in the Haymarket Theater. The hall was filled with a select company. (a) First part of the Military Symphony; Aria (Rovedino); Concerto (Ferlandy), the first time; Duet (Morichelli and Morelli) by me; a new symphony in D, the twelfth and last of the English; (b) second part of the Military Symphony; Aria (Morichelli), *Concerto* (Viotti), *Scena nuova* by me, Mad. Banti (*She song very scanty* [in English]). The whole company was extremely pleased, and I too. I made this evening four thousand gulden. One can do this only in England."[47]

Haydn added to his diary in English the following index of works that he had composed from January 2, 1791 to 1795 in England and had written out in his own hand:[48]

Opera seria l'Orpheo	110	Blätter
Sechs Symphonieen	124	"
Eine concertante Symphonie	30	"
Chor: der Sturm	20	"
Drey Symphonieen	72	"
Eine Arie für Davide	12	"

Gesänge für Gallini	6	"
Sechs Quatuor	48	"
Drey Sonaten für Broderiep	18	"
Drey Sonaten für Preston	18	"
Zwey Sonaten für Miss Janson	10	"
Eine Sonate in *F minor*	3	"
Eine in *g*	5	"
Der Traum	3	"
Dr. Harringtons Compliment	2	"
Sechs Englische Lieder	8	"
Hundert Schottische Lieder	50	"
Funfzig dergleichen (für Nepire)	25	"
Zwey *Divertimenti* für die Flöte	10	"
Drey Symphonieen	72	"
Vier Gesänge für Thallersal	6	"
Zwey Märsche	2	"
Eine Arie für Miss Poole	5	"
God save the King	2	"
Eine Arie mit vollem Orchester	3	"
Aufruf an Neptun	3	"
Die zehn Gebote Gottes	6	"
Marsch für den Prinzen von Wallis	2	"
Zwey *Divertimenti* mit verschiedenen Stimmen	12	"
Vier und zwanzig Menuets und Deutsche	12	"
Zwölf Balladen für Lord Avingdon	12	"
Verschiedene Gesänge	29	"
Canons	2	"
Ein Lied mit vollem Orchester	2	"
Für Lord Avingdon	2	"
Vier Contratänze	2	"
Sechs Lieder	2	"
Ouvertüre für Coventgarden	6	"
Arie für die Banti	11	"
Vier Schottische Lieder	2	"
Zwey Lieder	1	"
Zwey Contratänze	1	"

Summa 768 Blätter

Besides these observations written down by Haydn himself, I remember hearing the following from him about his stay in England.

I asked him once in jest whether it was true that he had composed the Andante with the Drum Stroke [Symphony No. 94] to waken the English who fell asleep at his concert. "No," came the answer, "but I was interested in surprising the public with something new, and in making a brilliant debut, so that my student Pleyel, who was at that time engaged by an orchestra in London (in 1792) and whose concerts had opened a week before mine, should not outdo me. The first Allegro of my symphony had already met with countless Bravos, but the enthusiasm reached its highest peak at the Andante with the Drum Stroke. Encore! Encore! sounded in every throat, and Pleyel himself complimented me on my idea."

Nepire [Napier], an English music dealer, had twelve children and was to be arrested for debts. Haydn arranged for him a whole hundred Scotch songs in modern vein, with accompaniment of a *basso continuo* and a violin, in many cases with the addition of a ritornello and the like. The sale of these songs was so good that Nepire was rescued from his money troubles, and instead of fifty guineas that he had paid Haydn for the first set, could afterwards offer double that for a second. For the music publisher George Thomson in Edinburgh Haydn arranged afterwards and on until 1803 two hundred and thirty such old Scotch songs in all, at one or two guineas apiece.[49]

Haydn had wished very much to hear something of his own work in the great London musicales arranged every year by the King, in which nothing but Handel's compositions was put on. He was given some hope of this, but a command soon appeared that at these musicales nothing composed less than thirty years ago might be performed. During his second stay in England, Haydn nevertheless succeeded.[50] One of his symphonies was put on, and was excellently played by the royal orchestra. The King then wanted Haydn to conduct a Psalm by Handel from the organ. Haydn, who had studied Handel's works diligently, executed this mission to everybody's satisfaction.

He had to perform for the Queen several times. She presented him with the manuscript of a German oratorio by Handel, entitled *The*

Redeemer on the Cross,* the only one that he had composed in that language. One evening when Haydn had been playing the pianoforte before the Queen for a long time, the King, who always spoke German, said he knew that Haydn had formerly been a good singer, and he would like to hear him do a few German songs. Haydn pointed to one joint of his little finger and said, "Your Majesty, my voice is now not even that big." The King laughed, and then Haydn sang his song *Ich bin der verliebteste.*[52]

The King and the Queen wished to keep him in England. "You shall have a place in Windsor in the summers," said the Queen, "and then," she added with an arch look toward the King, "we shall sometimes make music tête à tête." "Oh!" replied the King, "I am not worked up over Haydn, he is a good honest German gentleman." "To keep that reputation," answered Haydn, "is my greatest pride." On repeated urging to remain in England, Haydn claimed that he was bound by gratitude to his Prince's house, and that he could not separate himself forever from his fatherland or from his wife. The King offered to send for the latter. "She will not cross the Danube, much less the sea," Haydn replied. He remained unmoved, and he believed that on that account the King never gave him anything. Of the royal family, only the Duchess of York came to his benefit concert, and she sent him fifty guineas. He was very kindly received by her several times, for she knew that her father, the King of Prussia, thought a great deal of Haydn. For the Prince of Wales he directed twenty-six musicales, and the orchestra often had to wait several hours until the Prince rose from the dinner table. Since this effort remained wholly unrewarded, Haydn at the advice of his friends sent from Germany a bill for a hundred guineas when Parliament settled the Prince's debts, and he was sent this sum without delay.

It was ill received and attributed to greed that Haydn presented his claim. As though Haydn should have spent for nothing on the heir to the English throne the time and effort he could so well econo-

---

* Handel wrote this oratorio, the only one by him to a German text, in Hamburg. The text is by Brookes. It is in the possession of the Breitkopf and Härtel music dealer.[51]

mize! True delicacy will be less offended by the claim than by Haydn's having to claim what was his rightful due.

Dr. Burney first proposed to Haydn that he should be made a Doctor at Oxford. The ceremony of receiving the degree takes place in a cathedral with many solemnities. The doctors enter in procession and put to the candidates the question whether they wish to be admitted, and so forth. Haydn replied what his friend Salomon prompted. The election is put before the company from a platform. The speaker enlarged upon Haydn's merit, he cited his works, and at the question: Is Haydn admitted? there went up a general cry of assent. The doctors dress in a ruffle and a little mantle, and turn out in this costume for three days. "I really wished that my Vienna acquaintances had seen me in this outfit!" La Storace and several other musical friends waved to him from the orchestra. The day after the election Haydn directed the music. As soon as he appeared, everyone called: Bravo Haydn! "I thank you!" he answered [in English], raising up the ends of the little mantle. This caused a great jubilee. Handel had spent thirty years in England without being accorded the honor of becoming a Doctor of Oxford. It several times happened to Haydn that Englishmen walked up to him, surveyed him from head to foot, and left him saying [in English], "You are a great man."

Haydn received in London an ivory disk on a little blue ribbon with *Professional-Concert 1791* on one side, and with *Mr. Haydn* on the other; by showing this he was allowed free entry into the principal theaters, a courtesy never shown him in Vienna.

He earned in a three-year stay in England something like twenty-four thousand gulden, of which about nine thousand went for the journey, his support, and other expenses. He gave several persons lessons on the clavier, and each lesson was paid for with a guinea. "I opened my eyes wide at that!"

A lord took him to the great violin player Giardini. They stood in the antechamber, were announced, and heard very clearly that Giardini answered the servant, "I won't make the acquaintance of the German dog." The lord was extremely put out about it, but Haydn found the incident only comical, and he went soon thereafter to a concert to hear Giardini play.[53]

Through long practice he had learned in general how musicians must be handled and thus succeeded by much modesty, by appropriate praise and careful indulgence of artistic pride so to win over Gallini's orchestra that his compositions were always well performed.

Haydn oftentimes repeated that he had become famous in Germany only by way of England. The worth of his works was recognized, but that public homage which conspicuous talent usually enjoys came only quite late. Even Joseph II grew attentive to Haydn only during his journey. The Emperor wanted to hear his opera *La vera costanza,* but because of intrigue the roles were so badly assigned that Haydn took his score back again. Meanwhile he had the pleasure of hearing, after the return from his first journey to England, that a monument to him had been set up in his birthplace Rohrau. The donor was Karl Leonhard Count von Harrach, who had it erected in his tasteful garden at Rohrau on a charming knoll with the waves of the Leitha rippling around. The inscriptions on the monument—a four-sided column on which rests a musical trophy—are by the Abbé Denis. In the long rectangle of the main side, just below the trophy, the following verses, fitted to a Haydn composition, may be read:

Thou gracious Philomel, enliven now this shore,
A thousand throats let swell this song forever more.

The large tablet standing below contains the words:

TO THE MEMORY
OF JOSEPH HAYDN
THE DEATHLESS MASTER
OF MUSIC,
TO WHOM EAR AND HEART
CONTENDING DO HOMAGE,
DEDICATED
BY
KARL LEONHARD COUNT VON HARRACH
IN THE YEAR 1793

To the left on the area just below the trophy, fitted to another Haydn composition, stands:

A stone to Haydn's fame designed
consecrates this place enshrined,
and Harmony mourns in dismay.

On the lower marble plaque the following words are engraved, completed since Haydn's death:

ROHRAU
GAVE HIM LIFE
IN THE YEAR 1732, THE 1ST APR.
EUROPE
UNDIVIDED APPROVAL.
DEATH
IN THE YEAR 1809, THE 31ST MAY
THE ENTRANCE
TO THE ETERNAL HARMONIES.

Instead of April 1, March 31 should be named as Haydn's birthday. Haydn never neglected to make this correction when anyone examined the little model carved in wood that stood in his room.[54]

The following verse that a lady embroidered on a lampshade with which she honored Haydn, is also by the Abbé Denis:

Thou wert astonished that Orpheus' heavenly song
Once drew tears from the eyes of the mortal throng.
Today it is they who wonder so
That through thee their frequent noble tears must flow.

Haydn's situation became easier than before as a result of the savings made in England. He bought in Gumpendorf, a suburb of Vienna, near the Mariahülf line, the house at No. 73 in the lower Steingasse, together with the adjoining garden, approximately thirty paces square. Perhaps many a friend of art still makes the pilgrimage to a dwelling that the genius of harmony had so often glorified by its presence.[55] Here too it was that Haydn composed the oratorios *The Creation* and *The Seasons,* two works that crowned his reputation.

The first idea for the oratorio *The Creation* belongs to an Englishman, Lidley by name, and Haydn was to have composed Lidley's text for Salomon. He soon saw, however, that his understanding of the English language was insufficient for this undertaking; also the text was so long that the oratorio would have lasted close to four hours. Haydn meanwhile took the text with him to Germany. He showed it to Baron van Swieten, the royal librarian in Vienna, who arranged it as it now stands. Salomon was going to sue Haydn for this, but Haydn protested to him that he had used only Lidley's idea and not his words; Lidley moreover was already dead, and so the matter was dropped. Haydn had long been acquainted with van Swieten. "He patronized me occasionally with several ducats, and also gave me a comfortable traveling coach for the second journey to England." The violinist Starzer and the lute player Kohaut used to come often to Swieten's to perform Haydn's music,[56] and there also Handel's compositions were oftentimes given alternately under the direction of Haydn and of Mozart. Swieten himself had composed eight symphonies—"they were as stiff as he was"—and Swieten was the life secretary of a musical society in Vienna whose members (the Princes Lichtenstein, Esterházy, Schwarzenberg, Lobkowitz, Auersberg, Kinsky, Lichnowsky, Trautmannsdorf, Sinzendorf, the Counts Czernin, Harrach, Erdödy, Aponi, Fries) were accustomed to arrange several concerts a year. Only classical compositions were performed in these concerts, and the oratorio *The Creation* was likewise intended for them.

Haydn composed *The Creation* in 1797, thus in his sixty-fifth year, with a fire that usually animates only a young man's breast. I had the fortune to be a witness of the deep emotion and the most lively enthusiasm that several performances of this oratorio under Haydn's own direction wrought in all hearers. Haydn also confessed to me that he could not convey the feelings that mastered him when the performance wholly matched his wishes, and the audience in total silence listened intently to every note. "Now I would be ice cold in my whole body, now a burning fever would come over me, and I was afraid more than once that I should suddenly suffer a stroke."

The *Leipzig Musikalische Zeitung* turned out a review of the oratorio *The Creation* as thorough as it was appropriate.[57] Swieten and Haydn assured me that this critic had written to them from the bottom of his heart, and that they were incapable of expressing in more striking manner the feelings with which the poetry of text and music filled them.

Wieland's muse celebrated the praise of Haydn's *Creation* in the following verses,[58] which gave the composer much joy:

> How streams thy swelling song
> Deep within our hearts! We see
> Creation's great going-on,
> The breath of the Lord upon the waters breathe,
> Now through a lightning word the first light come to be,
> And the constellations on their courses first agree;
> How tree and plant begin, how mountains first arise,
> And glad to be alive the early beasts bestir.
> The thunder rolls in every ear;
> The rains drift down, and every being tries
> To come to life; appointed Creation's work to crown,
> We see the first-made couple pictured in thy sounds.
> O every noble feeling that once slept in the heart
> Awakes! who does not cry: how lovely is this earth!
> And, fairer still, their Lord to thee did life impart,
> That thou mightst thus perfect thy work.

Haydn's fortune was significantly increased by the oratorio *The Creation*. The musical society mentioned above made him a present of five hundred ducats. A benefit concert and the authorized edition of the score yielded him something like twelve thousand gulden. The plates of the score are in the possession of Messrs. Breitkopf and Härtel in Leipzig.

The unusual approbation with which the oratorio *The Creation* was everywhere received induced Baron van Swieten to adapt Thomson's *Seasons* and have Haydn set this poem to music to the same end as *The Creation*.

Baron Swieten, then nearing seventy years of age, was a man who took an interest in art and learning, and whose opinion carried weight in the circle of the great among whom he lived. The rules by which works of taste are to be judged were not strange to him; but in his own output he fell into all the faults and errors that he would have severely blamed in others. The best in his poems was not that which he expressed but rather that which he imagined, and it was amazing to find in his works none of the beauties by which, according to his intention and his emotion, they ought to have been distinguished.

Haydn often complained bitterly over the unpoetic text of *The Seasons,* and how hard it was for him to find inspiration to compose *Heysasa, Hopsasa, es lebe der Wein! es lebe das Fass, das ihn verwahrt! es lebe der Krug, woraus er fliesst!* and so on. [Long live wine! Long live the cask in which it's kept! Long live the pitcher from which it pours!] When he came to the place *O Fleiss, o edler Fleiss, von dir kommt alles Heil!* [Industry, noble industry, from thee comes all prosperity!], he remarked that he had been an industrious man all his life, but that it had never occurred to him to set industry to music. Haydn attributed to the strain that the composition of *The Seasons* cost him the weakness that grew ever greater from this time. He was seized with a brain fever shortly after completing the work, and at that time he described how his mind's incessant activity with notes and music was the cause of his greatest suffering.

If it were once decided to set to music a text of this sort, then Haydn surely did everything possible for it, and only a composer of genius could succeed in making such unlikely material less conspicuous by an attractive cover. Sentiments merely hinted at in flat, often ordinary prose are here by the magic of musical poetry really ennobled and idealized. In the spring of 1801 [on April 24] this work was performed for the first time under Haydn's direction in the Vienna palace of Prince Schwarzenberg, to the most undivided applause. In order to be relieved of the trouble of an authorized edition, Haydn turned over the score of *The Seasons* to the Breitkopf and Härtel music firm in Leipzig for the sum of a thousand ducats.

The Creation and *The Seasons* have been criticized for depicting objects foreign to the nature of music, which is inherently subjective and not objective, and this imitation is indeed not unconditionally commendable. In the midst of so many excellences, however, such passages are only minor blemishes, and Haydn himself set small store by them. When in correcting the clavier edition of *The Seasons* he found the croaking of frogs too strongly expressed, he observed that this place really belonged to Grétry, and Baron van Swieten wanted it that way. In the full orchestra this vulgar notion would disappear soon enough, but it would not do in the clavier edition. [See p. 186.]

In August, 1801, Haydn received a highly flattering token of the creditable reception of his oratorio *The Creation* in Paris. The assembled musicians of the great Opera in this capital sent him a large gold medal engraved by N. Gatteaux, with a lifelike portrait bust of Haydn on one side and on the other an antique lyre over which hovers a crown of stars. The inscription reads: *Hommage à Haydn, par les Musiciens, qui ont exécuté l'Oratorio de la Création du Monde au théatre des Arts l'an IX de la République Française ou MDCCC.* The medal was accompanied by the following letter:

De Paris ce 1 Thermidor an 9 de la République Françoise. Les artistes François réunis au théatre des arts, pour exécuter l'immortel ouvrage de la *Création du Monde* composé par le célèbre *Haydn,* pénétrés d'une juste admiration pour son génie, le supplient de recevoir ici l'hommage du respect, de l'enthousiasme, qu'il leur inspire, et la medaille qu'ils ont fait frapper en son honneur. Il ne se passe pas une année qu'une nouvelle production de ce compositeur sublime ne vienne enchanter les Artistes, éclairer leurs travaux, ajouter aux progrès de l'art, étendre encore les routes immenses de l'harmonie, et prouver, qu'elles n'ont point de bornes, en suivant les traces lumineuses, dont *Haydn* embellit le présent et sait enrichir l'avenir; mais l'imposante conception de *l'Oratorio* surpasse encore, s'il est possible, tout ce que ce savant compositeur avoit offert jusqu'ici à l'Europe étonnée. En imitant dans cet ouvrage les *feux de la lumière,* Haydn a paru se peindre lui même, et nous prouver à tous, que son nom brilleroit aussi long tems que l'astre dont il semble avoir emprunté les rayons.

Si nous admirons ici l'art et le talent, avec lequel le citoyen *Gateaux* a si bien rempli nos intentions, en gravant la medaille, que nous offrons à *Haydn,* nous devons rendre hommage aussi à la noblesse des sentimens, avec lesquels il s'est contenté pour son ouvrage de la simple gloire, qu'il récueille aujourdhui.

REY, *chef de l'orchestre du théatre des arts.* SEGUR LE JEUNE. AUVRAY. FR. ROUSSEAU. XAVIER. REY 3ME. SAILLAR. etc. etc., in all one hundred and forty-two signatures.

(Translation: The French artists brought together at the *Arts Theater* to perform the immortal opus *The Creation of the World,* composed by the celebrated Haydn, moved to a proper admiration for his genius, beg him to receive here the deferential respect and enthusiasm that he has inspired in them, and the medal that they have had struck in his honor. Not a year passes when a new production of this sublime Composer does not come to enchant the artists, to lighten their labors, to add to the progress of the art, to extend still more the vast roads of harmony, and to prove that these have no limits while pursuing the luminous trails with which Haydn embellishes the present and enriches the future. But the imposing conception of the oratorio surpasses still, if that is possible, everything that the learned composer has yet offered to an astonished Europe. In his imitation in this work of the fires of light, Haydn appeared to paint himself, and to prove to us that his name will be brilliant as long as the star whose rays he seems to have borrowed.

If we admire here the art and the talent with which Citizen Gatteaux has so well fulfilled our intentions in engraving the medal that we offer to Haydn, we should do honor as well to the nobility of sentiment through which he has been content, in return for his work, simply with the glory he receives today.)—Here follow the signatures.

Haydn was likewise elected a foreign member and honored with medals by the French Institut National, by the Conservatory of Music, by the Amateur Concert, and by the Societé Academique des enfants d'Apollon in Paris.

In a letter from Weimar on February 8, 1802, Herr von Kotzebue wrote to Haydn that in order to make his patriotic drama *Die Hussiten in Naumburg* as good as possible, he wished to have each chorus set to music individually by one of our best masters (Weber, Reichardt, Danzi, Schuster, Vogler, and so on), and he thus begged Haydn to undertake the last chorus of the first act.[59] Haydn answered that as an old fellow of seventy, and always more sickly, he did not dare to enter a contest with those great masters, in which he could easily be defeated.

As a matter of fact his health from the year 1802 grew always more precarious. He had to get for his composing a clavier that was very easy to play because the touch of an old pianoforte which he had used for many years already strained his nerves too much.[60] From time to time an old deep-rooted ailment caused him all sorts of trouble. Haydn suffered, to wit, from a polyp in the nose that, when it became embedded and threatened his breathing, a surgeon from the Order of the Brothers of Mercy in Eisenstadt had tied up, three times in thirty years, and had thus always rendered it harmless for a long time. The celebrated Hunter in London,[61] in whose family Haydn was well known, offered to cure this ailment completely; but the operation never took place, because the date for Haydn's departure from England happened to be put ahead, and more especially because Haydn was afraid it might have evil consequences. "I'll have to leave it to rot away under the earth now," he used to say; "anyway my mother suffered the same ailment, without ever dying of it."

The hours when Haydn was not depressed by bodily suffering he used for Thomson in Edinburgh, arranging and making palatable to modern taste old Scottish songs, whose melody is mostly crude and oftentimes offensive. At the request of his prince, who made the acquaintance of General Moreau and his lady in Paris, Haydn made a clavier sonata for the latter in the year 1803, and he received from her a very courteous letter of thanks for it. Haydn kept no copy of this sonata and in view of the known fate of General Moreau, perhaps it was never printed.[62]

About this time Haydn brought out through Breitkopf and Härtel in Leipzig his three- and four-part songs with pianoforte accompaniment. With the conviction that this work would bear the judgment of connoisseurs, he sent a copy of it to the widowed Empress of Russia, to whom, while she was a grand duchess staying in Vienna, he had the fortune to give several hours of instruction. The Empress mentioned this fact in a very gracious reply, and presented Haydn with a costly ring.[63] Haydn had the beginning of the tenth song, entitled *Der Greis* [The Old Man], engraved with his name on a

visiting card, and distributed to friends who inquired after him.[64]
Herr Maximilian Stadler in Vienna replied very appropriately to this
musical visiting card in the following little duet:

Since in the concerts that were given yearly for the relief of the
poor in Vienna, mostly Haydn oratorios were performed, the municipal council felt bound to reward Haydn's efforts with the great
civic medal of honor. Among all the marks of distinction he received,
this one was for Haydn one of the most flattering, "for it made me
think of this: *vox populi, vox Dei* [the voice of the people is the
voice of God]." The medal was accompanied by the following
letter: [65]

    Well born,
      Highly respected Sir!

After the many proofs of philanthropy with which, Sir, you have coop-
erated to alleviate the pitiable conditions of the aged, impoverished citi-

zens of St. Marx, the City Infirmary Domestic Economy Commission, instituted by the highest authorities, finds cause to call the attention of this Council to this magnanimous behavior, and to express the hope that these beneficent efforts might not remain unnoticed.

In view now of the fact that you, a most respected Doctor of Music in admiration for the master works of your genius, have on repeated occasions without pay personally undertaken the direction of those cantatas by which so many citizens are moved to charity and such important contributions to the poor citizens of St. Marx effected, the Municipal Council of this imperial and royal capital and court city, Vienna, having long looked for an occasion, seizes this opportunity to show in some manner its esteem for a man who is rendered by his talent immortal, who has already been marked for special honor by all civilized nations, who actively combines the excellences of the artist with the virtues of the citizen.

In order, however, to take also only the least cognizance possible, in view of this abiding merit, the Municipal Council has unanimously voted to add the present twelve-fold gold Citizens' Medal as a trifling mark of the gratitude felt by the comforted poor citizens of St. Marx, as whose agent we here do act.

May it gleam on your bosom as long as good wishes for your noble deed pour forth from thankful hearts, and may you deliver us the occasion to multiply the proofs of our most marked esteem, with which we remain, Sir,

yours most willingly,

Joseph Georg Hörl, *imperial and royal Lower Austrian Government Councilor and Burgomaster.*

Stephan Edler von Wohlleben, *imperial and royal Councilor and City High Chamberlain in Vienna.*

Joh. Bapt. Franz, *President of the City Infirmary Domestic Economy Commission.*

Vienna, May 10, 1803.

On April 1, 1804, Haydn was presented also with a diploma of honor as a citizen of Vienna by the municipal council.

Haydn sometimes said in jest that he was going to have his titles written in gold letters on a black signboard and hung before his house. The signboard would have been of imposing size, for Haydn was Kapellmeister to Prince Esterházy (March 19, 1760),[66] member of the Philharmonic Academy at Modena (May 14, 1780), a graduate as Doctor of Music from Oxford (in 1793), life associate of the

Society for Musicians' Widows in Vienna (December 11, 1797), member of the Academy of Sciences and Arts in Stockholm (September 5, 1798), of the Felix meritis in Amsterdam (May 4, 1801), member of the Institut National in Paris (5 *Nivôse* 1802), Citizen of Vienna (April 1, 1804), honorary member of the Philharmonic Society in Laibach (July 14, 1805), and member of the Société académique des enfans d'Apollon in Paris (December 30, 1807).

On July 25, 1808, Haydn received through the imperial Russian ambassador, Prince von Kurakin, in Vienna a gold medal of forty-two ducats' weight, which the Philharmonic Society in Petersburg had had struck as a proof of its esteem for Haydn. On one side of the medal is portrayed a lyre with four strings, above which hovers the name of Haydn, surrounded by a crown of laurel; below stands the date of the founding of the Petersburg Philharmonic Society: 1802. The other side of the medal has the inscription: *Societas Philharmonica Petropolitana Orpheo Redivivo;* below, the engraver's name, *Carl Leberecht F[ecit]*.

This honorable memento was accompanied by the following letter:

Well born Sir,
     Most highly respected Herr Kapellmeister,
The Directors of the Philharmonic Society of this city hasten to carry out a commission that they reckon among the pleasantest and most honorable in their life. They are to present to the immortal creator of the sublimest music a proof of the boundless respect that they, like all friends of music, experience at the name of Haydn; but at the same time as well of the gratitude that can seldom be more properly and never more sincerely and earnestly expressed.

The Philharmonic Society owes its institution to the philanthropic ardor of a few lovers of music. It was so fortunate as to see its boldest wishes fulfilled sooner and more handsomely than it had dared to hope; and thus arose an association to which a not insignificant number of widows already owes an old age free of care, and which, generously supported by our charitable imperial house and a beneficent public, may venture the brightest hopes for the future.

And this handsome success we owe to that musical masterwork, everywhere celebrated, we owe it to your *Creation*. Accept, then, venerable sir, the offering of most fitting, of greatest gratitude that this Society brings you with the accompanying medal. Receive it with the goodness of all great men, and yet so particularly your own, and send your good wishes and your interest for a society that you may consider your own work, and whose good works call down blessings on the serene evening of your life, which has made joy for mankind. We sign ourselves, with the deepest respect, Sir,

your most faithful servants,

Georg Johann Berwald. Epmatz. H. Czervenka. Dan. Gottlob Bachmann. Johann Gottfried Hartmann.

St. Petersburg, May 29, 1808.

Haydn had noted down the very considerable sums brought in for the benefit of the poor by performances of his oratorios, partly in Vienna, partly in other places. "This was not idle vanity, but the world may as well know that I had not been a useless member of the Society, and that one can also contribute to charity by music." The last of his musical compositions is the eighty-second (properly eighty-third) quartet, published by Breitkopf and Härtel in Leipzig and dedicated to Count von Fries in Vienna:

"It is my last child," said Haydn, as he handed over the score to me for further attention, "but it still looks like me." The quartet consists only of an andante and a minuet, which were both ready as early as 1803. Haydn waited till 1806 for the increase of strength and the right mood necessary to add an allegro, but in vain; and so it is that, instead of the missing movement, the visiting card quoted above was printed, but was incorrectly entitled a canon.

In the summer of 1806 even the little clavier was removed from Haydn's sitting room, because the doctor forbade him all exertion and wanted to deprive him of any temptation thereto. Haydn himself felt how necessary it was for the preservation of his health to follow this advice, for when he sat down from time to time at his English pianoforte to improvise, dizziness overcame him after a few minutes. "I never would have believed," he said on September 3, 1807, "that a man could collapse so completely as I feel I have now. My memory is gone, I sometimes still have good ideas at the clavier, but I could weep at my inability even to repeat and write them down."

How often one might have liked to speak to Haydn in the last years of his life the words of Agamemnon to Nestor:

The general burden of age weighs hard on thee. O gods!
Would that another bore it, and thou a youth shouldst go forth!

Only through rest, solicitous care, and strict conformity to his daily routine could he eke out the remainder of his strength. It was difficult for him to walk because his legs were swollen, and he often did not go from one room to another for months at a time. Then he spent his time in praying, in reminiscing about his earlier days, especially his stay in England, in reading the newspapers, and in going over his small household accounts. In the long winter evenings, he talked over the news of the day with his neighbors and servants, and sometimes he played cards with them and was amused at the pleasure they took in winning a few kreutzers.

After a long interval Haydn was again seen in a public gathering on March 27, 1808, to receive gratitude and honor for his artistic activity of many years. It was the day when a society of music lovers concluded their concerts in the University Hall with a performance of *The Creation* using Carpani's Italian text. Haydn, accompanied by many noble Viennese friends of art, was brought with the sound of trumpets and timpani to an easy chair in the middle before the orchestra. Sitting between his adored Princess Esterházy and several artistic ladies, surrounded by artists, pupils, gentlemen and ladies of the highest rank, and an extremely numerous company from cultivated society, Haydn received from all who could get near him the sincerest proofs of high esteem, of tender solicitude for his weak old age, and of joy that it was permitted him to live to see this day. German stanzas by Collin and an Italian sonnet by Carpani in praise of Haydn were distributed among the audience; Salieri had undertaken the direction of the music, and the performance was excellent.[67]

At that place which is imperceptibly prepared, and which suddenly surprises one, progressing with the brightest and most splendid harmonies: "And there was light!", the audience as usual broke into the loudest applause. Haydn made a gesture of the hands heavenward and said, "It comes from there!" For fear that a storm of emotions too long continued might endanger the health of an old man, he allowed himself to be carried away in his chair at the end of the first part. He took leave with streaming eyes, and stretched out his hand in blessing to the orchestra.[68]

Collin writes of this scene: [69]

> Loud are heard the frenzied farewell cries,
> Applause, compassion's calls to heaven strain:
> He, however, upward turned his eyes,
> Thinking thus his full heart to contain;
> Yet once aroused, the storm will not disband,
> And sweeps him on. He struggles all in vain.
> See, he leans forward now, the aged man;
> And drawing near the portals, only then
> In benediction stretches out his hand!
> All weep!—For he will never come again!

He did not come again.

Without being in any real sense ill, Haydn nevertheless felt more every day that old age was an illness in itself, and that nature was inexorably asserting her rights to his body. A spark of life so faintly glimmering was threatened by every ordinary occurrence, so events like those that the war in the spring of 1809 brought to Austria worked all the more injuriously on him.

Haydn loved his fatherland and his royal family with deepest loyalty. As often as warm weather and his strength permitted, he was taken, in the last two years of his life, to his innermost room for the sole purpose of playing his song *Gott erhalte Franz den Kaiser!* on the pianoforte. The Austrian defeats in Bavaria, which resulted in retreat, caused Haydn much sorrow. "This unfortunate war is bringing me ever closer to the grave!" he often repeated, with tears in his eyes, and it took many efforts to quiet him even a little.

In this humor I found Haydn on May 3 when, called away from Vienna, I took my leave of him. The following more intimate particulars of Haydn's last hours are an extract from letters of trustworthy correspondents.[70]

On May 10 in the morning a French army corps pushed on to the Mariahülf line, which is not far from Haydn's dwelling. They were just getting him out of bed and dressing him when four case shots fell, violently rattling the windows and doors of his house. He called out in a loud voice to his alarmed and frightened people, "Don't be afraid, children; where Haydn is, no harm can reach you!" But the spirit was stronger than the flesh, for he had hardly uttered the brave words when his whole body began to tremble.

From this hour on, physical weakness grew. Still Haydn played his Emperor's Hymn daily, and on May 26 even three times in succession, with an expressiveness at which he himself was amazed. On the evening of the same day headache and chill overtook him; they put him to bed early and called the doctors. Their help was fruitless. The patient lapsed into a state of total exhaustion and painless stupor in which, however, he gave signs of consciousness and perception even a few minutes before the end, which came on May 31 early in the morning toward one o'clock.

Haydn had lived for seventy-seven years and two months. His body lies in its own grave in his parish churchyard outside the so-called Hundsthurm Line in Vienna.

Had the great artist's death not come at a time when people in Vienna were stunned by the war and dulled to peaceful feelings, surely the great number of his admirers there would have organized a distinguished funeral. The French authorities announced the loss of Haydn in the Vienna newspaper in an honorable fashion, and on June 13 Mozart's *Requiem* was performed to Haydn's memory in the Schottenkirche.[71]

The whole church was decked with black hangings and ornamented with the intertwined initials of the name Joseph Haydn. The civic guard stood around the sarcophagus, and beneath, spread out on a cushion of black satin, lay all the medals and the ivory pass with which Haydn had been honored in London. The French general staff and the most distinguished residents and artists of Vienna were in the church.

Haydn received his last visit on May 17. It was from a French army captain, Italian by birth, who wanted to speak to him. When the servant told him his master was lying in bed, the captain begged that he might at least be permitted to see through the keyhole the man he esteemed so highly. Haydn, who was informed of this, had the officer come in. Enthusiastically the soldier described the feelings that Haydn's nearness gave to him, and the great pleasure that he owed to the study of his works. At Haydn's request he sang at the clavier in a neighboring room with great perfection the aria from *The Creation, Mit Würd' und Hoheit angethan* [In Native Worth and Honor Clad]. Haydn was deeply moved, the officer not less so, they embraced one another, and parted amidst the warmest tears. In a trembling and quite illegible hand the captain wrote down his name. Provided I deciphered it correctly, it was Clement Sulemy. Duty called him from Haydn's room directly to the Lobau, and from there to the melee of the battle of Aspern, where he was probably killed. Should he still be alive, he can boast of having been the last to give Haydn a few happy moments through music.

Haydn was small in stature, but sturdy and strongly built. His forehead was broad and well modeled, his skin brown, his eyes bright and fiery, his other features full and strongly marked, and his whole physiognomy and bearing bespoke prudence and a quiet gravity. The best busts of Haydn are unquestionably those that his friend, the capable modeler at the Vienna Porcelain Works, Herr Grassi (Haydn took his death on December 30, 1807, very hard) made from life. One of them is life-size in the antique manner with the inscription:

> *Tu potis tigres comitesque silvas*
> *Ducere, et currentes rivos morari.*
> [Thou canst lead beasts and companion forests
> And still the flowing streams.
>
> Horace, *Odes,* III, xi.]

The other, smaller in scale, portrays Haydn perfectly in wig and customary clothing, and Grassi placed below it:

Blandus auritas fidibus canoris ducere quercus.
[And blandish the listening oaks with your singing strings.
                                          Horace, *Odes*, I, xii.] [72]

Also of speaking likeness are the pictures of Haydn that an engraver named Ihrwach made in Vienna as wax cameos. Among the engravings known to me, the one at Breitkopf and Härtel in Leipzig appears to be the best, though not entirely faithful. Johann Elssler, for eighteen years Haydn's copyist and faithful servant, had a plaster cast of his master's head made after his death.

Lavater, who characterized every silhouette in his collection with a verse, wrote under Haydn's portrait:

Something more than the ordinary I perceive in the eye and the nose;
The forehead too is good; in the mouth something philistine.

The strong, somewhat heavy lower lip may have given rise to this opinion.

As a youth and a man Haydn loved hearty food, and he always rose early. From the age of seventy on he kept to a strict routine that had proved by experience to be the most advantageous. Specifically, he went to bed at eleven o'clock at night and arose at eight o'clock. He also rested for half an hour at six o'clock in the evening.[73] He almost always dined alone, and mostly on light and easily digested food. When one talked about his regimen, he usually concluded, "I am of no more use to the world. I have to be nursed and looked after like a child. It's high time that God called me to Him!"

Haydn spoke in broad Austrian dialect, and his conversation was richly endowed with that comic and naïve manner of speaking peculiar to the Austrians. He had little facility in the French language, but he spoke Italian readily and fluently. In English he had learned during his two journeys to express himself in a pinch, and in Latin he understood everything in that tongue in the Catholic ritual.

In 1807 Haydn had contracted on good terms that his books, music, manuscripts, and medals should go after his death to the Esterházy family. There are very few completed unprinted works except several church pieces among the manuscripts. The most interesting of these are forty-six canons, mostly to German lyrics, that hung framed in Haydn's bedroom. "I was not rich enough," he said, "to buy myself beautiful paintings, so I made myself a wallpaper that not everybody can have." Once his wife, complaining about the lack of cash, said to her husband that if he should die today or tomorrow, there would not be enough in the house to bury him with. "If that happens," answered Haydn, "take the canons to the music publisher. I guarantee you that they are worth as much as my funeral requires."

Prince Esterházy will keep the medals that Haydn received, his books on music, papers and manuscripts (fifty in number, of which, however, only a few are unknown) at Eisenstadt in Hungary. The Prince has also already made arrangements to have the remains of his great Kapellmeister brought in an iron casket to Eisenstadt, where he will be buried in the former vault of the Franciscans, now the resting place of Luigi Tomasini and of other deserving artists, both men and women, of Prince Esterházy's chapel.[74]

The Vienna public showed how highly it valued Haydn at the auction of his estate. Prince Johann von Lichtenstein paid more than fourteen hundred gulden for a parrot that Haydn had brought from England and had himself taught to speak.[75] Everybody wanted to buy a keepsake. Even people of humble position outbid one another and scrambled for the effects as if they were a saint's relics.

With this representation, as far as possible chronological, of Haydn's fortunes, we turn now to a summary of his conspicuous character traits and to a few of his opinions on art.

Haydn was very religiously inclined, and was loyally devoted to the faith in which he was raised. He was very strongly convinced in his heart that all human destiny is under God's guiding hand, that God rewards the good and the evil, that all talents come from above. All his larger scores begin with the words *In nomine Domini* and end with *Laus Deo* or *Soli Deo gloria* [In the name of the Lord, Praise to God, To God alone the glory]. "If my composing is not proceeding so well," I heard him say, "I walk up and down the room with my rosary in my hand, say several *Aves,* and then ideas come to me again." In religion also he found the greatest comfort for his physical infirmity. He was thoroughly reconciled in his last years to the thought of his death and made ready for it every day. Without speculation about the principles of faith, he accepted the what and the how of the teaching of the Catholic Church, and his soul found comfort therein. Thus in 1807 and 1808 at the Feast of St. Peregrinus, the patron of diseased limbs, he had himself taken to the Servite Monastery and had a Mass said.[76] An autograph draft of a will that Haydn drew up in 1809 [77] begins thus: "In the name of the Most Holy Trinity. The uncertainty as to when it may please my Creator in His boundless mercy to call me to Him from this mortal life has moved me while still in good health to declare my last will concerning my few remaining possessions. My soul I bequeath to its all-bountiful Creator. My body however is to be buried according to Roman Catholic usage in consecrated earth and with first-class rites. For my soul I bequeath 1) for holy Masses, etc." In England he noted the following in his diary: "On August 26, 1794, I went to Waverly Abbey, forty miles from London, to Baron Sir Charles Rich, a pretty good violoncello player. Here are the remains of an abbey of six hundred years' standing. I must confess that every time I contemplated this beautiful wilderness, my heart was oppressed to think that all this once stood under my religion."

This instance, however, does not indicate intolerant feelings. Haydn left every man to his own conviction and recognized all as brothers. In general, his devotion was not of the gloomy, always suffering sort, but rather cheerful and reconciled, and in this character, moreover, he wrote all his church music. His patriarchal, devout spirit is particularly expressed in *The Creation,* and hence he was bound to be more successful in this composition than a hundred other masters. "Only when I had reached the half-way mark in my composition did I perceive that it was succeeding, and I was never so devout as during the time that I was working on *The Creation*. Every day I fell to my knees and prayed God to grant me the strength for a happy completion of this work."

Who is not carried back by such expressions to the era of Albrecht Dürer and other artists of the German past? They too in their simple and straightforward way ascribed that which they accomplished not to the power of their own genius but rather to Him Who granted them the gift of accomplishment.

A natural consequence of Haydn's religiosity was his modesty, for his talent was not his own doing, rather a gracious gift from Heaven, to whom he believed he must show himself thankful.

Once the clavier-player ——— from P. visited him. "You are Haydn, the great Haydn," he began with theatrical bearing. "One should fall on his knees before you! One should approach you only as a being of the highest sort!"—"Oh my dear sir," countered Haydn, "don't talk to me like that. Consider me a man whom God has granted talent and a good heart. I push my claims no further."—"Do you know what bothers me?" ——— went on, when he had looked around the room. "You should live in the most splendid palace, your garden should be ten times larger, you should drive with six horses, live in the circles of the great."—"All that," countered Haydn, "is not in keeping with my wishes. I had a hard time in my youth, and I strove even then to earn enough to be free of care in my old days. In this I succeeded, thank God. I have my own comfortable house, three or four courses at dinner, a good glass of wine, I can dress well, and when I want to drive out, a hired coach is good enough for me. I have associated with emperors, kings, and many great gentlemen and have heard many flattering things from them; but I do not wish to live on an intimate footing with such persons, and I prefer people of my own status."

Of his humble origin, his poor relations, some of whom were shoemakers, farmers, and other common working-class people, Haydn was so little ashamed that on the contrary he himself often spoke of them. Of his own works he said, *"Sunt mala mixta bonis;*

there are good and bad children, and here and there a changeling has crept in."

No one also was more inclined to do justice to the merits of others than Haydn. He openly acknowledged that most of what he knew he had learned from Emanuel Bach. Likewise he always spoke of Gluck, of Handel, and of his earlier teachers with the most grateful respect. "Where Mozart is, Haydn cannot appear!" he wrote, when he was invited at the same time as Mozart to Prague for the coronation of Emperor Leopold II; and he repeated with deep emotion and tears in his eyes, "Mozart's loss is irreparable. I shall never in my life forget his clavier playing. It touched the heart!" When Cherubini returned from Vienna to Paris in March, 1806, he asked Haydn for one of his original scores. Haydn gave him the score of a symphony that is especially beloved in Paris, and said to him, "Let me call myself your musical father, and you my son." Cherubini melted into tears of sadness.[78]

In all modesty Haydn did not fail to perceive his own worth. "I know," he used to say, "that God has favored me, and recognize it thankfully. I also believe I have done my duty and have been of use to the world through my works. Let others do the same!" On another occasion he said, "If a master has produced one or two superior works, his reputation is established." His *Creation* would endure, and probably *The Seasons,* too. He once read the review of one of his compositions in which he was charged with a false fifth. "These gentlemen may think themselves very wise in such discoveries. Ach! if I wished to take up criticism, how much I should find to criticize!" He also told me that once, in the presence of K. and Mozart, he had one of his new quartets played over, in which several bold passages appeared. "That sounds strange," said K. to Mozart. "Would you have written it that way?" "Hardly," answered Mozart, "but do you know why not? Because neither you nor I should have come upon this idea." [79]

Haydn possessed a little casket filled with snuffboxes, watches, rings, medals, and other presents that he had received from the emperors and kings of Austria, Russia, Prussia, Spain, France, and Naples. "If life sometimes seems to vex me, I look at all this, and feel glad to be so honored in all Europe."

When Lord Nelson traveled through Vienna, he asked for a worn-out pen that Haydn had used in his composing, and made him a present of his watch in return. Haydn had Maret, Soult, and several eminent French officers who were in Vienna at the end of the year 1805, and visited him, inscribe their names in a book; and on days when he felt well, he generally welcomed visits from strangers traveling by.

I told him I was astonished that he could make up his mind, in view of his failing health, to attend the aforementioned scene in the University Hall on March 27, 1808. He answered, "Consideration for my health could not keep me back. It is not the first time that Haydn has been honored, and I wished to prove that I am still able to receive it."

It was hoped that the Order of Leopold, founded in 1808 for meritorious Austrians, would also be extended to artists, and Haydn was congratulated thereon in advance. This distinction would have given him much joy. "Then there would be a Chevalier Haydn just like the Chevalier Gluck! Only it is a pity that I have no children to whom it could be useful!" To the Emperor he would have said on this occasion that among the many songs he had written, *Gott erhalte Franz den Kaiser!* was always one of those he valued most.

A harmless roguery, or what the British call *humour,* was one of Haydn's outstanding characteristics.[80] He easily and by preference discovered the comic side of anything, and anyone who had spent even an hour with him must have noticed that the very spirit of Austrian cheerfulness breathed in him. In his compositions this caprice is most striking, and his allegros and rondeaux are especially often planned to tease the audience by wanton shifts from the seemingly serious to the highest level of comedy, and to be tuned to an almost wild hilarity. Likewise the earlier mentioned Farewell Symphony is an extended musical joke.

Even physical sufferings could seldom beat down Haydn's cheer-

ful nature altogether, and though one found him in an ill humor
at the beginning and took leave with downcast heart, he at least
would still call after as one went away, "Lots of love to all the pretty
women!" or some such droll notion contrasting with his own state.
To ladies he always had something gallant to say. It delighted the
old man, although quite within the bounds of modesty, to play the
role of an amorous sweetheart with them. Then he would add,
"It's all part of my métier!"

Here may be given several more lively anecdotes that Haydn had
entered in his diary from England.

When in a great concert the first piece was just about to be performed, the timpanist called loudly to the director to wait a moment
because his kettledrums were not yet tuned. The director, who
did not wish to delay any longer, answered that he should just
transpose.

"I stayed for five weeks on the estate of the banker Brassy, twelve
miles from London. N.B. Mr. Brassy swore once that things
worked out too well for him in this world." [See p. 150.]

Smorfie d'un Virtuoso
[A Musician's Grimaces]

Once when Tentucci was singing his favorite aria at the Lady's
Concert, he stopped to think an instant in the cadenza. During this
pause the night-watchman called out at the top of his lungs [in Eng-
lish]: "half part [sic] eleven o'clock." All burst into loud laughter,
and the aria ended.[81]

Haydn set great store by order and regularity in everything he did
and in all his surroundings. His rooms were always clean and neat,
everything stood in its place, and even the papers and music on the
pianoforte were not mixed up with each other. He dressed fully immediately upon arising in the morning, so that he need ask only for
hat and cane to be able to appear at once anywhere at all, a habit that
he adopted in earlier years when his Prince oftentimes called for him
unexpectedly. If he was anticipating visitors, he put a diamond
ring[82] on his finger and decorated his coat with the red ribbon on

which the Citizen's Medal is worn. Every evening he looked through his household accounts himself, "so that my people do not go beyond the bounds." To him, who with all his effort and diligence achieved some affluence only in advanced old age, unnecessary expense seemed a folly. He had few needs, a simple mode of life had been second nature to him from youth on, and he made it a point of honor always to limit his expenditures by his income. With a little extra money he aided his relatives. The French in the year 1800 had taken the little money and two silver watches of his brother Michael in Salzburg (d. August 8, 1806).[83] Haydn sent him a gold watch and snuffbox and promised money as well, as soon as his interest came in. To another brother [Johann], who was still employed as a tenor singer in Prince Esterházy's chapel when he was sixty years old, he contributed for twenty-five years toward a trip to take the waters at Baden. "I live less for myself," I once heard him say, "than for my poor relations, to whom I hope to leave something after my death. Today a shoemaker who wishes to marry my niece,[84] a widow with four children, appealed to me for a capital of a thousand gulden. I have promised it to him. If I had lived better than has been my custom, this would not be possible for me." In his will, all the descendants of his brothers and sisters were mentioned. The principal heir cited was the blacksmith Matthias Fröhlich, of Rohrau, a son of his sister Therese. To his servant Johann Elssler, the son of a music copyist for Prince Esterházy's orchestra, who had served him for eighteen years, he bequeathed a trust of six thousand gulden, and the same amount to his housekeeper. Among other legacies he set aside a hundred gulden for a young girl, Anna Buchholz, "because her grandfather lent me one hundred and fifty gulden without interest in the greatest need of my youth, which, however, I paid back fifty years ago." [See p. 95.]

If Herr Kapellmeister Reichardt had been more closely acquainted with Haydn's circumstances, he would probably not have charged him in his Letters from Vienna with suspected miserliness.[85] How little founded this reproof is, the following fact makes clear: in his will Haydn bequeathed a small sum to one of his nieces, the wife of a shoemaker, adding, "Should she by chance venture to produce a written claim against me, I declare it null and void, since I have paid debts of nearly six thousand gulden for her and her previous shiftless husband." Is a miser capable of such a sacrifice? And yet this niece was only one of the many poor relations Haydn had to assist, seldom a one of whom he sent away empty-handed.

In general, however, Haydn was not at all in a position to cover a large expenditure. It has been noted above that for all his marked talent, all his diligence and love of order, he had saved by his sixtieth year only 2,000 gulden! Until then he was paid for most of his compositions either not at all or only very moderately, and from a salary of 800 gulden, no great sum could be laid away. At his death there was a capital of 15,000 gulden, and the entire amount of the estate to be divided among the heirs did not come in full to 60,000 gulden in bank notes, thus at most to 12,000 talers in Convention standard.[86] Who still wonders that Haydn lived in no grand style on such limited means? He was too noble-minded to plunge into debt, to make a display of his quiet charity, or to misuse the generosity of his prince, who never denied him a request. A miser in Haydn's situation would probably have worked his pounds to far different advantage!

Haydn's aesthetic character was the work of a happy natural gift and of incessant study. Anyone hearing him speak of his art would not have guessed at the great artist in him, and in Haydn there was complete confirmation of Kant's observation "that the author of a product which he owed to his genius did not himself know how he found within himself the ideas for it, nor did he have it in his power to think out such at will or methodically and to instruct others how they might produce similar works." His theoretical *raisonnements* were very simple: namely, a piece of music ought to have a fluent melody, coherent ideas, no superfluous ornaments, nothing overdone, no confusing accompaniment, and so forth. How to satisfy these requirements? That, he confessed himself, cannot be learned by rules, and simply depends on natural talent and on the inspiration of inborn genius.

Someone told Haydn that Albrechtsberger wished to see all fourths banished from the purest style.[87] "What does that mean?" replied Haydn. "Art is free, and will be limited by no pedestrian rules. The ear, assuming that it is trained, must decide, and I consider myself as competent as any to legislate here. Such affectations are worthless. I would rather someone tried to compose a really *new* minuet."

Haydn always composed his works at the clavier. "I sat down, began to improvise, sad or happy according to my mood, serious or trifling. Once I had seized upon an idea, my whole endeavor was to develop and sustain it in keeping with the rules of art. Thus I sought to keep going, and this is where so many of our new composers fall down. They string out one little piece after another, they break off when they have hardly begun, and nothing remains in the heart when one has listened to it."

He also took exception to the fact that so many musicians now composed who had never learned to sing. "Singing must almost be counted among the lost arts, and instead of song they let instruments dominate." To Italian song Haydn granted precedence, and he counseled beginning artists to study song in Italy, instrumental music in Germany. Even the climate of Italy contributed to vocal flexibility. Italian singers employed in the chapel of Prince Esterházy altered their voices after a few years' stay in Hungary. Several returned to Italy, came back again, and lo, their voices had regained their former beauty.

Handel was great in his choruses but mediocre in song.[88] Gluck was to be preferred on account of his correct intentions and his power, Piccini on account of his grace and his charming song. In church music the works of his brother, Michael Haydn, deserved a first place; only it was a pity that this category was so badly paid, for one could earn more with a bagpipe than with offertories and masses.

From the quantity of his compositions, one might conclude that Haydn must have worked very easily. This was not the case. "I was never a fast writer, and always composed with deliberation and industry. Such works, however, are made to last, and this is at once revealed to the connoisseur by the score. When Cherubini looked through several of my manuscripts, he always hit on the places that deserve respect."

On each of the twelve symphonies that Haydn composed in England, he spent, of course amidst other occupations, one month, on a mass three months. He also remembered, however, having written one in one month, because he could not go out, on account of sickness.[89]

Haydn always worked out his compositions as a whole. He laid out the entire plan of the principal voice in each part, marking the main places by small notes or numbers; afterwards he breathed spirit and life into the dry skeleton through the other accompanying voices and dexterous transitions. His scores are clean and clearly written, and corrections are seldom found in them. "This is because I do not write until I am sure of the thing."

It would be very interesting to know from what motives Haydn wrote his compositions, as well as the feelings and ideas that he had in mind and that he strove to express through musical language. To discover this precisely, however, one would have had to lay before him one of his works after the other, and that proved irksome to the aged man. But he said that he oftentimes had portrayed moral characters in his symphonies. In one of his oldest, which, however, he could not accurately identify, "the dominant idea is of God speaking with an abandoned sinner, pleading with him to reform. But the sinner in his thoughtlessness pays no heed to the admonition." [Cf. p. 155.]

He set a mass, in the year 1796, when the French were in Styria, to which he gave the title *In tempore belli* [In time of war]. In this mass the words *Agnus Dei, qui tollis peccata mundi* are performed in singular fashion with accompaniment of timpani "as though one heard the enemy coming already in the distance." With the words immediately following, *dona nobis pacem,* he all at once pathetically interrupts all the voices and instruments. This mass is No. 2 in the printed scores.[90]

In the mass that Haydn wrote in 1801 it occurred to him in the

Agnus Dei qui tollis peccata mundi that frail mortals sinned mostly against moderation and purity. So he set the words *qui tollis peccata, peccata mundi* to the trifling melody of the words in *The Creation, Der thauende Morgen, o wie ermuntert er!* [The dew-dropping morn, oh, how she quickens all!] But in order that this profane thought should not be too conspicuous, he let the *Miserere* sound in full chorus immediately thereafter. In the copy of this mass that he made for the Empress, he had to alter the place at her request.[91]

Haydn sometimes said that instead of the many quartets, sonatas, and symphonies, he should have written more vocal music. Not only might he have become one of the foremost opera composers, but also it is far easier to compose along the lines of a text than without one. He complained, moreover, that our German poets did not write musically enough, for a melody that suits the first stanza will seldom do for the following one. Often the sense fits in one line but not in that which should correspond to it. They are also not careful enough in the choice of vowels. Haydn was only a little acquainted with the poets of the latest period, and he readily confessed that he could no longer find his way in their sequence of ideas and in their expression.

Haydn recommended to every composer not to abandon the practical side, because he knew from his own experience how much this added to theory. "I was a wizard at no instrument, but I knew the strength and the working of all. I was not a bad clavier player or singer, and could also play a concerto on the violin."

He used to praise Pleyel, Neukomm, and Lessel as his best and most grateful pupils.[92]

———————

In the end a letter of Joseph Haydn's may also find a place here, one already known, to be sure, but certainly not unworthy of repetition. It is from December, 1787, consequently from the time when Haydn had already produced several of his greatest masterworks and won a reputation throughout Europe. Mozart, however, had not yet attained his greatest height and had to struggle against envy and repression. The letter is to a friend in Prague who had requested an

opera of Haydn's composition for the theater there (from Mozart's
Life by Prof. Niemetschek):[93]

You request an opera buffa from me. Right gladly, if you want something from my vocal composition for yourself alone. But for performance
on the stage at Prague—in this case I cannot help you, because all my
operas are too closely tied up with our personnel (at Esterháza in Hungary), and besides the effect, which I have calculated for the local scene,
would never come off. It would be quite a different matter if I had the
invaluable good fortune to compose an entirely new libretto for the theater there. But then I should still be risking a good deal, since the great
Mozart can hardly have any rival.

For could I impress upon the soul of every friend of music, but especially the great ones, my own grasp and experience of the inimitable works
of Mozart, so deep and with such a musical understanding and sensitivity,
then would the nations vie with one another to possess such a gem in
their keeping. Let Prague hold fast to that dear man—and reward him,
too; for without this the story of great geniuses is a sorry one and gives
posterity little encouragement to further efforts, wherefore, unhappily, so
many hopeful spirits languish. It angers me that this unique Mozart is
still not engaged by any imperial or royal court! Your pardon if I have
got off the track: I dearly love the man.

NOTES
by the publisher of this book

In addition to that which Herr Legation-Councilor Griesinger says
of Haydn's modesty, of his manner of working, of his views of the
technical side of the art, and his partiality toward *The Creation*—let
a single example stand here instead of the many that could be given
from the master's autograph letters; not as though all that still required proof, but because it affords pleasure just to see this presented, as it were, in all the directions taken by such a pure, noble
spirit.

Thus Haydn wrote to the publisher of this book on June 12, 1799,
when he sent in his *Creation:*[94]

Unfortunately my affairs multiply with my years, *and yet it is almost as if with the decrease in my spiritual powers, my desire and the urgency to work increase. O God, how much is still to be done in this splendid art, even by such a man as I have been!* The world to be sure compliments me many times a day, even on the fire of my last works: no one, however, will believe with what toil and exertion I have to search it out, while on many a day my weak memory and flagging nerves so wear me down that I sink into the dreariest state and am thus in no condition for many days afterwards to find even a single idea, until finally, encouraged by Providence, I can sit down again at the clavier and there begin to hammer away. *Then everything is all right again, God be praised!*

Yesterday I received another parcel of *musikalische Zeitungen*. Your publication of this work does you great credit, etc. I only hope and pray, *old man that I am*, that the Herr Critics will not pounce too severely on my *Creation*, and thus wrong it. They will of course stumble at several points of musical spelling, and perhaps also at others that I have been accustomed these many years to consider mere trifles. The true connoisseur, however, will also see my reason for many of them and step over such stumbling-blocks with good will. But all this *inter nos; otherwise it might be set down as arrogance and conceit on my part, and my heavenly Father has kept me from these my whole life long.*

The catalogue of Haydn works as given on pages 7 and 8 has also appeared in print elsewhere, and, originating as it does with Haydn himself, is to be taken as definitive both in number and in genuineness of the works attributed to Haydn. It does an injustice to this exceptionally productive genius, however, in that many a work really belonging to him is not mentioned in the catalogue, and this leads me to impart the following.

Being very modest and (in an earlier day) totally unaware of the effect his works were having in the world, Haydn had never thought to make such a catalogue or even to keep copies of all his own work.[95] When the publisher of this book began in 1799 to plan a complete edition of Haydn's works and corresponded on the subject with the honored man, it appeared that he did not definitely recall half of his own works and at the inquiry after them was deeply troubled by their great number. So in order to lighten his task, the publisher of this book had a catalogue drawn up of all the Haydn works already in his collection at that time. This catalogue provided with the theme of every single work was sent on to Father Haydn, who then checked off those he recognized as genuine, added the date of composition as nearly as he could recall, crossed out what was wrongly attributed to him, and added on the masses, baryton pieces, and Scotch songs not given therein. This revised catalogue is the one now given here and in other places. And it may be relied upon to contain nothing falsely labeled with Haydn's name; but it can also be relied upon to contain far from everything that is rightly his. And if, as is everywhere the case, this list causes astonishment at the prolific nature of that creative genius, then it would cause far more astonishment to see all that he gave the world assembled—something no longer possible, to be sure. Thus the publisher of this book, for instance, possesses a not inconsiderable number of Haydn's compositions of various sorts, in some cases excellent, that were only acquired after the compilation of that catalogue, and that on the basis of interior and exterior evidence are surely by Haydn. Let it be taken, then, as it must be, that Haydn was by nature creative, that in most categories in which he worked, he blazed a wholly new trail and first trod it with success; but that he so uniquely smoothed and extended those paths that others had discovered, that one really hardly knows how to exalt sufficiently the power, the effectiveness, and the merit of this remarkable man.

Biographische Nachrichten

von

Joseph Haydn.

Nach mündlichen Erzählungen

desselben

entworfen und herausgegeben

von

Albert Christoph Dies

Landschaftmahler.

Wien, 1810.
Camesinaische Buchhandlung.

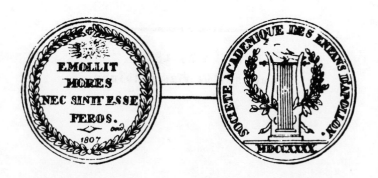

Biographical Accounts

of

JOSEPH HAYDN

ACCORDING TO HIS SPOKEN NARRATION

drawn up and edited by

Albert Christoph Dies

Landscape-painter

Vienna, 1810

CAMESINA BOOKSHOP

Sólo á tu númen, Háyden prodigioso,
Las Musas concedieron esta gracia
De ser tan nuevo siempre.

La Musica, Poema, por D. Tomas
de Yriarte [1]

Dedicated
to His Serene and Illustrious Highness,
the
reigning Prince
Nikolaus Esterházy von Galantha

Most serene Prince !
Gracious Sir !

hAYDN'S EXISTENCE in the world of art is the creation and sole property of His Serene Highness Prince Esterházy.[2] I venture to quote the words of the great composer himself:

"The friends of music often used to flatter me and to praise me unduly. Any distinction of praise that my name deserves dates from the very moment when the reigning Prince Nikolaus, among other instances of his magnanimity, made possible my greater freedom."

These words refer to that personage who with his own word created the most remarkable moment in Haydn's life, and to whom I most humbly make bold to dedicate this feeble sketch.

May Your Highness in his innate graciousness receive the same under his kind protection, and further permit me with deepest respect to name myself

Your Most Illustrious Highness'
most humbly obedient
A. C. Dies.

Introduction

I N   A   C O N V E R S A T I O N, one of my best friends, Herr Grassi,*
and I fell to talking of Joseph Haydn. My friend regretted that
this remarkable man would probably die without leaving any
materials for a biography. "So far," my friend continued, "he has
neither written any account himself nor been willing to permit a
scholar to write his life history. Although he takes pleasure in reminiscing among intimate friends and willingly tells his often comical
experiences, yet one must suppose that posterity will have to read
only hastily thrown together and perhaps inaccurate accounts of a
man who so deeply penetrated the secrets of harmony and who is
great and unique in his field."

"Don't you think," I asked my friend, "that Haydn might decide
to pass on to me the data for a future biography? Perhaps your long-
standing acquaintance with Haydn could prevail upon him to trust
my pen." "I doubt it; but I'll talk to Haydn about it and see what I
can do." It worked out that Grassi, having summoned all the arts of
persuasion during his visit, still was not going to achieve his purpose. Haydn stuck to his word that the story of his life could interest nobody. He paid no attention until he learned that I was an artist
who, courting more than one muse in an amateur way, had even
produced musical compositions myself.

---

* Anton Grassi, sculptor (brother of Joseph Grassi, court painter and professor at Dresden) and master pattern-maker at the Imperial Porcelain Works
in Vienna. He made a life-size and very faithful bust of Haydn, and died on
January 1, 1808. Herr Ihrwach [or Irrwoch] also struck a medal of uncommon
likeness.[3]

How many men might not have smiled at the word amateur, turning off the request with all manner of excuses! Haydn rather found in it sufficient reason to consent. "He must," said he, "be a man of feeling. His visit will be a pleasure for me."

In such a manner I became acquainted with Haydn, intending rather to collect some notes toward a biography than to produce myself a work of art that would satisfy all possible demands.

This account will justify to my readers the method that I have chosen. I present to them as many sections as Haydn permitted me visits and treat in each section the material which that visit yielded. My first visit decided me on this course; I would produce so faithful a representation that every contemporary of Haydn's might find again in the portrait, as if in a mirror, the characteristics of the original.

"But the mirror reflects ugliness with equal candor; we want no idealized picture! Everything must be perfectly natural!" I have written no idealization, so I have nothing to fear on this score from the enemies of the ideal. But I have written also no mere representation of nature that goes into the most insignificant details. Even the truest portrait has its eventual limits, and to attain these would truly require a great deal! Little as I hoped to achieve my purpose, I still strove to remain everywhere true to the predetermined goal, and carefully kept myself from immortalizing, like Denner's paintbrush, the wrinkles instead of the face.[4]

If I had made Haydn's acquaintance sooner, I would perhaps have been able to lay before my readers more abundant and better organized material. But in the years when weakness, hoarseness, and a failing memory tended to silence his tongue, I could only by repeated questioning and laborious probing bring about a sort of journal in which I entered events with strict fidelity.

I thought I should mention from my collection of biographical accounts only that which most concerns Haydn the man. I have permitted myself to say little about his musical genius. To judge this sort of thing properly, to follow his flights, to accompany him everywhere: this would require a knowledge often beyond my powers.

In order not to leave out of the picture the most interesting phase of Haydn's life, I meanwhile made unhesitating use of several articles from the *Leipzig Musikalische Zeitung*,[5] without entirely suppressing my own untutored opinions, but all with the sole intention of delivering for the critical and aesthetic evaluation of a worthy pen whatever materials I could gather. I have also considered that I have no right to present a characterization of Haydn modeled on my own whim. I have collected isolated vignettes. Let each reader assemble the whole according to his own abilities.

Vienna
April, 1810   Albert Christoph Dies

First Visit

April 15, 1805

GRASSI BROUGHT me to Haydn. I thought I did not displease him, for he came to meet me although he had been sick for a long time and both his legs were swollen. He gave me both hands, welcomed me with a cheerful countenance and with so keen a glance that I was quite taken by surprise. His lively look, ruddy-brown complexion, and extraordinarily neat clothing—Haydn was fully dressed—his powdered wig, his gloves and boots worn despite the swelling, banished all thought of illness and gave this old man of seventy-three the sound appearance of a man of fifty, of medium height, and still well-built. "You seem surprised to find me fully clothed," he said, "when I am still weak and sick, cannot go out, and breathe only indoor air. My parents taught me neatness and order in earliest youth, and these two things have become second nature to me." He also owed it to his parents that they had encouraged him in the fear of God and, of necessity because they were poor, in diligence and thrift. Plain virtues that you very seldom meet in our young geniuses. How often they hate order, even when the lack of it spells abortion for artistic production! They do not understand the importance of order and taste. According to Herder, "taste is nothing else than order in the service of genius."

The goodness of the Almighty frequently compensates for the lack of worldly goods through gifts of the spirit. He Who is everywhere was present in the little cottage in which Joseph Haydn first saw the light of day on March 30, 1732.[6] He it was Who presented him with a rare musical talent.

The father, an ordinary cartwright and justice of the peace [7] in Rohrau,* was married to a woman who had been in service as a cook with the gentry of the place. She was accustomed to neatness, industry, and order, which qualities she sternly required of her children from their tenderest years, thereby initially paving the way in the most expedient manner for further development of the talents of her six † boys, of whom our Joseph was the eldest.

In his youth the father journeyed about, following the custom of his trade, and reached Frankfurt am Main, where he learned to play the harp a little and, because he liked to sing, to accompany himself on the harp as well as he could. Afterwards, when he was married, he kept the habit of singing a little to amuse himself. All the children had to join in his concerts, to learn the songs, and to develop their singing voice. When his father sang, Joseph at the age of five used to accompany him as children will by playing with a stick on a piece of wood that his childish powers of imagination transformed into a violin.

Haydn still remembers those songs and innocent times with pleasure. His face lights up unusually when he tells about them. This time, in fact, he talked specifically that I might make use of it. "Young people," he said, "can see from my example that something

---

* The market town of Rohrau, from which the entire county takes its name, is not very important, and comprises only about 65 houses. Rohrau lies on the river Leitha on the Hungarian border north of Bruck, which small town would be some ¾ of a mile distant.[8]

The family of Count von Harrach, Bohemian in origin, bought the estate in ancient times and lives in the castle, which stands somewhat apart from the place and is almost entirely rebuilt. In 1732, Karl Anton Count von Harrach was imperial and royal chamberlain and privy councilor, chief master of the hunt for court and county, as well as royal master of the horse and holder of the fief of Rohrau. His consort Katharina (née the Countess von Bouquoy) was served by Haydn's mother as a cook.

† Three died in childhood.[9] Michael Haydn, Kapellmeister in Salzburg, is the author of many oratorios and of other church music, a field in which he is unique. Herr Neukomm is one of his pupils but finished his studies with Joseph Haydn. The second brother, Johann, was in the service of the Esterházy princes at Eisenstadt as a singer and died there on May 10, 1805, at the age of sixty-three.

still may come from nothing. What I am today, moreover, is the product of utmost poverty."

Doubtless we are to consider his father's love of singing as the first occasion when Haydn's spirit, already in earliest youth, entered its proper sphere. How easily the father could have set him to his own trade or dedicated him to the cloth, the heart's desire of both father and mother. This did not come about, thanks not a little to his concerts among the neighbors, by which he had won for himself a reputation in the whole town and even with the schoolmaster. And thus when the talk was of singing, all were unanimous in praise of the cartwright's son and could not commend enough his fine voice.

Since his father and the schoolmaster were close friends, it was natural for the latter to be drawn into consultation over Joseph's artistic destiny. The deliberations lasted a long time. The father still could not forget the priesthood. Finally, however, came the moment to decide. The various opinions converged. It was resolved that Joseph should stay with music and sooner or later, somewhere or other, perhaps as *Regens chori* [choirmaster] or even as Kapellmeister, earn an honorable living.

Joseph had passed the age of six when he had to leave his birthplace and travel to Hainburg,* a small town not far off. He was recommended to the care of the *Regens chori,* who undertook to guide the young boy on the virtuoso's course.

This good man, named Franck, was a distant cousin of Haydn. It was just then Rogation Week, a time of many processions. Franck was in great difficulty because of the death of his drummer. He cast his eyes upon Joseph, who would have to learn the kettledrums in a hurry and thus resolve the difficulty. He showed Joseph the elements of drumming and then left him alone. Joseph took a little basket of the sort country people use to bake bread, covered it with a cloth, set his invention on an upholstered armchair, and drummed away so enthusiastically that he never noticed what a dust was raised by

* The small town of Hainburg [Dies always writes Haymburg] lies on the Pressburg postroad between Deutsch-Altenburg and Wolfsthal on the banks of the Danube.

the meal in the basket, ruining the chair. He received a rebuke for
it, but his teacher was easily calmed when he observed with astonishment that Joseph was becoming a perfect drummer so quickly. The
circumstance, moreover, carried weight in the consideration of music
as his future career. Since Joseph was very short, he could not possibly in the procession reach as high as the former drum-bearer; so
they chose a little man who was unfortunately a hunchback and provoked the laughter of the onlookers.

"From that time on (Haydn's words) I have worn a wig. The first
one I got from my parents, a matter of neatness. But when I came
under the care of others, my few articles of clothing and one wig
were not enough. It pained me to note that uncleanliness was the
rule and, although I took great pride in my small person, I still could
not prevent occasional spots on my clothing about which I was sensitive and ashamed."

From his masters Joseph learned to know all the usual instruments
and to play several suitable to his age. His pleasant voice was a great
recommendation for him. He was praised for his studious diligence.
The parish priest knew him; this acquaintance soon proved important for Joseph, as I am about to tell.

The parish priest was a close friend of the imperial and royal
Court Kapellmeister Reutter [Dies always writes Reutern]; they
were intimates. It happened that Reutter traveled on business from
Vienna through Hainburg and stopped for a short time at the parish
priest's. On this occasion he spoke of the purpose of his journey,
namely, to find boys with good voices and ability to serve as choirboys. The priest immediately thought of Joseph and praised his
voice and his other musical abilities. Reutter wished to see the clever
boy and test his talents. Joseph was called in. He appeared. Reutter
asked him, "Well, boy,* do you know how to trill?" Joseph was under the impression that it was not permitted to know more than
other honest folk and answered the question accordingly: "Not even
the schoolmaster can do that."

"Look," said Reutter, "I will show you how to trill. Pay close at-

* [*Buberl*.] In what follows Reutter kept using this expression.

tention to the way I do it! Open your mouth only a little, hold your tongue still, no motion. Sing a note slowly and then, without stopping, the one next it; then again the first, and then the second; alternate the two notes always a little faster. Watch how I do it." Reutter then made a trill. Hardly had he finished when Joseph artlessly placed himself in front of him and after the second trial at most trilled so perfectly that Reutter shouted Bravo! in amazement, reached in his pocket, and gave the little virtuoso a coin [*Siebzehner*].

I was afraid the poor state of Haydn's health might prevent him from talking any longer. I bade him take care of himself, and my friend and I left him, since it was, moreover, almost time for his afternoon nap. They told me that for this nap, Haydn undressed completely, donned night clothes and dressing gown, and got into bed. He was strictly punctual in keeping, winter and summer, the time from half-past four to five o'clock, and thus slept no more than a half hour. The rest over, he dressed again fully, went downstairs with great difficulty, and proceeded to the housekeeper's room, where she brought some of the neighborhood children whose merry play gave Haydn pleasure and whose fun diverted him from his troubles. It must be a great blessing in advanced old age that the sense of failing bodily strength is lessened in most cases by a simultaneous failure of the memory and loss of the powers of imagination. This is the case with Haydn. He realizes himself that his spirit is weak. He cannot think, cannot feel, cannot write, cannot hear music! He would have died of boredom in this state if the memory of what he used to be were always present with him now, if his infirmity allowed him to compare the then to the now. The traces, however, are not all gone; they have only been long illegible except when through some accident the surface is lit up from behind. Then what is written in fire can be seen!—Haydn chances in his loneliness to open the drawers of a writing desk. The things inside call up the past for him. They are presents that high-born people made to their beloved Euterpe.—A rich and pleasurable variety, restoring to life the almost faded pictures. The spirit of living revives. Youthful strength floods the weakened body for a few minutes. In such moments Haydn seems to forget the words in the songs that he so inimitably set to music: *Und keiner nimmt des Irrthums wahr!* [10] At last the tension must break. With the letdown, joy gives way to depression. The oppressed heart seeks and finds release in an outburst of tears. The people who look after Haydn must take great care in trying with suitable measures to ward off such scenes, for if he once slips into depression, it is not then so easy to raise his spirits again.

Second Visit

April 24, 1805

I FOUND Haydn unusually weak. Only when I reminded him of the purpose of my visits did he recall what had passed before. He gave me his hand and made me sit beside him on the sofa.

"I am very weak today—old—haven't done anything—time hangs heavy!"

"Think," I answered, "of the truly renowned stretch of your life, and you can feel richly comforted."

The pictures I raised in Haydn's fancy by this dodge were too charming. They must have stimulated him sufficiently to increase the life-force. The process worked quickly. A friendly smile presaged a narrative based on the last thirteen—the most brilliant years of his life. Later I shall make use of this narrative; here it might intrude prematurely and upset the order.

I had to take advantage of Haydn's good will and his rekindled powers, so I bade him rest. Later I sought to tie together the threads of the narrative by the word *Siebzehner,* which my readers will recall from the first visit. Here is the burden of what followed.

After Kapellmeister Reutter had presented Joseph with the coin, he expressed a desire to speak to Joseph's father. The meeting was arranged as quickly as possible. Reutter gave the father the comforting promise that he would care for the boy's progress, but that he was still too young for this. He must wait till the end of his eighth year. Until then he must diligently sing the scales to cultivate a pure, firm, and flexible voice.

Joseph followed this advice. Since neither his schoolteacher nor anyone else in the little town was yet acquainted with the *do, re, mi,* and so on, of the Italian method, there was no one to instruct the eager boy. What does genius do in such a case? In these straits, it breaks forth and levels the most untrodden paths for itself. Joseph found out the most natural method, became his own teacher, and sang daily simply *c, d, e, f, g,* and so on,* observing all the rules of solfeggio without knowing it, and made such great strides that Reutter at the end of the appointed time was astonished.

Joseph had only his own self-instruction to thank when Reutter declared him ready for the job and took him without delay as a choirboy into the Choir School at St. Stephen's in Vienna.

My readers will perhaps be inclined to accord Reutter's behavior toward Joseph that praise which a patron of talent deserves. Only what follows can somewhat dim the fine light in which the man now appears. To be sure I had to guess at the circumstances, for Haydn spoke of his teacher with a care and caution that redound to his honor. All I could draw from him on this point was that the chapter of St. Stephen's paid the Kapellmeister for the board and tuition of each choirboy 700 gulden a year. The choirboys were six; he collected thus 4,200 florins.

As soon as Joseph in his newly achieved status had received as much instruction as he needed to fulfil the duties of choirboy, the

---

* I refuse to speak a word for the German method; there are important reasons why the Italian way of teaching is better. What is the use of having the pupil sing dry letters that do not occur in speech? At best the pupil learns to hit the notes, the letters, but not to articulate a single syllable. In words, not letters but syllables are heard. No song is spelled. In comic singing an extremely rapid articulation of syllables is called for. We wonder at the Italians for their fast articulation, and cannot imitate them for the simple reason that we did not in our youth practice articulating a fast string of syllables.

instruction came to an abrupt standstill, due perhaps to the very pressing affairs of the Kapellmeister.

Joseph was too young to understand that he would learn little from the abandoned instruction. If matters stood thus with his main occupation, can we not guess how little opportunity he was given to acquire either musical or other necessary knowledge?

Joseph's great bent for music would surely not have been lessened by grounding in a few languages on the side. He did learn a little Latin. Everything else went by the board, and one might venture to say that he lost ten of the youthful years best suited for study. Yet in this very neglect of his manifold capabilities and in their lack of direction at this time we may perhaps seek an explanation for the fact that musical genius utilized its full power to its own end, thereby growing into that gigantic stature we shall later remark in the man.

In the biographical sketch of Michael Haydn,[11] his intellectual development is placed in a good light. If one took literally everything said there on this point, one might be inclined to believe that Michael developed further than Joseph in everything except music. The latter had uncommon capabilities, but particularly a natural discernment that he began to make use of after his departure from the Choir School, but always in his own way; i.e., he easily and quickly acquainted himself with several branches of learning, never boasted of his accomplishments, and wholly avoided the wordy pomp of learned phrases, and so forth. That may be the reason why he suffered Mozart's fate in general and, like him, was taken for an empiricist. If this word is taken in its noblest sense, it is still not appropriate. Haydn and Mozart are extraordinary phenomena; it will always be difficult to express the worth of these extraordinary men in ordinary terms.

Meanwhile our Joseph was content with his place, but basically for this reason: Reutter was so captivated by the boy's talents that he declared to the father that even if he had twelve sons, he would take care of them all. The father saw himself freed of a great burden by this offer, consented to it, and some five years after dedicated Joseph's brother Michael and still later Johann to the musical

muse. Both were taken on as choirboys, and, to Joseph's unend-
ing joy, both brothers were turned over to him to be trained.[12]

Joseph was then already busy with composition in his spare time.
Reutter surprised him once just as he had spread out a *Salve regina*
in twelve parts on a yard-long sheet of paper. "Hey! what are you
up to there, boy?"—Reutter looked over the long paper, laughed
heartily at the copious sprinkling of *Salves,* still more at the boy's
preposterous notion that he could compose in twelve parts, and
added, "Aren't two voices enough for you, you little blockhead?"

Joseph knew how to profit from such lightly tossed off comments.
His compositions took on a less monstrous appearance, no small
gain for a genius who, left to himself and led astray by the passionate
powers of youth, could easily leap the confines of the straight and
narrow and beat about like an untamed stallion till he sank exhausted
to the ground. I speak here, to be sure, only of the youthful age from
ten to fifteen when no masterpieces are produced. But I am of the
opinion that the more creative talent a youngster shows, the more he
needs to learn that there is an intelligence that investigates the
mathematical principles on which art is based and that a structure
not erected according to these principles must soon fall to pieces.

Joseph had to content himself, until he was eighteen years old,
with the tossed-off comments of which the above serves as example. His spirit received no nourishment. What was a very sore point
with him, however, and at his age must have been agony, was the
fact that he seemed to be allowed on purpose to starve in body as
well as in mind. Joseph's stomach had to get used to an endless fast,
which for a time he sought to make up for at occasional musical affairs where the choirboys were paid with refreshments.

Joseph, once he had connected them with his stomach, developed
an incredible liking for these musical affairs. He concentrated on
singing as beautifully as possible so he would be known as a good
singer and—his secret motive—be in demand everywhere, thus finding opportunities to satisfy his nagging hunger. Who would have
thought that the old saying "Make a virtue of necessity" might apply
even to a genius? But what am I saying? Does not each day's ex-

perience show that the goddess of hunger seeks out genius everywhere and unbidden forces herself upon him as companion and teacher throughout youth, often through the whole of life?

Haydn had as a choirboy many funny adventures. Once, when the court was building the summer palace at Schönbrunn, Haydn had to sing there in the choir during Whitsuntide. Except when he had to be in the church, he used to play with the other boys, climbing the scaffolds around the construction and raising a regular row on the staging. What happened? The boys suddenly beheld a lady. It was the Empress Maria Theresa herself, who ordered somebody to get the noisy boys off the scaffolds and to threaten them with a thrashing if they dared to show up there again. The next day Haydn, driven by curiosity, climbed the scaffold alone, was caught, and sure enough collected the promised reward.[13]

Many years later, when Haydn was in the service of Prince Esterházy, the Empress came once to Esterháza. Haydn presented himself before her and thanked her most humbly for the reward he had received. He had to tell the whole story, which occasioned much laughter.

In nature there is no standing still. Haydn now had to find out that he was not destined to remain a choirboy forever. His pretty voice, with which he had so often sung for his supper, all of a sudden betrayed him. It broke, and wavered between two pitches.

The following anecdote Haydn told me at a later time, but it belongs in the period when his voice was breaking. At the ceremony undertaken every year at Klosterneuburg in honor of St. Leopold, the Empress Maria Theresa customarily appeared. The Empress had already let it be said in jest to Kapellmeister Reutter, "Joseph Haydn doesn't sing any more; he crows." So Reutter had to replace Joseph with another soprano for the ceremony. His choice fell upon Joseph's brother, Michael. The latter sang so beautifully that the Empress had him called before her and presented him with twenty-four ducats.

"Michael," Reutter asked him, "what are you going to do now

with all that money?" Michael thought a moment and said, "One of our father's animals just died, so I shall send him twelve ducats. You please keep the other twelve for me until my voice breaks, too." Reutter took the money, but he forgot to give it back again.

Since Haydn because of his cracked voice was unfit to be a choirboy any longer and thus had no further monetary value for Kapellmeister Reutter, the latter found it only fair to discharge him.

A piece of mischief on his own part hastened Haydn's dismissal. One of the other choirboys, contrary to the usual costume of a choirboy at that time, wore his long hair in a queue. Haydn out of sheer mischief cut it off for him! Reutter called him to account and sentenced him to a caning on the palm of the hand. The moment of punishment arrived. Haydn sought every means to escape it and ended up declaring that he would rather not be a choirboy any more and would leave immediately if he would not be punished. "That won't work!" Reutter retorted. "First you'll be caned, and then get out!" *

Reutter kept his word, and thus the cashiered choirboy, helpless, without money, outfitted with three miserable shirts and a worn-out coat, stepped into the great and unknown world. His parents were very upset. The tender-hearted mother especially showed her anxious cares with tears in her eyes. She implored her son that he might still give in to the wishes and prayers of his parents and dedicate himself to the priesthood! This wish that had lain slumbering for ten years awoke now undiminished. The parents left their son no peace. They thought they had to prevail, but Haydn remained unshakable in his purpose, and paid no heed. He had, to be sure, no grounds on which to oppose his parents' wishes. He thought he explained things clearly enough when he compressed the surge of genius, mysterious even to himself, into the few words, "I don't want

---

* Both Joseph and Michael Haydn appear to have stirred the anger of Kapellmeister Reutter rather often, and he never allowed them to go unpunished. When Michael was in Vienna in 1801, he once went by the Choir School in company with close friends. Here he stopped and, smiling, said, "In that dear house for many a year I collected a thrashing every week."

to be a priest." But how could this answer satisfy his parents? How were they to imagine the development of their son's talents, or the happy and celebrated future it would give rise to, when Haydn himself thought of no such thing, when he understood as little as his parents what genius is, knew nothing of the pride that usually masters the youthful genius, and was capable himself of no insight at all?

How little Haydn ventured to exploit his own knowledge my readers will recognize from the following account. When occasionally in company with his two musical brothers he visited their parents in Rohrau, they would have songfests just as they had ten or twelve years before. The father persisted in accompanying his old favorites on the harp. It was just like old times with one exception, that now the three sons often thought their father made mistakes and sought to correct him accordingly. Little arguments usually ensued wherein the father always cited someone who had taught him this or that song in his youth; and each time he stoutly declared, "There was a man who really knew." On the other hand the sons always cited Kapellmeister Reutter who "said so, and he ought to know." Neither party would give in, each reiterating his proof till the father, wrought-up, ended the dispute with the mighty pronouncement, "You're all asses!"

Joseph kept quiet not merely to honor his father but because he mistrusted his own knowledge. This torment of mistrust arose from Haydn's new situation. He saw himself sunk in poverty and found it hard to come by even the barest necessities. He naturally cast searching glances on other young musicians, compared their ostentatious dress with his own worn-out clothing, and was led to ask, "Why the great difference between them and me?" Such a youth, endowed with so great a musical nature and possessing besides so much natural intelligence, could not long hunt the answer to this question without coming on some clue. Pride was a stranger to him, nor had it ever yet allowed him to dream up imagined merits, so he stood in no danger of self-deception. Blinded neither by self-love, by pride, nor by prejudice, the truth-seeker happened on an important revelation: [14]

Perseverance in diligence brings to the wise their goal,
Where at last we must recognize ourselves.
Oh, lordly is the reward. Believe, we have learned much,
If we remark that we know nothing at all.

Haydn made this important discovery in a dark little attic five floors up under the eaves of the Michaelerhaus, in the Kohlmarkt.

The bitter loneliness of the place, the total lack of anything to bolster up an idle spirit, and his altogether miserable situation led him into meditation often so gloomy that he was obliged to take refuge in his worm-eaten old clavier or his violin to play away his cares. Once these thoughts grew so gloomy, or more probably hunger plagued him so strongly, that he determined against all inclination to enter the Servite Order just to have enough to eat. But this was only his first impulse and could never, with his disposition, become a reality.[15] Only melancholy minds, overcome by the coincidence of many outward events, can become the unhappy victims of their irritated feelings. Haydn's happy and naturally cheerful temperament always kept him from violent outbreaks of melancholy. If the rain of summer or the snow of winter drove through the chinks in his attic and he awoke soaked through or covered with snow, he found such things quite natural and made a cheerful joke of it all.

The following merry scenes belong pretty much to the time shortly before or after Haydn's departure from the Choir School. The telling will acquaint my readers still more with Haydn's cheerful youthful humor.

For some time after his departure Haydn did not know which way to turn. He had a thousand projects that he discarded almost at the beginning. If he now and then made a sudden resolve, the motive was hunger, which on one occasion determined him to make a journey to Mariazell. Haydn went at once upon his arrival there to the choirmaster, announced himself as a pupil from the Choir School, produced a few compositions he had brought along, and offered his services as a singer. The choirmaster did not believe him, turned him down, and, when Haydn persisted, sent him off with these words, "All kinds of riffraff show up here from Vienna pretending to be discharged choirboys till it turns out they can't hit a single right note."

In this way, then, nothing was to be accomplished. So Haydn went into the church next day, turned up in the choir among the singers, struck an acquaintance with one of them, looked through the music he had in his hand, and asked to keep it so he could sing it. The young man apologized, saying he did not dare to. Haydn made another attempt, pressed a piece of money into his hand, and kept standing near him until the music began and the young singer finally had to sing. Suddenly Haydn tore the part from his hands and sang so beautifully that the choirmaster was struck with wonder and apologized to Haydn when the music was over. The clergy sent to inquire who the good singer might be, and to invite him to dine. Haydn accepted the invitation with alacrity, stretched it out for a week, and—as he said—filled his stomach for some time to come.

Haydn once took a notion to invite a lot of musicians for a serenade at an appointed hour. The rendezvous was in the *Tiefer Graben*. There the musicians were to dispose themselves in front of some houses and in corners. There was even a drummer up on the high bridge.[16] Most of the players did not know why they were there, and each had received orders to play whatever he wanted. Hardly had this frightful concert begun when the astonished residents of the *Tiefer Graben* opened their windows and began to scold, to hiss and whistle at the accursed hell-music. Meanwhile the watchmen, or, as they were then called, the *Rumorknechte* [riot squad], had also come around. The players escaped just in time, except the drummer and a violinist who were both led away under arrest. Their freedom, however, was restored again after several days since they could not name the ringleader.

The well-known Ditters and Haydn were young friends. Once the two were roaming the streets at night and halted outside a common beer hall in which the musicians, half drunk and half asleep, happened to be fiddling miserably away at a Haydn minuet. The dance-hall pieces that Haydn of course used to compose at that time found much favor on account of their originality.

"Come on, let's go in!" said Haydn.

"In we go!" Ditters agreed.

Into the taproom they go. Haydn places himself next to the lead violin and asks, very offhand, "Whose minuet?" The latter answers, still drier if not indeed snapping him off, "Haydn's!" Haydn moves in front of him and says, feigning anger, "That's a stinking minuet!" [17] "Who says?" cried the fiddler, now angry himself, jumping out of his seat. The other players follow suit and are about to break their instruments over Haydn's head; and they would have if Ditters, a big fellow, had not shielded Haydn with his arm and shoved him to the door.

Today's visit was almost too long, for Haydn's poor health did not allow him to talk any more. He ended the conversation with the words, "I can't go on any longer now!" and so asked to be excused. I broke in, and even drew a smile from him as I said, "This time I leave you in the attic. There I shall find you again later."

Third Visit

May 5, 1805

MY VISIT today was fruitless; Haydn asked to be excused. The cold, stormy weather worked on his weakened nerves and made him cross.

"Come later," said the housekeeper, "when the weather is warm, between eleven and twelve o'clock. Then he is in best spirits and glad to talk. He is always depressed by cold, windy, rainy weather."

Fourth Visit

May 9, 1805

I REMINDED Haydn of the attic and asked him to tell me how he got away from it.

"I chanced," Haydn began, "to become acquainted with the celebrated Kapellmeister Porpora, who was a much sought-after teacher, but who, perhaps on account of age, sought a young helper and found such in me. Among Porpora's students was a young girl between seven and nine years old. The famous Metastasio was the benefactor of this girl and her mother, was educating her at his own expense, and gave her singing lessons with Porpora." [18]

At these lessons old Porpora made use of young Haydn, who undertook the task gladly, regardless of the distance, and now was so fortunate as to earn two gulden a month. While Porpora taught the girl singing, Haydn, who had to accompany on the piano, found an excellent opportunity to gain a perfect knowledge and practical use of the Italian method of singing and accompanying.

Porpora was a man of strictest discipline with Haydn, who for his part put up with everything and bore the pokes in the ribs or the epithet *Bestia! C[oglione]*! with submission. He even cleaned the shoes when he had to accompany Porpora to the country during the summer months. Haydn took it all well enough because he also learned a lot from the man.

Haydn's fortunes seemed now to take a turn for the better. He became acquainted with Metastasio, who gave him much useful advice, and in whose house he rapidly learned the Italian tongue. He also made about this time the acquaintance of an honest, middle-class family, engaged in the stocking business, who, without being well-to-do or even assured against all want themselves, nevertheless were so charitable as to assist Haydn according to their means. Haydn told the mother about the holes in the roof he slept under and joked about the snow on the bedclothes. But while he had only meant to laugh at his troubles, the good woman took a more serious view. She was moved to offer young Haydn her own room to sleep in in winter. Haydn agreed to the offer, with the secret hope that he would soon be in a position to pay back with thanks this great service.* Since the poor woman, however, was provided with only the most necessary furniture, the floor had to take the place of a bed, and thus Haydn found at least a warm place to lie down ready for him on any winter evening.[19]

Haydn was pleased to see the improvement in his situation. What lay closest to his heart, though, was to do something with the important discovery I mentioned above, and enable himself through a serious study of theory to bring order (which he loved above all, as we already know) into the outpourings of his soul. He decided to buy a good book. But what? That he could not tell, and he had reasons for not asking advice. Since he did not know how to choose, he left it almost to chance, planning first to leaf around in the book a little and size it up before uselessly spending perhaps the income of an entire month for it. Haydn ventured to walk into a bookstore and ask for a good textbook of theory. The bookseller named the writings of Carl Philipp Emanuel Bach as the newest and best.[20] Haydn wanted to look and see for himself. He began to read, understood, found what he was seeking, paid for the book, and took it away thoroughly pleased.

That Haydn sought to make Bach's principles his own, that he studied them untiringly, can already be noted in his youthful works of that period. Haydn wrote in his nineteenth year quartets that made him known to lovers of music as a profound genius, so quickly had he understood. As time went on, he procured Bach's later writings. In his opinion Bach's writings form the best, most basic and useful textbook ever published.

* Haydn's wish was soon realized. When the woman grew poor, Haydn assisted her, and settled on her a monthly pension, which, even after her death, her daughter enjoyed for some thirty years until her own death. Not Haydn, but his servant, gave me the particulars of this.

As soon as Haydn's musical output became known in print, Bach
noted with pleasure that he could count Haydn among his pupils.
Afterwards he paid the latter the flattering compliment that he was
the only one to understand his writings completely and to know how
to make use of them.

Haydn had left a lot to chance in the purchase of the work. Fortune was especially kind to him. It played into his hands the winning
ticket among so many blanks, but proceeding in this way is not to be
recommended and may in most cases cancel out the hoped-for advantage forever. Haydn's procedure, however, was not so altogether
blindly undertaken. He did not buy until he had inspected, and could
then trust to his own sound judgment for a correct decision. Still his
natural judgment could have led him astray if fortune had dealt him,
instead of Bach's, works like Kirnberger's, which must also have
pleased him and still would have been in a certain way bad for him.[21]
But far from finding fault with Kirnberger's writings in general, I
here set down Haydn's own opinion. He described them as a "basically strict piece of work, but too cautious, too confining, too ever-
lastingly many little restrictions for a free spirit." I agreed and
added, "Like tight clothes and shoes, in which a man can neither stir
nor move." "That's it exactly," was Haydn's answer.

The second textbook Haydn subsequently bought was Mattheson's
Der vollkommene Kapellmeister [1739]. He found the exercises in
this book nothing new for him, to be sure, but good. The worked-
out examples, however, were dry and tasteless. Haydn undertook for
practice the task of working out all the examples in this book. He
kept the whole skeleton, even the same number of notes, and invented new melodies to it. Haydn now added to his library the textbook of Fux. He found nothing in it that could enlarge the scope
of his knowledge; still the method, the approach, pleased him, and
he made use of it with his current pupils.[22]

My readers can easily imagine that our friend Haydn now had not
much spare time left. His hours passed with lessons to give and with
studying. Everything was tied up with music, and never another
book came into his hands during this time; only Metastasio's poems

were an exception. And even they cannot be called an exception, for Metastasio always wrote poems for music, made a sensation, and consequently was of necessity known to a Kapellmeister who intended at some time to try his own hand at an opera.[23]

It is quite natural that in a country bordering on Italy, the Italian opera flourished while no care was bestowed on the German tongue. North Germany wrote, to be sure, a purer tongue and possessed great poets, but how long a time went by before the South took note, acknowledged, and followed the example? It is thus not to be wondered at that Haydn was not quick to acquaint himself with the German poets and writers of the day. But that he possessed a sense and feeling for qualities of seriousness, greatness, beauty, wit, and simplicity in German poetry can be seen in the choice of German songs that he set to music in later years.

Haydn, when he was about twenty-one years old, set to music a comic opera in German. This first piece for the stage bore the title *Der krumme Teufel* [The Crooked Devil], and came about in an odd way. Kurz, a genius of the German theater, performing at that time at the old Kärnthnerthor Theater, was delighting the public in the role of Bernardon. He had heard a great deal spoken in praise of the young Haydn; this drew him to seek an introduction. A happy chance soon created an opportunity for him to satisfy his wish. Kurz had a beautiful wife who was kind enough to receive serenades from young musicians. Now young Haydn brought her a serenade, which Kurz took to honor himself as well as his wife. He sought a better acquaintance with Haydn. The two came together; Haydn must go home with Kurz. "You sit down at the piano [*Flügel*] and accompany the pantomime I will act out for you with some suitable music. Imagine now that Bernardon has fallen in the water and is trying to save himself by swimming." Then he calls his servant, throws himself flat on the stomach across a chair, makes the servant pull the chair to and fro around the room, and kicks his arms and legs like a swimmer, while Haydn expresses in six-eight time the play of the waves and swimming. Suddenly Bernardon springs up, embraces Haydn, and practically smothers him with kisses. "Haydn, you're the man for me! You must write me an opera!" So began *Der krumme Teufel*. Haydn received twenty-five ducats for it and counted himself rich indeed.

This opera was performed twice to great acclaim, and then was forbidden because of offensive remarks in the text.

Fifth Visit

May 11, 1805

SUCH A bright day as today encouraged me again to visit Haydn. By ten o'clock I was there, and learned that the Princess Esterházy had sent word she would visit Haydn in company with the Princess her daughter.

I was pleasantly surprised by this intelligence, and comforted with the century in which lofty, princely persons seek out Merit in its own abode and thus reveal that they know how, through a lofty nobility of spirit, to raise high birth still higher.

Haydn allowed me to use the short time.[24] The content of his narrative was the following.

My readers are already acquainted with Haydn's mode of living and daily affairs up to now. He gave music lessons and spent the remaining time in study of his own, and in the special concern of perfecting his knowledge of instruments. He developed under the guidance of a celebrated virtuoso,[25] whose name has escaped me, into a good violin player; for quite a while filled the post of organist in some outlying church or other; wrote quartets and other pieces that won him increasing favor with music lovers till he was known all over as a genius.

Finally the moment arrived in which Haydn's fortunes should improve. He was about twenty-seven years old when the goddess of Fortune once again took a fancy to raise up the deserving. The Bohemian Count von Morzin, a passionate lover of music, maintained a number of bachelor musicians. The position of chamber composer fell vacant, and this Haydn received in the year 1759 with a salary of six hundred florins. "My good mother," said Haydn, "who had always the tenderest concern for my welfare, was no longer living, but my father experienced the pleasure of seeing me a Kapellmeister." These chance words let me see deep into Haydn's heart and revealed it to me in a most lovable light.[26]

Haydn was now a Kapellmeister with a sure income and was content with his situation, except for the fact that he had to live unmarried. It was not to be expected of an ardent young man that he would heed that ban very long. His natural urge only grew all the stronger because of the ban, and Haydn could not withstand it any longer. Since he was living in the house of a wig-maker who had two daughters, and this man once jokingly said to him, "Haydn, you ought to marry my eldest daughter!" he married her (in spite of his inclination, for the younger was the real object of his love) just to have a wife at once.[27] Later, however, he must have deeply regretted the ill-considered step, as Haydn's words, "We became fond of each other, despite which I soon discovered that my wife was very flighty," * and his subsequent silence on that score leaves us to suppose.

I am no friend of what "they say" and will introduce no unauthenticated rumor into this account when I cannot discover the pure truth at the source. It seemed to me that Haydn held the tale of his domestic woes unworthy or too commonplace to find room in his biography. I therefore asked him nothing more and resolved to await further clarification from Haydn of his own free will.

A year went by without Count Morzin's knowing of the marriage of his Kapellmeister, but something else came up to alter Haydn's situation. The Count found himself obliged to reduce his heretofore great expenditures. He dismissed his musicians, and so Haydn lost his post as Kapellmeister.

* [*dass meine Frau viel Leichtsinn besass*] The word *Leichtsinn* is capable of various, even offensive meanings that are not all involved here. According to the most credible testimony, Madame H. was a domineering and jealous woman, injudicious, and deserving the name of spendthrift.

Meanwhile Haydn had the great recommendation of a public reputation; his amiable character was known; Count Morzin was moved to be useful on his behalf—three circumstances that combined so fortunately that Haydn soon after he ceased to be Kapellmeister to Count Morzin (in 1760) was taken on as Vicekapellmeister, under the direction of Kapellmeister Gregorious Werner,[28] in the service of Prince Anton Esterházy de Galantha at Eisenstadt, with a salary of four hundred florins.* The latter gave Haydn the four times of day [*Tagszeiten*] as a theme for a composition; he set these to music in the form of quartets, which are very little known.[29]

Haydn's latest good fortune was this time of short duration. Prince Anton died after a year [March 18, 1762], at the age of fifty-two, and Haydn was taken into the service of the succeeding Prince Nikolaus, brother of the deceased, at a starting salary of 400 florins. This was subsequently raised to 700, and later to 1,000 florins.

It would be very interesting to trace more accurately from the time Haydn entered the service of Prince Nikolaus Esterházy the circumstances attending each and every composition. But how could I manage this when age had weakened Haydn's memory and when he often forgot the most remarkable details, or purposely said nothing about them because he held them not worth mentioning? Haydn would have passed over in silence the following story, so often and so variously recounted. I reminded him of it and asked for an explanation.

Prince Nikolaus Esterházy spent the whole summer at Esterháza in a new palace that he was then building and that later became his favorite residence. His court had to attend him there. The palace, only partly built and furnished, was not yet roomy enough for such numbers; so a selection was made, and the musicians who had to accompany the Prince to Esterháza found themselves obliged to do without the companionship of their wives for six months. They were all spirited young men who looked longingly toward the last month, the day, the hour of departure, and filled the palace with

* Persons in princely service enjoy, besides salary, other benefits as well, such as free dwelling, firewood, and so on.

lovelorn sighs. "I was then young and gay and consequently no better than the rest," said Haydn with a smile.

Prince Nikolaus must long since have guessed the secret wishes of his musicians. The comic goings on must even have amused him. Otherwise how could he have taken it into his head this time to lengthen by two months the usual six months' residence?

This unexpected order threw the ardent young husbands into despair. They stormed Kapellmeister Haydn, they begged, they implored: he must, he should do something!

No one could sympathize with the desperate case of these married men more than Haydn, but this was not enough to find a good way out. How should he go about it? Should he present to the Prince a petition in the name of the orchestra? This would only invite laughter. He put to them a host of similar questions, but found a satisfactory answer to none.

An ordinary man in such cases plays a silly prank; a man of talent finds a way out. Haydn had recourse to his muse, and sketched a sextet of a new sort.*

On an evening soon after, Prince Nikolaus was surprised in the most wonderful way with this music. Right in the middle of the most passionate music, one voice ends; the player silently closes his part, takes his instrument, puts out the lights, and goes off. Soon after, a second voice ends; the player behaves the same as the first, and withdraws. Now a third ends; a fourth voice; all put out their lights and take their instruments away with them. The orchestra grows dark and increasingly deserted. The Prince and all the audience maintain a wondering silence. Finally the last man but one, Haydn himself, puts out his lights, takes his music, and withdraws. A single violinist is left.† Haydn had picked him to be last on purpose, because his solo playing pleased the Prince greatly, and he would be almost forced by the art of this player to wait for the end. The end came, the last lights were put out, and Tomasini also went off.—The

---

* This sextet in *F♯ minor* is also known as a symphony .

† Luigi Tomasini, later concertmaster, whose two sons, likewise musicians, are now in princely service. Luigi died some time ago [April 25, 1808].

Prince now stood up and said, "If they all go off, we must go too."

The musicians had meanwhile collected in the antechamber, where the Prince found them and smiling said, "I understand, Haydn; tomorrow the men may all leave," whereupon he gave the necessary orders to have the princely horses and carriages ready for the journey.*

The truth of the tales of the ancients concerning the wondrous workings of music upon the emotions has often been doubted, but I do not understand the basis of this doubt. The instrumental music of the ancients always served as accompaniment to singing or to mimic dancing. One would have to cast doubts, as well, therefore, on the powerful workings of song and of dance, and so on, which, after all, experience still bears out every day.

Had Haydn undertaken without singing, without dancing, without acting, solely through the power of melody and harmony to work on the Prince's feelings, to make himself understood, and to accomplish his purpose, it seems to me he would have undertaken an impossibility. Granted that instrumental music stirs the emotions. What language then can boast of having found words for those emotions? Music without the addition of words, of dancing, or of acting is a riddle to the intellect, capable of an infinity of meanings. Thus Haydn wisely had recourse to acting. The putting out of the lights, the going away, and the like, were actions that spoke to assist the music and earn it the nickname Farewell Symphony.

Haydn wrote at a much later time the celebrated oratorio *The Seven Last Words of the Saviour on the Cross.* I doubt that a more expressive utterance were possible. Our whole nature by the power of melody and harmony is attuned to the loftiest sentiments, to the tenderest sorrow. And yet the mind would not comprehend the source of those feelings. It would wander around amongst an infinity of meanings, not grasping the true one, were not each Adagio superscribed with the key words. We should, for example, take the modu-

* My readers will find an entirely different version of this incident in the *Musikalische Zeitung* for October 1799, page 14, an example of the changes such incidents must undergo when repeated from mouth to mouth.[30]

lation from minor into major for a usual phenomenon of the century and at most believe that it was intended to indicate a transition from a sad into a happy state of mind. But that is much too indefinite. Haydn wanted in the oratorio to express such a state of mind as rises above earthly imperfection to heavenly bliss. The words *Hodie mihi,* and so on, are the theme.[31] What a great uplift is thereby given to the above-mentioned shift from minor into major that he makes use of toward the end of the Adagio! He lifts us suddenly from the vale of tears into the Elysian fields. Enchanting and solemn melodies melt the heart. We experience bliss no language may tell. We know what we hear. The words say it clearly. They steer perception on the right road.

Sixth Visit

May 17, 1805

HAYDN HAD received the sad news of the death of his brother Johann in Eisenstadt and was most grievously concerned.[32] My readers will be pleased to learn that Princess Esterházy and the Princess her daughter, whom I mentioned in connection with the previous visit, wished to give Haydn the news of the death themselves. With delicate care, they feared, and rightly, that such a message of sorrow from any other lips might easily shatter the frail old man, so together, by their own bearing of the news, they took away the bitterness of it, and by their humane behavior perhaps lengthened the days of the venerable Haydn.

Chance led today's talk again to the *Seven Words of the Saviour on the Cross.* Although I have spoken prematurely of this great work of art, a strict account of how it came to be was still of the greatest importance to me. So I will impart the story to my readers without troubling myself about the exact year in which the oratorio first saw the light.[33]

Haydn received a letter in Latin from a canon of the cathedral church of Cadiz in Spain. They wanted from Haydn a solemn oratorio for Good Friday. The ceremony with which the oratorio was to be given was described in great detail, and Haydn was asked to take it into account. They had deliberated over the text a long time and finally believed no more fitting words could be found than the last words of the Redeemer on the Cross. First of all Haydn should lead the way with an Introduction to announce the ceremony. Then a canon would mount into a pulpit specially erected in the cathedral, speak with loftly expression the *Pater dimitte illis,* and so on,[34] and interpret the words in a talk (lasting at most ten minutes), then step down from the pulpit and devote himself to kneeling before the life-size image of the Crucified, specially erected on the cross. Now would come the first Adagio, which (like all the others) should last at most ten minutes. The canon would rise when the music ended, mount into the pulpit again, and discourse briefly as before. So words and music would alternate throughout the oratorio. The end would come with the musical representation of the earthquake following the crucifixion.—The entire church, even altars and windows, all would be draped with black. A single large lamp in the center would light the mourning place. The oratorio would begin at the stroke of the noonday bells. The church, once it could seat no more hearers, would be closed before the beginning of the ceremony.

It was to be expected that an oratorio taking its words and its lofty material from religion, suitably supported by the power of harmony, would work powerfully on the hearers; all the more since several arts were in a friendly way united and might secretly help to enhance the effect.

The entire outlined plan does great credit to its Spanish author. He must have had the sensitivity of a great poet to know that short, expressively spoken words would move the heart; moreover, so that the words might be clearly understood, he did not have them sung, but spoken, and even clarified in a short talk. Thus the music might readily move hearts already worked upon into a state of utmost melancholy and keep them there. The dark, poorly lit church offered the eye no distracting object.—Christ on the cross was the single visible object on which it must fix.—The outward pomp that otherwise always accompanies the Catholic church service has disappeared entirely. The hearer will be taken unawares by a truly awful simplicity, and his sense of the religious will be engaged.

This oratorio is presented every year on Good Friday in the cathedral at Cadiz under the circumstances just described. The German spirit of enterprise soon gave the work the form of a pianoforte arrangement and of quartets. A text was even fitted to the music. Whether it has thereby gained or lost, I will not venture to decide. But this much is clear, that as soon as the above-mentioned circumstances are foregone, and the music robbed of an important part of its existence, it can no longer make the great effect that it has on its hearers in Cadiz.

Just as that still, solemn church setting in conjunction with the music makes a whole, so, if the two are separated from each other, the music alone remains a possibly incomprehensible fragment. Haydn saw very well that in Germany the music might appear alone as a fragment and, as such, most probably would be boring, as might well be the case with slow movements only, following one after the other. He therefore added a text and undertook other suitable alterations, but, as I have said, I do not venture to decide whether the music works better alone or with the text.

Later Addition

Several reviews that have been published concerning the *Seven Words* prove that the writers have not been able to take the only standpoint from which the work must be viewed if it is to have the afore-mentioned effect.

Nothing may be lacking in the circumstances described, not even religiousness, and yet the critics take not the least account of all this. They even commonly make the error of supposing that Haydn was trying to solve the problem of expressing clearly in instrumental music, without words, the meaning of the words.

My readers have seen above that it is just the other way round. It was not expected that Haydn should go beyond the limits of musical art. The idea was to stir the listener's feelings. It was up to the spoken words to guide those feelings in the right direction.

The critics, however, may easily be led to false opinions by the simple clavier edition or by the quartet arrangement. These editions appeared without a word of further explanation, a sufficient excuse for the candid critic. Now that the whole story of the origin of this work is told in a short preface to the newest edition with words, this excuse ceases to be valid.[35]

This introduction was surely not known to Herr G. Nägeli when he mentioned this work of Haydn's in passing (*Musikalische Zeitung,* Vol. 5, No. 14) and called it—the original instrumental composition, that is—an unfortunate experiment.[36] I grant that I might likewise have thought this if I were less informed as to the meaning of the work. And by the repeated examples of so many composers who purposely choose their material outside the province of music, in order to surprise by novelty, I might have been led to believe that such was the case with Haydn.

Haydn was not always the editor of his own compositions. Much of his output, even the earliest pieces, suffered the fate of metamorphosis at the hands of speculators into all sorts of shapes. Even today Haydn is at odds with someone unnamed who came by several works from Haydn's early period without ever restoring them to the true owner. These works, for the baryton, were among the favorite pieces of the late Prince Nikolaus Esterházy.

The name of that wholly forgotten instrument, the baryton,[37] gave me an opportunity to lead today's talk back to the time where Haydn ended his story at my previous visit.

The so-called Farewell Symphony had increased Prince Nikolaus's affection for Haydn. The Prince loved music, and himself played the baryton, which in his opinion should be limited to only one key. Haydn could not be sure about this, because he had only a very superficial knowledge of the instrument. Still, he believed it must lend itself to several keys. While Haydn, unbeknown to the Prince, was conducting an investigation into the nature of the instrument, he acquired a liking for it and practiced it, late at night because he had no other time, with a view toward becoming a good player. To be sure he was often interrupted in his nocturnal studies by the scolding and quarreling of his wife, but he did not lose patience and in six months attained his goal.

The Prince still knew nothing. Haydn could resist a touch of vanity no longer. He played openly in the presence of the Prince, in several keys, expecting to earn no end of applause. The Prince, however, was not at all surprised, took the thing as a matter of course, and said merely, "You're supposed to know these things, Haydn!"

"I understood the Prince perfectly," Haydn told me, "and although at first I was hurt by his indifference, still I owe it to his curt reminder that I suddenly gave up the intention of being a good barytonist. I remembered that I had already gained some note as a Kapellmeister and not as a practicing virtuoso, reproached myself for half a year's neglect of composition, and returned to it with zeal renewed."

The Prince soon after assigned Haydn's talent a worthier occupation. He had to write an Italian opera for the Prince's theater in the castle at Eisenstadt. *Acide e Galatea,* an opera for four singers, presented on the occasion of the marriage of Count Anton Esterházy de Galantha to the Countess Theresia Erdödy on January 11, 1763, received general applause. The word was quickly spread abroad and awakened sleeping Envy. That this monster awoke, the following will show. The operas *Acide e Galatea, Lo Speziale,* 1768, *Le Pescatrici,* 1770, *Philemon und Baucis,* a marionette opera, 1773 (favorite of the Empress M. Theresa), *Il Mondo della Luna,* 1777, and several other marionette operas (all produced at Esterháza) were so generally talked about with approval that the court at Vienna desired an opera by Haydn for the Court Theater. He undertook the work with pleasure and set to music *La vera Costanza, Dramma giocoso* [1776].[38]

The opera was completed. As a matter of course Haydn had weighed the capabilities, likewise the vocal range, of each singer and arranged the voice parts accordingly, so they would be suitable. How great then was his astonishment to see his distribution of the parts overruled and to be informed that he had no right to assign parts according to his own opinion. They wished now to impose upon him another distribution. Haydn replied, "I know what and for whom I wrote," would not be imposed upon, and took his case to the Monarch. Emperor Joseph understood Haydn's rights, sought to mediate, but found unbelievable opposition so that Haydn declared that he would sooner not have the opera produced than struggle any longer against the cabal. Haydn concluded today's account with the words, "I did not give the opera. I packed up, went home to my Prince, and told him the whole story. The Prince did not condemn my course of action but had the opera given at Esterháza in 1779. The great Emperor Joseph was in the audience." [39]

Seventh Visit

May 23, 1805

THE THREATENING rainy weather today got on Haydn's nerves. During the night his rheumatism had bothered him, and he had slept little. This made him all the weaker. He begged me to spare him today as much as possible. I asked leave to pick up the story where it had ended the last time, but in vain! Haydn would not be cheered. His memory busied itself only to recall long-forgotten unpleasantness and thus to nourish his bad temper.

I heard in this way an interesting incident, and only regret that I may make no use of it because Haydn did not give his permission. I will not, however, suppress the observation that the noblest actions take place in secret, and lose much, nay, cease to be noble, if their author's vainglory spreads them about intentionally.

Here it is a question of a truly noble action that probably will remain a secret so long as it remains improbable that several persons still living will come forward to indict themselves and confess: we wronged Haydn in the worst way, and he knew no revenge but beneficence.[40]

I sought to change the direction of the conversation. "Have you ever made a system, or rules," I asked, "with the help of which you could extort the certain approval of the public?" Haydn was silent, so I went on. "You know," I said, "that our philosophers analyze everything and are not long satisfied with 'this pleases' until they have found the reason *why this pleases?* Once they have discovered the reason, they then know the component parts of the beautiful and can govern the latter by rules which anyone who means to produce something that will please must observe as strictly as possible."

Haydn answered, "In the heat of composition I never thought about that. I wrote what seemed to me good and corrected it afterwards according to the rules of harmony. Other devices I have never made use of. Several times I took the liberty not of offending the ear, of course, but of breaking the usual textbook rules, and wrote beneath these places the words *con licenza.* Some cried out, 'A mistake!' and tried to prove it by citing Fux. I asked my critics whether they could prove by ear that it was a mistake? They had to answer No."

"My own ear," Haydn went on, "hears no mistake in those places; on the contrary, I seem to hear something beautiful, so I begged leave to sin against the rules."

Haydn's *con licenza* earned him the plaudits of all music connoisseurs abroad while many a home composer smiled at the liberties taken. I used to hear Frenchmen and Englishmen speak of it with the wonder that only the sight of a work of genius will produce. Haydn seems to have thought of Horace's lines:

> *Fingere . . . non exaudita . . .*
> *Continget, dabiturque licentia sumpta pudenter* *

Indeed, he could ask with Horace:

> * A new-discover'd theme
> For those, unheard in ancient times, may claim
> A just and ample licence, which, if us'd
> With fair discretion, never is refus'd.
> [tr. Philip Francis]

Ego, cur acquirere pauca
Si possum, invideor? *

And the following words of Schiller (*On Naïve and Sentimental Poetry*) are the best commentary on Haydn's *con licenza:* "If the academic, always fearful of error, hangs his words like his ideas on the cross of grammar and logic, is hard and stiff lest he be vague, uses many words to say not much, and sooner than mislead the careless robs his thought of power and sharpness, then the genius gives to his with a single happy brush-stroke an outline forever fast and clear and yet wholly free."

Eighth Visit

May 28, 1805 [42]

OUR FRIEND was in a better humor today and told the following comic incident with surprising liveliness. Haydn's customary winter abode was at Eisenstadt. He had been about fourteen or fifteen years in princely service when, as sometimes happened, he had to journey on business to Vienna. It was winter and Haydn had thrown on, over a rather worn suit of clothes, a fur coat whose age was plain to be seen. This outfit, good enough for the journey, was fittingly completed by an unkempt wig and an old hat. So great a friend of neatness as Haydn on this occasion was scarcely to be recognized; it was as though he were masked. Clothed thus he entered Vienna by the Kärnthnerthor. In the Kärnthnerstrasse he heard music in the residence of a count, one of his own symphonies in fact. The orchestra was well-provided with good players. Suddenly Haydn called out, "Stop! Driver, stop!" The driver stopped. Haydn sprang out of the carriage, dashed into the house, rushed up the steps, opened an antechamber on the second floor where just then there was no serv-

* . . . Why am I now envy'd so,
If I can give some small encrease? . . .
[tr. Ben Jonson] [41]

ant, and hearing the music in the next room, laid his ear to the door in order to listen in peace. Without Haydn's noticing, a servant came then by a side door into the room, paused to reflect behind Haydn, measured him with a searching glance from head to foot, and finally thundered out the words: "What is the man doing there?"

"I only wanted to listen a little."

"This is no place for listening; let the man be on his way."

Haydn pretended he did not hear the servant's rudeness,[43] stuck to his place, and noticed that the servant watched him attentively—as if he had perhaps come to steal—but finally proved so uncivil as to seize Haydn by the fur coat and say to him, "The man has heard enough. I tell the man to clear out now or he'll be shown the door."

This was so clearly spoken that Haydn had to understand. To avoid being longer exposed to the servant's rudeness, he felt in his pocket and gave him a couple of coins. This was a different matter; Haydn received permission to hear the first Allegro to the end.

The end came. "Now the man must really go away, I truly can't allow him to listen any longer." Haydn intended to purchase permission to listen to the Adagio with the persuasive power of more coins when, luckily for him, the door opened and a musician noticed him. In a moment the whole concert room was talking. Haydn's name was on everybody's lips. They tore open the door. Twenty persons and more streamed out, surrounded Haydn, pulled him forcibly into the room, and closed in a tight circle around him, some to greet him as an acquaintance, others who did not know him or had never even heard of him, to make his acquaintance.

Into the midst of this chatter a voice penetrated as if from above: "That's not Haydn—it can't possibly be! Haydn must be a fine, big, handsome man and not the insignificant little man you've got there in the middle."

Everybody laughed.

They all looked up, and Haydn, more astonished than anybody, looked around to see who wanted to contest his very existence. There was in the group an Italian priest who had been in Vienna a short time, had heard much about Haydn and loved his music. When this man understood that Haydn was in the room and he had come too late to push himself into the circle, he had the idea of climbing on a table in order to see. The picture of Haydn that he had imagined beforehand did not match the reality, and now egotism and prejudice led him sooner to charge nature with an error than to recognize that he had deceived himself. This man seems to have belonged to the numerous class of people who are accustomed to mistake the clothes for the man. The earnestness with which he showed his doubt about Haydn's person, as I said before, made everybody laugh. This lasted until the Adagio of the symphony put them into another frame of mind and banished the urge to laugh. Haydn stayed till the end of the symphony and then took leave of the company.

Once when a *Landtag* was held at Pressburg, Prince Nikolaus took his whole orchestra along. There were parties with the Empress Maria Theresa present.

At one such party Haydn conducted a concert (with the violin as usual) in which four amateurs of gentle birth played. The Empress jokingly said that it would be fun to see what would become of the music if the professionals suddenly left the dilettantes in the lurch.

Haydn had keen hearing, intercepted in mid-air the words of the Empress, and immediately arranged with Tomasini (who is already known to my readers [see p. 101]) that he should, as soon as he saw Haydn going off, break the E-string of his violin and not worry himself about the consequences.

The symphony began. At the point of greatest complication Haydn, unnoticed, broke his own E-string. Unfortunately, however, the amateur playing next him immediately offered him his own violin. Haydn found a suitable pretext for not taking the violin by holding a handkerchief to his nose, saying, "Nosebleed!" and going off. Then Tomasini snapped his E-string and played his role well. The symphony began to go as if on stilts, staggered, stumbled, and after a few measures fell to earth.

Thus quickly did Haydn's wit bring to reality the wish of the Empress and provide the whole assembly with a good laugh.

Ninth Visit

June 1, 1805

ALTHOUGH IT promised fine weather, Haydn had nevertheless had
a very restless night and felt in advance the stormy weather to come.
Weakness kept him from talking much, so I thought it better to
spare him my visit this time and went into the little garden behind
Haydn's house. From there I looked over the back of the tidy dwelling and decided to inform myself on this matter in order to be able
to acquaint my readers in the future with house and garden.

Tenth Visit

June 10, 1805

I HAD never seen Haydn so lively as I found him today. The conversation lasted longer than ever before, but I can for the most part
insert the material later in the course of the story.—Haydn did tell
me one anecdote that I think deserves to find a place here.

I have already said that Haydn, while he served Prince Nikolaus,
often had to travel from Eisenstadt to Vienna and to stay on there
for several weeks. Because he did not travel in company with his
wife, he had a servant [Johann Elssler] possessed of sufficient skill to
see to breakfast and other things of this sort that comfort demands.
This man loved his master beyond words. He had observed him
thoroughly and anticipated his every wish. To be sure the observations were of a thoroughly singular sort and for the most part naïve.

Haydn was in Vienna on this occasion and as usual kept every
morning a period for work behind closed doors. The servant meantime sat guard in the anteroom, going on tiptoes to anyone who

came, gesturing not to make any noise, and then saying very softly, "Sh! Sh! the master is studying."

Three strangers who wished to make Haydn's acquaintance were received by the servant in the above manner and had to put up with waiting for the end of the work period. They remonstrated several times, to be sure, and supposed that an occasional exception to the rule might be made, but the servant would not be persuaded. He more than once laid his ear to the closed door with a significant look, and put off the strangers from one quarter-hour to the next. Finally he said with a kind of certainty, "It will surely be soon now, the master has worked down to the bottom." The servant had remarked that Haydn at the end of his fantasies liked to run down to the bass and ended there.—The strangers were now let in. They told Haydn of the preceding scene, and the naïveté of the servant enlivened the interview with frequent loud bursts of laughter.

This same servant, when he had to fumigate Haydn's room and believed himself alone, used to stand with the censer before Haydn's picture and cense him by way of expressing his veneration. (He was seen at it.) As insignificant as this incident may be, it still serves to acquaint us with the philanthropic nature of Haydn's character, caught here, as it were, in the act. Dissimulation often plays an assumed role in company, and by this hypocrisy it earns the name of amiability, while it appears unmasked to its servants at home and is detested by them. Haydn's philanthropic bearing toward high and low is natural. Only jealous artists dare secretly smile at him, beloved by every one.

I am all the more willing to make room in the narrative for the following incidents because they enlarge upon the relationship between Prince Nikolaus and Haydn.

Haydn owned in Eisenstadt a little house that twice fell prey to flames. The generous Prince Nikolaus both times hurried thither, found Haydn in tears, comforted him, had the house rebuilt, and provided the necessary furnishings. Haydn, deeply moved by the

Prince's generosity, could repay him only with love, attachment, and with the offspring of his muse. Touched to the heart, he wished to prove his gratitude. He swore to the Prince to serve him till death should resolve the life of the one or the other, and never to leave him though he be offered millions. [See p. 220 note.]

This last addition might seem superfluous, but it was not, for Haydn was practically besieged on all sides by his friends. No words of persuasion were spared in placing before his eyes the most glittering prospects in England, France, and Russia. Haydn entered into no inquiries, was satisfied with his fortune, and, being grateful, remained true to his intention.

The Prince knew how to treasure Haydn's worth. At every opportunity he overwhelmed him with proofs of his liberality. Haydn was even permitted in the most pressing straits to borrow against the Prince's credit; straits he sometimes entered perforce, because, as we know, his wife loved to spend. Haydn, however, had recourse to this remedy as seldom as possible; or, if the need were too pressing, acquiesced in small sums in order not to abuse the goodness of his Prince.

I have until now kept secret from my readers the words Haydn uttered at my first visit: his need had continued up to his sixtieth year.

I confess that the expression seemed to me at that time a riddle that could not be solved until the persons appearing in this work should be known by their deeds. We know by this time the magnanimous generosity of Prince Nikolaus. We know Haydn as a man who at all times loved order, was never a spendthrift, and with all the marks of his generosity, had nothing more to show than the above-mentioned house and 500 gulden in cash.[44] Is one not forced to the conclusion that Haydn's wife was a spendthrift person who must be held basically responsible for Haydn's pressing need?

I refrain from all further comments on this subject. That which I have said, I had to say because Haydn's words otherwise might easily be misconstrued.

We have already seen by several examples how much Prince
Nikolaus treasured and loved his Haydn. Thus as Haydn's fame
spread ever more abroad, the Prince valued his man all the more. He
was proud of his possession, and rejoiced with Haydn when the
Philharmonic Academy of Modena in 1780 gave proof of its esteem
for Haydn's merits by receiving him into membership, surprising
him with its diploma. Several years later Haydn set to music for this
Academy a four-voice cantata by Metastasio, which bore the title
L'Isola disabitata and was presented at the Academy in 1785.[45] I will
make mention here of several musical products that flowed from
Haydn's pen during the lifetime of Prince Nikolaus:

Hexenschabbas, a marionette show, presented at Esterháza, 1773
L'Infedeltà delusa, a burletta, presented before the Empress Maria
     Theresa at Esterháza in September, 1773
Genofevens 4ter Theil, a marionette operetta, at Esterháza in the sum-
     mer of 1777
Dido, a parody marionette operetta, at Esterháza, 1778
La Fedelta premiata, Drama giocoso, at Esterháza, 1780
Armidà, Dramma eroico, at Esterháza, 1784
Il Ritorno di Tobia, Azione sacra, for the licenced theater in Vienna,
     1784.[46]

Lovers of music know that it is not usual to designate symphonies
and quartets by the year of composition, so nothing can be certainly
said on this score. The following letter from Prince Henry of Prussia
to Haydn, however, fixes the date at which these six quartets appeared:[47]

I thank you, Sir, for the quartets you sent me, which give me great
pleasure. Please accept the accompanying trifle as a mark of my especial satisfaction. I remain, moreover, with regard
                                        most cordially yours,
Berlin, February 4, 1784   HEINRICH

This letter was accompanied by a gift, a gold medal with the likeness
of Prince Henry.
     I append here likewise a letter of His Majesty the late King of
Prussia, in order to bring together as much as possible those matters

that belong in the time of Prince Nikolaus:

To His Majesty of Prussia the repeated attention that Herr Kapell-meister Haydn has wished to pay to His Highness by the sending of six new quartets is an especial pleasure,[48] and it is a fact beyond doubt that His Highness has ever known how to treasure and always will treasure the work of Herr Kapellmeister Haydn. That the latter may the more effectively be shown this, we send him the accompanying ring as a sign of our royal satisfaction, being always graciously disposed toward him as well.

Potsdam, April 21, 1787   F. WILHELM

Eleventh Visit

November 21, 1805

THE LONG interval separating the previous visit from today's was occasioned by an illness that befell me. Haydn suffered a similar fate. Illness twice sent him to bed, but the last attack was of a beneficent sort. The accumulated morbidity was fortunately diminished, per-haps entirely cleared away, as may be supposed from his subsequent well-being. Even the swelling of his legs, the visible proof of illness and weakness, disappeared. This circumstance had no little to do with Haydn's being in a happy frame of mind and even, as far as age allows, becoming active again. The following circumstance stirred Haydn to test whether he could still exploit his strength a little. Chance brought to his hands a short time ago one of his youthful compositions that he had forgotten all about. This work is a four-voice short mass with two obbligato sopranos. The recovery of this child, lost fifty-two years before, gave the parent great joy. He ex-amined it attentively, conducted an investigation, perceived it was not unworthy of him, and determined to dress it in modern clothes.

"What specially pleases me in this little work," said Haydn, "is the melody, and a certain youthful fire, and this stirs me to write down several measures a day in order to provide the voices with a wind-instrument accompaniment."[49]

We know that Haydn passed his whole life hitherto in ceaseless activity. He made good use of every minute. How painful then he must have found the loss of time since advanced age and its usual concomitants forced him to inactivity. And how pleasant on the contrary to feel of late his powers reviving within him. He informed me of this fortunate alteration with eyes sparkling happily, hoped to be so fortunate as soon to end the aforesaid mass, and had on that account already written to Breitkopf and Härtel (publisher in Leipzig) to bespeak them for its publication.

Today's visit was lengthened by the events of recent days (entrance of the French troops into Vienna) which provided rich material for conversation. To be sure it dealt neither with the political situation nor with the presence of the French troops; rather the mention of wartime recalled to Haydn a visit that he had received from two musicians of the French Imperial troops.[50]

I now led the talk back to the purposes of this work and urged Haydn to continue the account of his life.

I have already repeatedly spoken of the kind and magnanimous behavior of Prince Nikolaus toward Haydn, who, as often as he spoke that name, poured out with his words the thankfulness of a heart brimming over, although the beneficent Prince had long since passed on to eternity. His departure occurred in 1790; Haydn had served this Prince for thirty years.[51] His diligence was noticed in the will, and a peaceful old age was provided him by the assurance of a lifelong pension of 1,000 gulden yearly.

Prince Anton, son of the deceased, followed him in the succession. This Prince thought proper to reduce the customary expenditures of the previous régime. Since he did not particularly love music, the orchestra was disbanded, and the musicians were discharged. Haydn and the aforementioned Tomasini, however, received an additional allowance; the former had 400 gulden for life and was to keep the title of Kapellmeister to Prince Esterházy. The Prince required no services of him.

The discharged musicians sought and easily found further prosperity; it was a big recommendation for them to have perfected themselves under Haydn's direction. Haydn himself was approached on behalf of Count Grassalkovics about entering his service as Kapellmeister. On this occasion, however, he showed his attachment to his Prince and turned the proposal down, and an unusual occurrence provided him the occasion to prevail upon Prince Anton to reverse his decision and to take into service anew the whole wind section of the dismissed orchestra.

Haydn now found himself in a comfortable and carefree situation. He could dedicate himself entirely to his art and busied himself with plans for making the best use of the future. While he was thus occupied a strange man one day walked unexpectedly into his room and said bluntly, "I am Salomon from London and have come to fetch you. Tomorrow we shall conclude an agreement."

This Salomon was a German, born in Cologne on the Rhine, and a celebrated violinist, previously in the service of Prince Henry of Prussia, who had been living in London for several years and whom Gallini, manager of the new theater in the Haymarket, had commissioned to undertake a journey to Italy in search of capable singers for the theater. Salomon was known by name to our Haydn, for the former had already been commissioned by Gallini a few years earlier to write to the latter and induce him to travel to London.[52] At that time, however, Haydn would not break his word to Prince Nikolaus. Now news had spread of the death of the Prince just as Salomon was en route to Italy. Hardly had he heard the news when he hastened to Vienna and surprised Haydn with the afore-mentioned visit and the blunt address that followed. "If it pleases my Prince," said Haydn, "I'll go with you to London."

Prince Anton granted permission for the journey at once, but it was not all right as far as Haydn's friends were concerned, the ones who had so often before tried to persuade him to leave Vienna. They reminded him of his age (sixty years),[53] of the discomforts of a long journey, and of many other things to shake his resolve. But in vain! Mozart especially took pains to say, "Papa!" as he usually called him, "you have had no training for the great world, and you speak too few languages."

"Oh!" replied Haydn, "my language is understood all over the world!"

The pointed expressions of both composers, the unrestrained utterance of the truth, many readers might take for intentionally offensive raillery; for, in the usual course of events, two artists like H. and M. ought to hate and persecute one another. No doubt, too, both would have indulged in fury if they had been ordinary men. Nature, however, was pleased to make, as it were, extravagant use of the harmonic stuff necessary in the formation of two such superior beings, so I find it no wonder that they valued one another highly and were joined by a bond of sincere friendship.

Haydn's tender character and love of his fellow men are already known to my readers from several places in this account. Hopefully, I shall find in the future still more occasion to speak of the same, so I save my further remarks in order not to interrupt the narrative here with a digression.

We saw that even the remonstrances of a Mozart could not shake Haydn's firm resolution. Once Prince Anton had granted permission for the journey, Haydn thought of nothing but what was connected with it. Money was the most urgent point. In order to get such quickly, he sold his house in Eisenstadt (which is known to us as the gift of Prince Nikolaus) for 1,500 gulden. His additional cash consisted of 500 gulden. This last sum was the entire fruit of his life up to then that he could consider as truly his own property; for everything else he looked upon as proofs of his Princes' magnanimity, and made use, in reference to the 500 gulden, of the joking expression, "I was a poor devil." It was his wish to possess a capital with which he could discreetly do something for his relations and leave them something after his death. To be sure he enjoyed a yearly pension of 1,400 gulden, but still he was not master of the capital that produced the 1,400 gulden, and thus could not satisfy his wish. This vexed him, but his hope of gratifying his praiseworthy desires by the journey to England seemed all the more likely because Salomon, an honest man, was empowered to conclude the agreement with Haydn. He thus set his sights upon his own honor and that of art, upon his own profit, and above all upon security. Salomon had to agree to deposit in the Fries and Company Bank 5,000 gulden as indemnity for any untoward event. When Haydn had settled this and his household affairs, he fixed his departure and left on December 15, 1791 [for 1790], in company with Salomon. Mozart on this day never left his friend Haydn. He dined with him, and said at the moment of parting, "We are probably saying our last farewell in this life." Tears welled from the eyes of both. Haydn was deeply moved, for he applied Mozart's words to himself, and the possibility never occurred to him that the thread of Mozart's life could be cut off by the inexorable Parcae within the following year.

Twelfth Visit

November 29, 1805

WHILE THE chief aim of Haydn's journey was to arrive in London without great loss of time, he never begrudged the time if he found occasion to become acquainted with great composers. Thus his acquaintance with the concertmaster Cannabich, made in Mannheim,[54] was even now a pleasant memory.

In the capital, Bonn, he was surprised in more ways than one. He arrived there on a Saturday and intended to rest on the following day.

Salomon took Haydn on Sunday to the court chapel to hear Mass. Hardly had they entered the church and found themselves a good place, when the High Mass began. The first sounds announced a work of Haydn's.[55] Our Haydn supposed it a coincidence that was so obliging as to flatter him, but it was very pleasant to him to hear his own work. Toward the end of Mass, someone approached and invited him to go into the oratory, where he was expected. Haydn went there and was no little astonished to see that the Elector Maximilian had summoned him there, took him immediately by the hand, and presented him to his musicians with the words, "Thus I make you acquainted with your much-cherished Haydn." The Elector gave both parties time to get acquainted, and, to give Haydn convincing proof of his esteem, invited him to his own table. Haydn was not a little embarrassed by this unexpected invitation, for he and Salomon had arranged a little dinner in their rooms, and it was already too late to make a change. So Haydn had to make his excuses, which the Elector accepted. Haydn thereupon took leave and went back to his rooms where he was surprised by an unexpected proof of the Elector's good will. His little dinner was transformed by the quiet order of the Elector into a large one for twelve persons, and the ablest of the musicians were invited to it.

Thirteenth Visit

December 9, 1805

HAYDN FOUND nothing remarkable on the rest of the journey to London. He arrived there, as he had hoped, safely, and found several rooms ready at Salomon's, which he occupied. Subsequently Haydn rented for himself in an outlying suburb a little place where he daily spent several hours in order to have the necessary quiet for composing.[56] He found himself obliged to escape the constant visits of the curious.

Gallini was highly delighted with Haydn's arrival. He closed an agreement with him, the details of which would not interest my readers, so I pass them by in silence.

The *Opera seria, Orfeo e Euridice,* was the first of Haydn's output in London. I do not know whether he will impart to me a closer account of this opera in the future. I did not see fit to remind him of it and interrupt the talk, because he happened on a subject in which the experience of many years had made him an infallible instructor, although at first glance it might seem of no great importance.

Seldom will a Kapellmeister reach his goal of hearing his work performed as perfectly as possible if he has not previously sought in rehearsals to win over to himself the performing artists (singers and players). If he neglects that, then even the best orchestra will give the work, at most, the correct notes. The whole perhaps sounds correctly together, despite which the audience thinks it is hearing the lifeless playing of clockwork because the whole is not inspired with charm or grace. These qualities must join with the correct, the strict form if the latter is to work on our sensibility, if rather than merely pleasing, it is to charm and to enchant. I do not speak here, moreover, of the graceful charm that a composer weaves into his harmonic texture, and that remains forever his own, but of that charm that the singer or player while he performs the piece will exercise, if lack of feeling, intrigue, egotism, or some other violent emotion does not keep him from it.

Gluck's *Iphigenia* failed utterly to please the ears of the Parisians at its first performance because the singers and the orchestra had not previously been won over, and hence performed the music like a machine. Gluck sought to change this mistake, even making use of force (it is said), and only after many vexations attained the goal that he could have won by kindness in a much easier and surer fashion.[57]

Haydn's conduct toward the orchestra that could make or break his opera was captivating and kind; he won them over to his side at the first rehearsal. He had set out a symphony that began with a short adagio, three identical-sounding notes opening the music.[58] Now when the orchestra played the three notes too emphatically, Haydn interrupted with nods and "Sh! Sh!" The orchestra stopped, and Salomon had to interpret for Haydn. Then they played the three notes again but with no happier result. Haydn interrupted again with "Sh! Sh!" In the ensuing silence, a German cellist quite near to Haydn expressed his opinion to his neighbor, saying in German, "If he doesn't like even the first three notes, how will it be with the rest!" Haydn was happy to hear Germans speaking, took these words as a warning, and said with the greatest courtesy that he was requesting as a favor something that lay wholly within their power, and that he was very sorry that he could not express himself in English. Perhaps they would allow him to demonstrate his meaning on an instrument. Whereupon he took a violin and made himself so clear by the repeated playing of the three tones that the orchestra understood him perfectly. Haydn did not in the future let the matter rest there. He implored, as small children do, by holding up both hands, called now this one, now that one "my treasure" or "my angel." He often invited the most important players to dinner, so that they appeared gladly for private rehearsals in his home. He praised them and interwove reprimand, when it was necessary, with praise in the subtlest fashion. Such behavior won him the affection of all musicians with whom he came in contact, so that out of love for him they rose to the level of inspiration required for performance of a Haydn work, and which generates the charm and grace we are speaking of here. Who is not here reminded of Aesop's fable where the storm wind and the sun test their powers to compel a man to take off his coat?

Haydn saw with much pleasure that even the Italian singers, although from tender childhood on they had accustomed their ears and throats to the opera style of their fatherland which, though always melodic, avoids all complications and dissonances, nevertheless took pains not to bungle his (very often) surprising modulations and intonations, but to perform them gracefully. Of course, the Italian singers often let him see that as a special favor to him they submitted to such difficulties. Even the most famous, indeed, were no exception, and if Haydn progressed from ordinary to less ordinary harmony, if he portrayed a shocking situation not merely with clamorous music but with a surprising, shocking modulation, they remarked that such places were very hard to sing.

Haydn knew how often singers in Italy force a Kapellmeister to avoid difficulties of every sort in his compositions. The broad scope of harmony, however, is thus shrunk very narrow and by this shrinkage a monotony produced that easily bores the listeners. In such straits the composer has only one way out: he must think up a light, flowing, pleasant, enticing melody and try as much as he can to touch the heart. This is all very commendable and will, to be sure, tickle the public's fancy and set its emotions to work. Perhaps the composer is so fortunate as to comply with both requests, but the true connoisseur soon notices that, though the enticing melody seeks to lull to sleep and, by its magic, to corrupt the intellect, such music is empty of inner content because the intellect on closer inspection finds little, often enough only trivial, nourishment that shows not the slightest trace of ennoblement.

All these remarks, which I introduced into the conversation, Haydn did not gainsay; but he added further that "the age must be taken into consideration; for, lately," he went on, "several of the Italians have rebelled against the common shopworn ways of their country. They move with ease, as the need arises, in all spheres of harmony, as, for instance, Cherubini."

Haydn's initial aim (this much follows from his vocal compositions) was always first to engage the intellect by a charming and rhythmically right melody. Thus he secretly brought the listener to the ultimate aim: to touch the heart in various ways; and finally, when this effect has long since passed, and when, even after centuries, the critical understanding wishes to analyze the work of art, to transmit to it material rich in satisfaction.—He wished to be a correct author, but (by his own admission) he did not count this so important that he would sacrifice initial and ultimate aims to pedantic niceties. "If I thought something was beautiful, and it seemed to me likely to satisfy the ear and the heart, and I should have had to sacrifice such beauty to dried-up pedantry, then I preferred to let a little grammatical blunder stand."

The powerful magic of grace exercises an irresistible power over the feelings even when not coupled with a strict form. This can be seen every day in people who, though they are not well-made or are even ugly to look upon, nevertheless possess much charm and know how to be very gracious. How much more must the pleasure increase if the imperfection in form strikes neither the eye nor the ear but can be uncovered only by the critical mind—and that only with much time?

I must inform my readers of another arrangement which Haydn contracted that first year with the manager of the Musicians' Concert (Professional Concerts).[59] These concerts were given once a week in the new concert hall in Hanover Square, and Haydn had committed himself to deliver a new work for each concert, in all twelve pieces of different kinds, adding the stipulation that his works should always be performed in the second half. On the one hand, Haydn thereby took upon himself a considerable obligation, for, to gain applause, he had to surpass in beauty the pieces presented in the first half. On the other hand, he had this advantage in return, that if he over-shadowed the first half, his work remained in the memory all the longer and all the more glory would be his. This too, though, could misfire, for he naturally ran the risk that failing to equal the beauties of the first half, he would have to endure reproof all the more biting and sink ever so much lower.

Salomon occupied the post of first violinist in this Musicians' Concert. Haydn, kept busy with his art, did not notice that quarrels were beginning between Salomon and the other managers that resulted in a separation, whence came into being a second weekly concert series given in the New Theater in the Haymarket. Gallini and Salomon were the entrepreneurs, and reckoned on Haydn's fame as a sure thing, nor were their expectations betrayed.

The Musicians' Concert, meanwhile, was intent upon maintaining and where possible increasing its previous renown. After Salomon's departure the celebrated Cramer became first violinist. Men of distinguished reputation, as for example Clementi, and so on, were handsomely recompensed for their compositions. In general, nothing was omitted whereby the rise of the new concerts might be hindered. But the public, following the general acclaim, crowned Haydn with laurel, thronged the theater, and seldom visited the Musicians' Concert, which very soon felt the loss, and plotted some means by which best to assert its former reputation. They would almost have wrung a victory from Haydn by violence. Clementi, probably without knowing the purpose, had to compose a symphony that turned out worthy of the celebrated artist. With this symphony the first half of a concert

Haydn in Esterházy Court Uniform.
Portrait by Johann Basilius Grundmann, *ca.* 1768.

Joseph Haydn.
Bust by Anton Grassi, 1799.

Photograph from the Picture Archives of the Austrian National Library.

Courtyard of Haydn's House in Gumpendorf.

Staircase Lantern from the Esterházy Castle at Esterháza.

The Esterházy Castle at Esterháza.

Photographs by Carol Joyce Gotwals.

was opened; the audience showed its noisy approval. Haydn knew nothing of the plan and had to forego the advantage of entering the lists with a specially prepared symphony, which justice would have demanded; but since the purpose was to diminish his renown, they put on an already known Haydn symphony in the second half and believed thus to obtain their end. This expectation came to nothing. The applause was unbelievable. Clementi grew pale and expressed in a few words his indignation over the choice of a Haydn symphony which proved so unfortunate for himself. This occurrence could not long be kept quiet. It ran from mouth to mouth and served no little to make Haydn's name more celebrated than ever.

The manager of the Concerts proceeded now to other means. Convinced that without an arrangement with Haydn they would not get the public to grant first rank to the concerts, they decided to send six deputies to Haydn to offer him profitable terms and through their entreaties to incline him to an agreement. The deputation did its best. Haydn, however, would not break his word to Gallini and Salomon, or harm them through his own base greed. Since they had undertaken so much and had assumed such great expense on his behalf, he believed it only fair not to begrudge them their profit.

The deputation was soon after dispatched a second time to Haydn. They repeated the same terms as on the first mission, and added that they had full power to offer him 150 guineas and even more over the agreement existing between him and Salomon if he would enter into a contract with the managers of the Concerts. To this Haydn gave the same answer that my readers have already heard before.

Some time later Haydn was apprised by his friends of a newspaper account that concerned himself. I regret that I do not have the page before my eyes and cannot state in which newspaper the article was inserted. Haydn recalled only that he was pictured in it as old, weak, and incapable of producing anything new. He had long since written himself out and was forced by failing wits to repeat himself. On this account an agreement had been entered into with Haydn's noted pupil, I. Pleyel,[60] who was soon coming to London where he would compose for the Musicians' Concert.

Haydn saw clear through the malicious plot and did not doubt that they had used all their tricks to persuade Pleyel to come to London. Since they dared to picture Haydn in public newspapers as a worn-out old man, it was safe to suppose that in the letters directed to Pleyel still more exaggerated pictures were drawn, the more surely to lure him into the trap. Such were the deductions Haydn made, and he regretted that his pupil should serve the intrigue as its pawn, which last he might easily have prevented if it had occurred to him to inquire of Haydn himself about the state of things. Probably this would have happened, too, if Pleyel could have taken more time; but from his sudden arrival in London, the opposite was to be expected.

After Pleyel's arrival Haydn could clearly see by his behavior that he had in his pupil an opponent who wished to contend with him for the prize. Haydn felt none of the imputed weakness, so he remained on this score calmly composed and trusted to his genius and his taste. But when he thought he noticed that his former pupil behaved toward him with a certain reserve and even failed to seek out his company so frequently as before, he was sad and embittered toward the intriguers through whose machinations Pleyel was duped and forced to play the role of ingrate toward his teacher.

As soon as Pleyel set out on his new course, his fame and the novelty of the thing were bound to prove propitious to the Musicians' Concert. That much I could gather from Haydn's account. But in order to leave no gaps in the story, I suppose that connoisseurs soon noted that Pleyel despite his pleasant melodies still could not venture to compete with Haydn's complete grasp of the art, especially since Haydn continued to bring out a new masterpiece every week in the New Theater. It may be further supposed that the Musicians' Concert could not gain the victory over the series in the New Theater but had to content itself with second place. Here my suppositions end, and I can assert with certainty that Pleyel finally came across the scent of the intrigue, recognized the injustice done his teacher, and took the occasion of a banquet that he specially arranged for the purpose to ask for Haydn's forgiveness. I will impart to my readers verbatim the few quiet words with which Haydn closed today's conversation: "I gladly forgave my pupil, and since then we have been friends again just as before."

Fourteenth Visit

December 21, 1805

I HAVE already said many times to my readers that Haydn in his conversations suffers a certain excitement which, since his powers of memory have weakened, usually leads him astray from a strict chronological ordering of his account and causes him to pass over events that, if he indeed considers them insignificant, nevertheless have interest for some readers. Many of these events Haydn told in earlier times to his friends, who told them around. Thus they came into the public domain and gradually lost their original form. But even in garbled form every anecdote is welcome to me, because I can separate at the source the true from the untrue and can cast out the latter.

In today's visit Haydn was not so cheerful as I found him the last time, so I tried to abbreviate as much as possible and contented myself with the correcting of several incidents that belong to the period of eighteen months he spent in London the first time and that should have taken their place in the previous account.

Haydn's arrival in London caused a considerable stir among all cultivated persons. The well known Dr. Burney, author of the musical journey, celebrated it in a little poem that appeared under the title *Verses on the Arrival in England of the great Musician Haydn, January 1791.*[61]

Haydn observed at the very first of the Professional Concerts that he had done well to stipulate second-half performances of his works. The first half was usually disturbed in all sorts of ways by the noise of latecomers. Not a few people came from well set tables (where the men, after the custom of their country, stayed sitting and drinking after the women had proceeded at the end of the meal into another room), took a comfortable place in the concert hall, and there were so overpowered by the magic of music that a deep sleep overcame them. Now imagine whether in a concert hall where not a few but many persons with their snuffling or snoring or hanging of heads present the true listeners with something to chatter about or more probably to laugh at, whether quiet can reign there? Haydn noted with annoyance that even in the second half the god of sleep kept his wings spread over the assemblage. He saw it as an insult to his muse, vowed to have revenge, and composed to that end a symphony [No. 94] in which he placed the softest piano in contrast with fortissimo where it would be least expected, in the Andante. To make the effect as surprising as possible, he accompanied the fortissimo with kettle-drums. Hard upon the preceding Allegro, the Andante began *con sordino* and pizzicato. If I were to make a comparison with the soft whispering sounds of the first eight measures, or theme, I should say one supposed he heard the footsteps and whispering of a ghostly choir. This almost inaudible harmony of muted instruments brought on the full orchestra without mutes and fortissimo amid the terrible thunder of kettledrums and contrabasses. Haydn had particularly bidden the timpanists to take thick sticks and drum away without mercy, and they fully matched his expectation. The sudden thunder of the full orchestra startled the sleepers, who all woke and looked at one another with disconcerted and wondering counte-nances. They understood the reprimand that Haydn employed to wake them from their stupor and were fair enough to treat the incident as an original stroke of genius and to praise it. When, how-ever, during the Andante a sensitive young lady, carried away by the surprising working of the music, could not face it with a sufficient display of strong nerves and so fell in a faint and had to be carried into the fresh air, then some used the incident to find fault, and said that Haydn had always surprised us up to now in courteous fashion but this time he grew very coarse.

Haydn troubled himself little with this fault-finding; his purpose —to be heard—was fully attained, and for the future as well.

This Andante, which all amateurs know in the edition for pianoforte (in C), is called the Andante with the Drum Stroke.[62]

Haydn's muse was already revered long before he arrived in London in person, but once he was actually present, the veneration increased with each day. Everybody wanted to see and to hear and, to satisfy his curiosity, thronged into the concert hall or into the New Theater. Here in the second year an accident occurred that could easily have been tragic, but by good luck it was not.

When Haydn appeared in the orchestra and sat down at the pianoforte to conduct a symphony himself, the curious audience in the parterre left their seats and crowded toward the orchestra the better to see the famous Haydn quite close. The seats in the middle of the floor were thus empty, and hardly were they empty when the great chandelier crashed down and broke into bits, throwing the numerous gathering into the greatest consternation. As soon as the first moment of fright was over and those who had pressed forward could think of the danger they had luckily escaped and find words to express it, several persons uttered the state of their feelings with loud cries of "Miracle! Miracle!" Haydn himself was deeply moved and thanked the merciful Providence that had allowed him in a certain way to be the cause for or the means of saving the lives of at least thirty people. Only a couple of persons received insignificant bruises.

I have heard this incident related in various ways and almost always with the addition that in London they conferred on the symphony the flattering name "The Miracle." It may be that such is the case, but when I made inquiry of Haydn about the matter, he said, "I know nothing about that." [63]

Fifteenth Visit

January 14, 1806

THE TALK happened today upon the opera *Orfeo e Euridice*. I was very pleased to find an opportunity to learn something about this subject. I redoubled my attention in order to absorb every word and thus truly concentrated. Now my readers can imagine my surprise when Haydn, in place of a narrative, finished with these few words: "The opera was not performed."

And why not?

Gallini had entered into an agreement with several persons to bring about the construction of the New Theater. The contractors had then, whether from ignorance or upon the counsel of false men Haydn did not know, disregarded a necessary point and undertaken the construction without permission from the King and Parliament.

The theater now stood there completed and the orchestra was already assembled to rehearse the opera *Orfeo*. Haydn had distributed the parts, and hardly had forty measures been played through when official persons entered and in the name of the King and of Parliament ordered that the opera should under no circumstances be played, not even once in rehearsal, and so on. Even single arias might nowhere be sung or played. *Orfeo* was, so to speak, declared contraband, and what was worst, the playing of all operas in the Theater in future was forbidden.

This unexpected blow dismayed not only Gallini but also the whole orchestra. Gallini, however, did not let the matter lie, but rather did what a sensible man must, and sought by all reasonable means to render the incident as harmless as possible. By his activity he soon brought things to the place where he was allowed to give concerts and ballets in the New Theater.

We know how very useful Haydn was to him in bringing the

Theater into favor. The former did not want for musical output, since he had been in earlier years a very diligent composer in secret and kept under lock and key many completed works that until then no one had ever heard. Now his early diligence stood him in good stead. For he could, since the previous sacrifice of time on the opera *Orfeo* had been in vain and he would have required time to produce another new work, he could, I say, have recourse to the output already at hand and thereby avoid haste in work.[64]

Haydn mentioned his wife today, in this way. He received from her in London a letter in which she informed him that she had seen a pretty little one-story house together with a little garden in the suburb Gumpendorf, No. 73 in the *kleine Steingasse,* which had pleased her very much since it could be bought at a fair price. She wished therefore that he would do her the favor of sending her 2,000 florins, for which she would buy the house to occupy in the future when she was a widow.[65] I had difficulty in suppressing a smile at the naïve candor of the woman's expression. Whether Haydn noticed it, I do not know. He went on, "I did not send her the requested money but waited till my return to Vienna. When this time came, I inspected the little house myself. Its still and solitary situation pleased me. I bought it, and during my second journey added a story to it. My wife died about seven or eight years afterwards (1800), and I have been occupying it ever since as a widower."

The days of sentimental journeys and all, too, that belongs with sentimental beings are gone by. They were pushed away by gigantic events that worked powerfully indeed on our way of thinking, so powerfully perhaps that we shall soon begin, perhaps have long since begun, in the presence of sentiments of sheer power and exaggeration to be ashamed of our sensibility. Did I not fear this to be the case, I should, while we talk still of Haydn's house, lead my readers into that house, into every room, and show the furniture that can be found there, the musical library, and a splendid English and a French pianoforte. I should open many a drawer, take out watches, snuff-boxes, rings, and the like, show off everything costly and gorgeous, and I could tell many things about the occasion that produced each one of these presents.

I should bring my readers before Haydn's clavier. They would, if sensibility were still the fashion, summon up Haydn's muse at the sight of it, wishing perhaps to buy it, as a priceless treasure, for a great sum.*

Even the yard behind the house would be sure to amuse my readers. A parrot that in its iron cage in warm weather is guard of the yard might prove interesting. To be sure it does not speak like Yorik's starling: "I can't get out of here!"; [67] but it still keeps the sparrows out. And if a handful of them fall to quarreling on the neighboring roofs, it joins in the quarrel with a wonderful gift of mimicry and outcries them all. Sometimes it imitates a flute and runs through a whole octave, or it speaks the words, "Come Haydn Papa to the pretty little parrot."

What a delightful little garden! Thus my readers would exclaim with me in our enthusiasm. Here it was that the great composer warmed himself in God's sun and pondered *The Creation!* Or—and how often did this not happen!—he yielded to the beneficent impulses of his heart and, when a tree in his little garden was full of fruit, had the neighbors' children called in, amused himself with them, since he was uncommonly fond of children, and distributed the ripe fruit among them. But all this is no more the fashion, otherwise I should have said with pleasure at least as much on these matters as was once said and written on Rousseau's cottage.

* In earlier years Haydn regularly used a harpsichord (clavecin). For several years he noticed that the sharp tone of the harpsichord produced a truly cutting sensation in his brain. Since the painful sensation kept growing, he found himself obliged to exchange the harpsichord for a clavier.[66]

Sixteenth Visit

January 24, 1806

IN ONE circle appeared now a man, whom I shall not identify more closely, who seemed to pride himself on his reputation as a critic of Haydn's muse. His criticism dealt particularly with the church works, which, he maintained, were not perhaps merely theatrical, but were better fitted for a dance hall than for a church. He finds in them contradances, minuets, and the like, but nothing of the dignity that should belong to that sort of music.*

I had for a long time intended to inquire of Haydn himself about his principles for composing sacred music and incidentally to investigate in careful terms the above-mentioned harsh criticism. I had, with regard to the second point, to go to work especially cautiously because I did not wish to be cruel and to hurt Haydn. My intention succeeded as I hoped. Haydn remained calm, and passed on to me, with regard to the first point, a letter from Herr Assessor Zelter in Berlin,[68] from which my readers can see that Haydn in the opinion of a musical scholar knew how to give to his serious vocal

---

* Many critics in general, but the Italians particularly, find fault not only with Haydn's and Mozart's vocal music, but with everything German in that category, always excepting the case where the imitation in German works of Italian taste is markedly to be heard. Many critics though are fair enough to allow that instrumental music is well understood by Germans. Haydn's symphonies in 1795 were still known little or not at all in Rome. About that time a traveling virtuoso gave a concert in Rome and announced he would open it with an excellent symphony of Haydn. The symphony in E flat did not please. A voice in my vicinity even said half aloud, *"O che roba del diavolo!"* [O, what devilish stuff!] Such expressions will be heard among any and every people that particularly loves folksong (which is always extremely simple). No harmony of a higher order can lightly venture to penetrate such ears. What puzzles me, however, is that we woo vulgar approval in our works of art, for is the verdict of the ignorant worth so much that their majority can pass sentence?

music a fitting dignity and was incapable of such gross mistakes as those of which he was accused by the unnamed critic.*

Berlin, March 16, 1804.

I can find, honored master, no words to express to you the joy that your friendly letter of February 25 has given me. I shall leave it as a relic, as a patent of nobility, to my eleven children. I know that I must attribute such praise more to your kindness and love than to my merit, but your praise is so sweet that I shall also earnestly endeavor in all seriouness to deserve it.

You may know that the review of your masterwork is by me,† and that for a very long time now, I have respected you deeply. But I should never have fashioned it as you did, great master, nor could I ever do so. Your spirit has penetrated into the sanctuary of godly wisdom; you have brought fire from heaven, with which you warm and enlighten earthly hearts and lead them to the infinite. The best that we others can do is simply this: with thankfulness and joy to worship God Who sent you that we might perceive the wonders He has revealed in art through you.

What I hoped to receive from you, dear man, for my Singakademie (which now consists of two hundred singing voices, of which 160 may be considered active and useful), to wit, a sacred work by you, I have, to be sure, long been hoping for, but it has taken 15 years to put the treasury of the Institute in a position to be able to defray the cost of such a master-work. I feel only too deeply how trifling the price is for a work of yours, which no money can pay for, and thus have reckoned, of course, more on your love for art and on the glory of God than on our trifling money.[71] So I pray you, if the state of your health permits, to undertake this work, that your great name too resound to the glory of God and of art in our circle, which has as its sole purpose the reawakening and maintaining of church or sacred music, presently so neglected.

Simply to possess something of your work, I had taken the liberty of arranging for our chorus the two songs of Gellert, *Herr, der du mir das Leben* and *Du bist's, dem Ruhm und Ehre gebühret.* Your wish has thus

---

* In the sixth volume of the *Leipzig Musikalische Zeitung,* number 51, it is reported of Johann Adam Hiller: "J. Haydn's masses also were very dear to him. In particular he copied with his own hand a score from the parts of the one published as No. 4,[69] and from this, in order to make it wholly his own, copied out the parts again. On the score he printed in large capitals: *Opus summum viri summi I. Haydn.*" [Greatest work of a very great man.]

† The review appeared in the *Leipzig Musikalische Zeitung,* 1807 [*for* 1801], number 17, letter 6.[70]

already been fulfilled for longer than seven months, but whether I have done it correctly you will discover from the enclosed scores, and I heartily urge you to tell me what you find in them to improve.[72]

If only I could grant you the joy of hearing us do your choruses, of edification at the calm, devotion, purity, and sanctity with which your chorus *Du bist's dem, etc.* is sung here! The finest and best youth of Berlin join here with fathers and mothers, as if in a heaven filled with angels, celebrate in praise and joy the glory of the most high God, and train themselves in the works of the greatest masters of art whom the world has seen. O come to us, come! You shall be received like a god among men. We will sing for you a Gloria, etc. that will make you raise your gray and honored head, and raise it to the laurel, for our master Fasch has taught us how to honor masters.[73]

Farewell, dear, beloved man! May God still keep you, long, long! You have not produced a work in which your great age is to be noticed. Your *Seasons* is a work youthful in power and old in mastery. God be with you!

Your

ZELTER

Among the letters and papers that Haydn passed on to me, not one was to be found in which was not expressed the esteem that rightly belongs to genius ennobled. But it is particularly striking in the above letter that our Haydn (despite the charge of the unnamed person) is requested by a musical scholar to oppose the decline of church music. If Haydn were really considered the man to meet the above challenge successfully,* then the charge of the unnamed falls to pieces, a charge that may be attributed by careful investigation not to Haydn's inventive spirit but rather to the lively tempi in three-four and three-eight time, because one is reminded by these tempi of minuets and of waltzes. Nowhere else as in Italy have I heard in the

---

* Readers who are interested in more information than space permits here will find such in an excellent review in Volume 4, Number 44, of the *Leipzig Musikalische Zeitung*.[74] It is there very correctly remarked that in Haydn's masses "not the gloomy devotion and ever penitential piety of the great old masters of Italy, but a more serene and reconciled devotion, a tenderer sorrow, and a fortunate awareness of heavenly goodness prevail."

Hence certain passages appear to him who takes no account of the above too brilliant for the place, or if he judges less fairly, he will call them theatrical.

churches not so much opera as true dance music. During my twenty-one years' residence in Rome, I often had opportunity in churches to meditate upon the degenerate music, and I always observed that the aim of many Kapellmeisters there must have been to tickle the ear, which they succeeded in doing, too, because the people (in churches where the organ was built opposite the high altar) turned around when the music began, and, their backs to the high altar, behaved almost as if in the theater.* Theatrical arias with obbligato instrumental accompaniment, and at the end a concerto *a solo*,† are daily occurrences in the Roman churches, and with their immoderately sensual and trifling performances can very easily scare away devotion but never awaken it.

In today's conversation the words "faultfinder" and "critic" were often pronounced. Haydn thus recalled the following anecdote.

During his first eighteen months' stay in London he sought (as we know) to become acquainted with celebrated musicians. Among these was known to him the name of Giardini, who had won signal honors as a violinist. Haydn wished to know him in person. He spoke his wish in the presence of a lord who offered to present him to Giardini. It was a pleasant business for the lord to make two celebrated men acquainted with one another. The lord and Haydn went along together, had the servant whom they found in the anteroom

* In Dupaty's Letters on Italy he says, in Forster's translation (Letter 37): "I heard the vesper opera, etc.

"The whole office was music; people went in and out, chatted, laughed; they crowded around the orchestras."

In Letter 102 he says of Naples: "People go into the churches only if illuminations are to be seen or music is to be heard there; in a word, if there is opera in the church."

I was long an eyewitness of this and certify that the picture is without exaggeration and is literally true.[75]

† If it is moreover the custom everywhere to play a concerto at the end of the church music, still it is not to be contended that a choice must be made. Rondos in somewhat the style of *Marlborough s'en va, etc.* I have often heard played in Roman churches. Then the venerable shades of the Bachs, of Handel, and of other great masters presented themselves to my imagination, and I fancied I read in their mien righteous indignation at this wrong.

announce them. The door remained open a little. The lord and Haydn clearly heard the answer that Giardini gave his servant in a loud voice and that may be literally translated thus: "I do not want to know that German dog."

The lord was extremely put out at the rudeness of the virtuoso and thereafter avoided his company. Haydn, on the contrary, thought only of the comic aspect of the scene, and this makes him laugh even now whenever the name of Giardini occurs. Nor did the untoward behavior of the latter keep Haydn from seeking an opportunity to get to know him on artistic grounds. Giardini soon after gave a public concert. Haydn was unrecognized among the audience, and admired the skill of the virtuoso who in old age still played with the fire of youth. In the Adagio the violin gave forth the tenderest tones, thus winning the audience. So Haydn gladly forgave him his bad temper and attributed the outbreak to great age.[76]

Haydn had once made mention to a friend of mine of some thoughts he had during the composition of a church piece.[77] The matter seemed important to me and today the proper time to make inquiry, so I then brought our talk to the *Agnus Dei* of the Mass No. 4. I have already pointed out in a previous note [p. 136] how greatly Hiller revered this mass. In the review of it in the *Leipzig Musikalische Zeitung* [cf. p. 137] the said *Agnus Dei* is extolled as a masterpiece of aesthetic procedure and is given in score. The reviewer rightly accords the greatest praise to the build-up observed therein.

Now let us hear how Haydn in his own personal way achieved all these perfections. He spoke to himself during the composing. "I prayed to God not like a miserable sinner in despair but calmly, slowly. In this I felt that an infinite God would surely have mercy on his finite creature, pardoning dust for being dust. These thoughts cheered me up. I experienced a sure joy so confident that as I wished to express the words of the prayer, I could not suppress my joy, but gave vent to my happy spirits and wrote above the *miserere,* etc. Allegro."

If, led on by Haydn's words, one should draw the conclusion that he perhaps developed every consequent more happily than the antecedent seemed to warrant, then this would be a perfection not understood by many critics, one which, if only a wise use be made of it, will certainly be in keeping in church pieces. The wise composer will never offend the dignity of circumstance and place, and this Haydn never did.[78]

In order more and more to win Haydn's confidence in my singleness of purpose in writing these accounts and to render him fully certain that he could trust my pen completely without fear of being mistreated, I begged him to name me one of his friends who might at the same time serve as judge of my manuscript, and I assured him that I should willingly submit to the friendly pronouncements of such a person. Haydn was touched and said to me in the fullness of his heart many things that I cannot tell without blushing. The main point of his words was a refusal inasmuch as he had never doubted my sincerity and moreover never would. I kept urging him, and said that he might rightly doubt, since I had read so few places aloud to him thus far, but that many I could not read to him because they contained partly praise, partly descriptions of his illness, and I would not poison the happy moments in which he could forget old age and weakness by recalling both. His answer was, as he took my hand and pressed it, trembling and weak, "Thank you, thank you!"— Thereupon he named the Saxon Legation Secretary, Herr Griesinger, who has been his friend for some seven years now. When I afterwards became acquainted with this worthy man, it was soon revealed that he quite quietly and without Haydn's knowing it had for several years been collecting materials for Haydn's biography, which is one day to appear in shortened form in the *Leipzig Musikalische Zeitung*.

Seventeenth Visit

February 19, 1806

SEVERAL DAYS ago Haydn sent to ask me the name of his greatly esteemed and learned friend in Berlin. It struck me as strange that he should have forgotten the name of an honored friend, so I asked the person sent to me how Haydn was. "Dear God," was the answer, "he is extremely weak and has lost all patience because he has been hunting the whole forenoon for a letter from the Kapellmeister and can't find it." I named Zelter's name and the servant ran off in a hurry.

With this visit I found Haydn really weak, so I hoped to net only a little for these accounts.

Haydn excused himself for having sent to me. "I didn't know any other way out because it upsets me fearfully when my memory fails. I wanted to converse in solitude with a friend and could find neither letter nor name.

"—I must have something to do.—Usually musical ideas are pursuing me, to the point of torture, I cannot escape them, they stand like walls before me. If it's an allegro that pursues me, my pulse keeps beating faster, I can get no sleep. If it's an adagio, then I notice my pulse beating slowly. My imagination plays on me as if I were a clavier." Haydn smiled, the blood rushed to his face, and he said, "I am really just a living clavier.—For several days now an old song in E minor has been playing inside me, one that I have often played in my youth, *O Herr! wie lieb' ich dich von Herzen*. [O Lord, with all my heart I love thee.] Wherever I go or stay, everywhere I hear it.— But curiously, when I am so deeply upset that nothing helps me to escape the torment, and my song *Gott erhalte Franz den Kaiser* once occurs to me, then I feel easier; it helps."

"That doesn't surprise me," I said, "for, flattery aside, I consider the song a masterpiece."

"I almost think so myself, though I shouldn't say it."

My readers will be inclined with me not to consider this expression of Haydn's about one of his own works an outburst of vanity, as some critics will charge. I see in it a certain self-confidence that pleases me, and indeed pleases me more than the often too great modesty with which Haydn usually meets praise and which, if someone wants to criticize, can easily be criticized, because a man possessed of so much love of fame, even if he had the purest of hearts, cannot possibly remain indifferent to praise. And since he cannot do so, why should he appear to in his words? Why should he belie, with words that are not spoken from the heart, the fleeting blush praise brings to his cheek and the brightening countenance? What right do the critics have to call such rare expressions of self-confidence vanity? —And rare indeed! It was the first expression of this sort that I had any occasion to remark and I, moreover, drew him into it.

I now return to the interrupted conversation. It was of no importance to these accounts, so I contented myself with verifying several anecdotes that I found related in the M[usikalische]. Zeitung in the second volume and that belong to Haydn's first London sojourn.

In the fourth number of 1799 the following is related: "When J. H. went to London in 1791 and was received and treated honorably not only by all music-lovers (a certain party excepted) but also by all cultivated people, the national temper of the great rough mob showed itself very clearly in the following incident. Haydn entered the orchestra of the theater. It was just time to begin. The musicians stood up to welcome him. The connoisseurs in the upper gallery were astonished at this courtesy. But when they heard that it was shown to an artist, and what was more, to a foreigner, they fell to hissing, whistling, and crying, "Fiddler! Fiddler!"

Haydn said, "The musicians in the orchestra did me great honor; but I don't believe I heard the hissing, whistling, and calls of 'Fiddler! Fiddler!'"

The second anecdote (fifth number, 1799) Haydn wholly confirmed.

He found, as it happened, a strong opposition party in London, mainly the Italians, whose guiding spirit was Giardini, whom we already know. Giardini, in an attempt to make Haydn's music ridiculous, brought out two trios in which he characterized the Italian taste by long meaningful notes and expressed the German by short, endlessly chopped up little notes. The author identified himself only as a dilettante. An organist in the Imperial German Chapel, thinking he must avenge the insult to German music, engraved an answering cartoon in which the names of the best known German composers were placed in a sun and in the surrounding rays. J. S. Bach stood in the center and close around him Handel, Graun, and Haydn. In each of the farther sunrays was the name of another German composer. Beneath the sun was an Italian owl abhorring the light of the sun. To the side, however, an Italian capon and a German hen stood ready to fight. It is true that Haydn saw this sheet, and was well pleased with the place accorded him.

Once this was cleared up, the talk turned to the state of Haydn's health. To give it a pleasant turn, I led it to other subjects. I told him how I had mentioned his house in these accounts; that I had not forgotten his clavier; that I had spoken of the parrot watching over the yard, and had said a few words about the little garden and above all much in several places about his patriarchal way of life and household management. His features brightened and he said, "I guess my way of life deserves no criticism."

"One might wish," I replied, "that your housekeeping might be generally imitated. The consequences could only be good."

It seemed to amuse him especially that I had said a few words about his clavier. He found it comical that I should have called it a "priceless treasure," giving such an unambiguous hint to the lovers of curiosities. "But haven't they," I said, "offered the surgeon who owns the bullet that killed Nelson 100 guineas for that miserable little lump of lead? Now isn't your creative clavier worth as much as that destructive bullet?"—"In London," said Haydn, "they care for such stuff! I actually saw Handel's clavier at the Queen's, who bought it from the family and kept it as a relic."

Eighteenth Visit

March 15, 1806

HAYDN'S WEAKNESS, though he looked quite well, did not permit him to add more materials to these accounts. He could not speak without effort, and he had to use his strength economically because he had already received several visits today and now Herr ———— was announced.

"My lawyer," Haydn said to me.

"Surely you don't have a lawsuit?"

"Not that, but now and then a few small additions to be made to my will."

"What? Your will is already made?"

"A long time since. I am ready for death at any moment." [79]

Haydn now with difficulty rose from his chair, trotted to the writing table, took a calling card, gave it to me, and said in a tone of calmest composure, "See what I've been busy with since your last visit. I've had a calling card printed. There, read for yourself Gellert's words applied to myself: [80]

Hin ist alle meine Kraft, alt und schwach bin ich.
[Gone is all of my own strength, old and weak am I.]

I do not deny that I was moved, and to conceal my emotion I took my leave.

On the way home I ran the gamut from tears to laughter. I have often had to laugh over an epitaph, but today for the first time in my life a visiting card put me in the opposite humor. Nevertheless, the emotion could not last long, for I soon realized that so long as one can perceive, admit, and in the admission joke about one's feebleness, the mind must still retain its vigor. Woven into Haydn's character is a genial, witty, teasing strain, but with it always the innocence of a child. His musical output attests to this (as several critics have already remarked), and now still in old age, his behavior in company often gives rise to the above observation. He seems, for example, to find pleasure in painting his state of health worse than it really is. On such occasions I usually make answer that in his appearance not a trace of indisposition is to be seen. The brightness which then spreads over his face confirms that one has guessed the truth, although he pictured the opposite.

Later Addition

I ventured to question Haydn on the subject of teasing [*Neckerei*] in his musical output. He admitted to me that it was a characteristic of his that used to be due to an abundance of good health. "Perhaps," I said, "like merry boys, who from sheer soundness of health don't know what to do with themselves and romp about in innocent mischief, now rolling around in the grass, now teasing one another in all sorts of ways."—"Exactly!" Haydn replied. "One is seized by a certain humor that will not be tamed."

Nineteenth Visit

May 12, 1806

THE BENEFICIAL influence of spring air could be noted in Haydn's whole being. His spirit, which at my previous visits seemed to be heroically intimate with death, today was pleased to declare its presence in the living body. I wished good father Haydn long enjoyment of such days and years.

"Only not at the cost of your own life," he replied, "as so many people keep doing. They protest they would gladly see their own life shortened if mine might be lengthened by it. I can never believe that, and I can't allow it, because life is too costly a thing."

Haydn found pleasure today in speaking of comic events. I expressed a wish to hear more of the London goings on, but when he once gave out another theme, I did not want to confuse him.

Sometime ago by a peculiar chance a song had come to hand that Haydn had set to music some twenty years ago and that he no longer recalled at all. The sight of it renewed the memory of the occasion that gave rise to this song. The story amused me, and I trust that my readers have not that gloomy character which, like Heraclitus, will grumble at everything; so I shall tell them the whole business.

Haydn received from a young woman, unmarried and a foreigner,* a letter phrased as intimately as if both parties had already known one another for twenty years. It began, "Dear, good Haydn, best of men" [*Lieber, guter, bester Haydn*]. The young lady explained that she was a captain's daughter and in love with an officer. He, however, would not marry her unless her dear Haydn, who, she well knew, could refuse nothing to a well-behaved young gentlewoman (Haydn could not tell this without a smile), did her the favor of assisting her with his divine music in getting the officer as her husband. Now the young lady analyzed in detail how and why Haydn should do so. I beg leave of my readers to tell as much of this as is necessary to understand the story.

The young lady had sent Haydn some verses which she had written herself and for which she wanted a beautiful melody. With this melody the maiden would surprise her music-lover by singing him the song. She hoped he would surely be moved by it and would marry her.

No doubt my readers will have formed a high opinion of the content of the text submitted and also believe the young beauty must have sung at the least like an angel. Concerning the latter point it

* I suppose Haydn used the word "foreigner" on purpose to render investigation idle.

can only be supposed that her voice was pathetic when she begged Haydn in the same letter not to expect too much of her feeble bosom and to allow her to rest often. Concerning the textual content my readers will doubtless be amazed merely by reading the title and will comprehend, as little as I, how "the sly and ever helpful poodle" could bring a music-lover to resolve to hasten into marriage. Perhaps the poodle's history will explain this.

The tale is true. The poodle was the music-lover's property, truly beloved, and had a most perfect poodle-intelligence.

On a little walking tour that the officer had undertaken in company with a friend, he said much in the poodle's praise that the friend doubted. It came to a wager. The officer buried a taler in the earth under a bush, with the assurance that he would call out, after they had gone on a great distance, "Lost! go find it!" and the poodle would bring the taler back again. The agreement was punctually carried out, but the poodle kept them waiting till the next morning, having undergone a peculiar adventure in the meantime.

A young journeyman had come in his travels to the bush and being tired out lay down beneath it, toyed with the grass, found the taler, and, delighted, stuck it in his pants pocket. Not long afterwards the poodle came along, and not finding the taler, followed the scent of the journeyman, whom he soon overtook and joyfully sprang upon, fawning on him like a master. The happy fellow considered himself doubly fortunate and was already reckoning how much money he would get for the poodle. The beast followed him right into the next village,—right into the inn,—right into the bedchamber, and lay down by the bed where his new master slept. The following morning the journeyman, whom sweet sleep had overpowered, was awakened by a maid. The chamber door being open in the meantime, the poodle deliberately took the journeyman's pants, rolled them into a ball, slunk through the door with this burden in his mouth, and brought back to the officer the pants and the lost taler in them.—With inquiries they tracked down the truth, and after the complete unraveling the poodle meant even more to the officer than a sweetheart.

The young lady thought to conquer the heart of the officer by per-
petuating in verse the deed of the poodle. And to stimulate Haydn to
the manufacture of a truly beautiful melody, she had enclosed several ducats in the letter begging him not to despise this small sum;
straitened circumstances prevented the lady-donor from repaying
him as she might have wished.

Haydn composed the music (in B flat major) [see p. 21 n], sent it
together with the ducats to the beauty, and asked her whether she
considered him such a stingy old skinflint that he doted on ducats?
—As punishment she should make for him with her own hands a
pair of garters as a keepsake.

The beauty took this in earnest. Shortly after she sent the garters,
reported that she was ill, and added to this that if Haydn received no
further news of her within the fortnight, he might count her soul
among those of the departed. No news came, and it is probable that
the young lady, inclined to consumption, grieved herself to death
over the failure of her marriage scheme.

Later, today's conversation gave me an opportunity to ask about
the ties of friendship between the deceased Swieten and Haydn. I
shall subsequently combine and lay before my readers all I learned
about this one point.

Twentieth Visit

May 17, 1806 [81]

HAYDN GAVE me proofs that he loved me as a friend and that he had
no fear of trusting that friend completely. I believed up to now—because I was told so—that Haydn had never set down in writing anything about the periods of his life. He now convinced me to the
contrary by taking out of his writing desk several pocket notebooks
in which are recorded short accounts covering both London jour-

neys. He started to leaf through these and found various incidents that I can now add to my accounts of the first London journey. "I will," he said, "pass these books on to you shortly, only I must first point out what is suitable, for there are some things as well that are not for the public." I thanked him for his trust, and he then told me with his former liveliness several anecdotes that follow here.

Not long after Haydn's arrival in London, he received a visit from an officer who was, to be sure, very polite but no friend of small talk, and who briefly stated the purpose of his visit. He wished that Haydn might compose two military marches for him. Haydn excused himself, saying that the opera *Orfeo* left him no extra time, that he only wrote when he was in the right humor for it, and could not know whether the *estro musicale* [musical inspiration] would take him early or late. He would—if it were agreeable—get a competent composer to write them under his personal supervision.[82]

"The marches must be by you. If I had wanted what you are proposing, I should not have come to you." While the officer was saying that, his hand played with the guineas in his pocket, now and then gathering up a handful and letting them roll back again in the pocket.

"The sound of the gold," said Haydn, "reminded me that England was to be my land of opportunity, so I asked him how much time he was allowing me to wait for the *estro.*"

"A fortnight. And the price?"

"Fifty guineas."

"Here is my hand on it; I shall come on the appointed day."

Haydn completed the marches. The officer came, Haydn sat down at the pianoforte and played the first march (E flat major) with his usual expressive performance. The officer, motionless as a statue, listened.—"He doesn't like it," thought Haydn. The playing ended. —The officer said as coldly as possible, *"Ancor una volta!"* [Play it again!]

Haydn, not knowing what to make of it, played the march a second time, and redoubled his powers in the playing, while casting a furtive glance toward the officer's countenance in the hope of reading approval there. Not a trace of it! When he had ended, the officer stood up. Haydn thought, "He will not hear the second march even once." Meanwhile the officer brought a roll of fifty guineas out of his pocket, handed it over to the astonished Haydn, and still saying nothing took the one march and started to go away.

"Don't you want to hear the second march too?"

"No," the officer replied, "it can't possibly be better than the first. Farewell! Tomorrow I sail for America." [83]

The banker [Brassey] begged Haydn in the most flattering way to give his daughter music lessons. He had undertaken her instruction, and everyone in the [Brassey] house paid him the most distinguishing honor. The banker's entire family went once for several weeks into the country. Haydn was invited to go, and often entertained the company with descriptions and stories of his experiences that must not seldom have made a striking contrast to the splendid circumstances of the banker.

Once when Haydn and [Brassey] were alone together, the latter listened attentively to such a story. Suddenly he sprang up as if possessed, uttered the most frightful oaths, and swore that if he had a loaded pistol, he would shoot himself on the spot.

Haydn too had sprung up in the meantime and cried, "Quick, help; quick: don't shoot me!" He thought he had only one life and it was too soon to lose it.

The banker's wife and several others hurried thither in alarm. The banker called out to them, "Bring the pistols! I'm going to shoot myself." The people who had hurried in sought to calm his trembling and to discover the cause of his murderous intent. The banker long refused an answer. When they finally implored of him with tears in their eyes, he repeated again the strongest oaths, and protested that he was going to shoot himself, because he had never known misfortune. Grief, misery, and need he did not know, could speak nothing of them from his own experience, but, as he now observed, was still not happy, because he knew only eating and drinking; he knew only superabundance and hence detested it.

Haydn finished his story here. But not to leave my readers in sorrow on account of the banker, I can give them assurance that he did not shoot himself.[84]

Haydn enjoyed the friendship of a distinguished friend of music and was present at a concert which the latter gave at his house.[85] Among the people invited was a clergyman. Haydn performed one of his symphonies. During the Andante the listeners noticed that

the clergyman fell into the gloomiest depression. His friends there asked him the reason for this fit of melancholy. His answer was that "the Andante announces to me the coming death that I dreamed of last night." He thereupon left the concert, went home, took to his bed already ill, and expired several days afterwards.

"Isn't that an amazing occurrence?" Haydn said.

"No more," I replied, "than if a blind hen finds a barleycorn. I should think it amazing, even a miracle, if among all possible dreams none ever came true; if three numbers were never guessed in lotto."

Haydn's good humor still continued. He told the following anecdote to which I yield space here, though it seem to the eyes of my readers nothing more than a funny story. It is of importance, however, where Haydn is concerned because it deals with his nasal polyp.

Haydn had several times already submitted to surgical operations and, even under the hands of the celebrated Brambilla,[86] had been so unfortunate as to forfeit a piece of the nasal bone without being wholly freed of the polyp.

In London Haydn chanced on the acquaintance of the celebrated surgeon H[unter]; "a man," said Haydn, "who undertook surgical operations almost daily and always successfully. He had inspected my polyp and offered to free me of this complaint. I had half agreed, but the operation was put off, and I finally thought nothing more at all about it. Shortly before my departure [in 1792] Mr. H[unter] sent to ask me for pressing reasons to come to him. I went. After the first greetings several big strong fellows entered the room, seized me, and tried to seat me in a chair. I shouted, beat them black and blue, kicked till I freed myself, and made it clear to Mr. H[unter], who was standing all ready with his instruments for the operation, that I would not be operated on. He wondered at my obstinacy, and it seemed to me that he pitied me for not wanting the fortunate experience of his skill. I excused myself for lack of time, due to my impending departure, and took my leave of him."

Twenty-first Visit

May 27, 1806

THE FOLLOWING anecdote will serve to show how much Haydn's art was extolled in London, and his person honored.

Haydn received from Mr. S[haw], a member of Parliament with whom he was not previously acquainted, a courteous invitation to dinner.[87] The carriage was sent for him at his lodging, and Mr. S[haw] paid him the honor of receiving him at the house door and presenting him to his assembled family. It was winter and they were sitting around the open fire, on either side of which, in the English custom, stood a row of chairs, one for the ladies, the other for the gentlemen. The place in the middle before the hearth invariably remains unoccupied.

Haydn already knew the local usage and was about to sit down on the men's side. He was at once prevented, however, and made to take the most honored seat in the middle before the hearth.

Gradually it became apparent to him that all the women were wearing white, and the men brown; moreover he was surprised to see that the women had tastefully fixed in their hairdresses wide pearl-colored ribbons on which could be read the name J. Haydn in gold embroidery.

Haydn could say not a word for surprise, looked now at the women, now at the men, and so discovered that the latter were wearing his name in steel beads as a decoration on the collars of their suits. Haydn's embarrassment mounted greatly and disappeared only at the table. The company dispersed late at night. At Haydn's departure Mrs. S[haw] undid the ribbon * in her hair and presented it to Haydn as a pledge of eternal friendship.

Some time later Mr. S[haw] chanced to see that Haydn occasionally took snuff. The snuffbox was only made of brown paper and had two lids with Haydn's name engraved on a little silver plate. Mr. S. asked Haydn for the box as a keepsake, had a silver case made to protect it, and engraved on the cover a lyre of Apollo around which were the words *"Ex dono celeberrimi J. Haydn."* [Gift of the most renowned J. Haydn.]

Rauzzini, a celebrated singer, likewise a composer, lived, after he had retired from the theater, at Bath and invited Haydn to honor him with a visit. Dr. Burney conducted Haydn thither, and both were Rauzzini's guests for three days.

Rauzzini had placed in his garden a monument to the honor of his best friend, whom death had snatched away from him. He lamented, in an inscription, the loss of a friend so true, and so on, and concluded his lament with the words: "He was not a man—he was a dog."

Haydn copied the inscription in secret, and made a four-part canon to which he set the words. Rauzzini was surprised. The canon pleased him so much that he had it carved on the monument to the honor of Haydn and of the dog.[88]

Haydn gave me today a pocket notebook from the year 1792. He

---

* Haydn's autograph account says pin; my readers will excuse his failing memory.

leafed through it and found only one entry that seemed to him not unworthy of being made known. Here it is.

In Whitsuntide in St. Paul's Church in London the charity children sang with only organ accompaniment. The children were all newly dressed and marched in a kind of procession to the church. Inside the church a platform had been erected in the dome on which on this occasion 4,000 children assembled. On the platform stood the organ, also. The audience were below in the church, and heard the children's singing as some unearthly music. The organist first played the melody with no harmonizing bass or inner voices; then the children joined in *unisono,* slowly, solemnly with the organ accompaniment and sang a sacred song to the following melody:

Haydn wrote in his pocket book, "No music moved me so greatly in my whole life as this, full of devotion and innocent." He told me in addition, "I stood there, and wept like a child." He remarked that the voices sounded like angels' voices; that the descent in the first three measures to the low B worked in a dread, heart-gripping way whilst the notes of the tender young voices died away, and the B sounded only like a hovering breath; that in the continuation of the melody the ascending tones gradually gained in life and strength and that thus the melody took on light and shadow which worked powerfully on the feelings.

Haydn's pocket book contains many things of no importance to my readers that I pass up as much by my own choice as in keeping with Haydn's wishes. Yet it seems to me the following anecdotes may give my readers some pleasure, although they have no bearing on Haydn's person and should find no place per se in these accounts.

Haydn was present at a great concert when all the musicians were ready to begin. Only the timpanist had not yet tuned up and called out to the orchestra leader that he must still wait a moment, he had to tune the kettledrums. "Ach!" the leader answered, without stopping to think,—"What do you mean, tune?—You'll have to transpose."

I had already resolved a long time ago to ask Haydn how much truth there was in the assertion (which I had several times heard and also read) that he sought in his instrumental pieces to work out some verbal problem or other selected at will? Whether, for example, he had never thought of expressing in a symphony movement a coquette, a prude, and so on? "Seldom," answered Haydn. "In instrumental music, I generally allowed my purely musical fantasy free play. Only one exception occurs to me now, in which in the Adagio of a symphony, I chose as a theme a conversation between God and a heedless sinner."

On a later occasion the talk turned again to this Adagio, and Haydn said he always expressed the Deity by love and goodness.

I begged Haydn to designate to me the theme of the Adagio, because it would be sure to interest most readers, but he no longer remembered in which symphony it is to be found.[89]

Twenty-second Visit

June 9, 1806

At today's visit I was eyewitness to an interesting scene. Haydn showed me a portfolio of copper engravings, part of them purchased in London, part received as gifts. Many of them are portraits of celebrated musicians whom Haydn knows personally. While we were leafing through the engravings, Prince Paul, son of the reigning Prince Esterházy, was announced as a visitor to Haydn. It was a truly moving sight to see the venerable old man, the great artist esteemed by a prince with the one word, "Merit," and embraced and covered with kisses to the accompaniment of the words, "My good Haydn, may God keep you for many years yet!" Haydn himself was deeply moved by the tenderest interest of the Prince in his well-being, by such genuine wishes for the preservation of his life.[90]

Even during the Prince's visit Haydn was complaining that he had not been really well for several days, for which he blamed a continuing annoyance. I asked him after the departure of the Prince to explain more clearly, and learned that twelve years before in London Haydn had lent sixty guineas to a German whose name he did not reveal. Out of consideration of the family name the man bore, Haydn did not require a receipt for the sum and trusted to the well known old German honesty. The debtor never paid back this sum. Haydn finally sent for him; he came. Haydn referred in the matter of the debt to a note in his own hand as the sole existing document. On this sheet were written the names of several debtors, the amounts were shown, and also stricken out. Only the name of the debtor mentioned stood uncanceled, but he *could not remember* this debt. Haydn was astonished at his faithless memory. He could sue for the amount, but since he shied away from the trouble that inevitably accompanies such suits, he preferred to give up the whole business. This much Haydn told me of the questionable case, concerning which I cannot pass judgment, although it seems impossible to me really to be able to forget such a considerable debt and all circumstances connected with it.[91]

Twenty-third Visit

June 18, 1806

HAYDN CONTINUED to feel well during the warm weather. He took some exercise daily. Yesterday several friends invited him to go along with them to a famous instrument-maker's to inspect a newly invented musical instrument with organ pipes [*Orgelwerk*]. Haydn let himself be easily persuaded although the artist's lodgings lay some distance from Gumpendorf. When the coach came to a stop, the younger men sprang quickly out, made Haydn's descent easy, and then carried him several flights up to the artist's lodgings. The organ-work even played a Haydn composition. Haydn listened with pleasure, and this pleasure gave his will-to-live new force.[92]

Haydn showed me another little book of notes. I opened it and found a couple of dozen letters in English in it. Haydn smiled and said, "Letters from an English widow in London, who loved me; but although she was already sixty years old, she was still a beautiful and amiable woman whom I might very easily have married if I had been free then."

This woman is the widow, still living, of the celebrated clavier player Schröder,[93] whose melodious song Haydn emphatically praised. In the letters of the widow, who was a musician herself, one sees that this woman loved Haydn's genius. Often she cannot find words to interpret the feelings that Haydn's music awakes in her. Joined to this is the greatest respect for the man whose genius-laden works are the wonder of the entire world of culture. Haydn enjoyed very pleasant hours in the company of the widow. When he was invited nowhere else, he generally dined with her.

Because I found Haydn in such a good humor for speaking of women, I threw out in jest some searching questions. He frankly admitted that he had welcomed the sight of pretty women, but he could not understand how it came about that he was loved in his life by so many a pretty woman. "My good looks," he added, "cannot have led them into it."

"You have," said I, "a certain genial something about you, in face and figure, that people like to see and to which they must be good."

"They can see in me that I mean well towards everybody."

"That must have placed you open to many an advance?"

"Oh, many! but I was prudent!"

I pray my readers not to believe that I would lead you back unawares to the times of the *Confessions à la Jean Jacques*. I have told
enough to preserve truthfulness and to show that Haydn fancied
himself made of no better stuff than other men, and sought by feigning purity to put himself on no higher plane of morality than in his
own opinion he deserved.

The talk turned to Haydn's doctorate. He regretted having mis-
laid or lost a little pocket book in which he had noted down details
of the whole procedure by which he had been graduated Doctor of
Music from Oxford University.[94]

Dr. Burney was the instigator. He persuaded Haydn to this
course and even traveled with him to Oxford. At the ceremony in
the University Hall, the company present was stirred by an address
to honor with the doctorate the service of a man who had risen so
high in music. The whole assembly gave Haydn an ovation. Then
Haydn was dressed in a white silk gown with sleeves of red silk and
small black silk hat, and thus arrayed he had to sit in the doctor's
seat. After this function, there was music and our own Mara, who
was then in England, sang. They begged Haydn to give something
of his own composition. He climbed up to the organ gallery in the
hall, turned around to face the assembly with every eye fixed on him,
gripped the doctor's gown on his breast in both hands, opened it, let
it fall closed again, and said as loud and clear as he could [in Eng-
lish], "I thank you." The assembly well understood this unexpected pantomime; Haydn's thanks pleased them and they answered
[in English], "You speak very good English."

"I looked quite funny in this gown, and the worst of it was, I had
to go about the streets in this masquerade for three days. Still, I
owe much in England, in fact I might say everything, to this doctorate. Through it I became acquainted with the foremost gentlemen,
and gained entrance to the greatest houses."

Haydn said this with his characteristic naturalness, so that I can
scarcely imagine how it is possible for a genius like him to be so
completely unacquainted with his own power and to attribute every-

thing to the doctorate and nothing to his art. No complacency showed in these words, much less any concealed pride, for how easily might he not have framed the words to satisfy complacency, pride, and boastfulness? He, who paid the doctorate the greatest honor in accepting it, admitted with natural modesty (or should the word be worldly wisdom?) that he owed it everything, and that even in his case, the clothes had made the man.

Twenty-fourth Visit

August 17, 1806

A LONG continuing warm spell delayed this visit. I found Haydn unexpectedly weak. His formerly sparkling eyes were dull, his complexion very yellow; he complained besides of headache, deafness, forgetfulness, and various ills. With difficulty I concealed the degree to which I felt sorry for him and sought to bring up pleasant topics of conversation. What can amuse a Haydn more than music? I was lucky enough to disperse the clouds on his countenance a little, and at the question, "How long is it since you have touched your pianoforte?" he sat down to it, began slowly to improvise, struck some wrong notes, then looked at me, corrected the false notes, and struck some new ones in the correcting.

"Ach!" he said after a minute (the playing lasted no longer), "You hear for yourself, it is no good anymore! Eight years ago it was different, but *The Seasons* has brought this evil on me. I never should have written it! I overworked myself at it!"

Haydn stood up, and we went slowly up and down in the room. Deep gloom settled again on his brow; no brighter glance found a way through this dark cloud. "You see," he said, "I live out my few remaining days alone like this."

"You shouldn't; you should always have a friend around to cheer you up."

"Even that tires me out. I often receive visits, but the talking, even giving short answers, confuses me so that I end up not knowing where I am and long for peace."

I suppose that Haydn had learned of the death of his brother Michael, which occurred on August 10, 1806, in Salzburg, and this sad news had caused the melancholy to which he almost succumbed. His faded eye did not please me at all; it boded an approaching end. May the spirit of death one day take him away in a soft embrace without suffering!

Autumn's hastening on makes it probable that the decline in his powers will increase with the raw weather, so I fear I shall find rare occasions for adding new material to these accounts.

The small notebooks which Haydn gave me contain little that is useful. He noted down, for instance, visits that he made or received, journeys to places around London, descriptions of these, many anecdotes, accounts of the theater, verse, curiosities, in short, many things that would strike a stranger in London. The few accounts that concern Haydn personally are sketched there briefly. They served him merely to recall the circumstances to memory, and left such to be embroidered in the telling by his sense of humor, which, suddenly breaking out, often rendered the theme with variations. Thus it can happen that one sometimes hears an anecdote related in various ways, for which Haydn, who liked so well to please other men, was certainly responsible.

Neither from the little notebooks nor from Haydn's spoken accounts to me would I know how to select material having further bearing on his first stay in London, so I hurry on to a conclusion of the accounts of it. Haydn did not remember the day of his departure, and said every time I asked him about it that he had been in London the first time one and one half years, and because his wife urged his return, and he too wished to enjoy Vienna and, in general, the atmosphere of the fatherland, he had decided to quit London.[95]

Here I must make mention of an incident that again obliges me to retrace my steps chronologically. To wit: Haydn, not long after his arrival in London [in the summer of 1791], was called back by

Prince Anton to write an opera for the occasion of some celebrations to be given at Esterháza. But Haydn was bound in London by contract and hence was obliged not to obey his prince. Upon his return, now too late, he prepared himself for a reprimand, which to his surprise consisted only of the words, "Haydn, you could have saved me 40,000 gulden!"

After Haydn's arrival in Vienna, the music-loving public was rightly full of expectation to hear the first six symphonies of the famed collection and other pieces written in London, so Haydn got up at his own expense a great concert in the Redoutensaal whereby his earned fortune was increased by several thousand gulden.[96]

It could not fail that while Haydn was acquiring such signal fame during his first stay in England, this fame should create the greatest sensation in Haydn's fatherland. I will not be needlessly circumstantial on this point, and will only say that every cultivated man pronounced the name Haydn with a tone that revealed a feeling of national pride.*

The imperial chamberlain and privy councilor, Karl Leonhard Count von Harrach, proprietor of the domain of Rohrau (Haydn's birthplace), decided to erect there a monument to our Haydn.†
The Count wrote:

The reason for my placing a monument to Haydn in my garden was simply that, having come of age, I wished to transform the formal and kitchen gardens, the orchards and the pheasant preserve around my castle, which incidentally occupied forty yokes of land,[97] I dare not say into an English park, but still into an orderly promenade, not without some measure of economy.

I considered it fitting and proper, as well as an honor for my park, to erect in the castle precincts surrounding his birthplace a stone monument to the laudably celebrated J. Haydn. Haydn himself was then in England,

* I honor national pride if it recognizes, honors, and rewards living merit in the fatherland; if, however, it delays in these three things till death has long since claimed the person, then it loses much if not all its worth.

† At my request, Herr Count von Harrach imparted these accounts to me in writing.

was only slightly known to me, and knew nothing of my undertaking; moreover, he learned only two or three years later by chance that this monument was standing in Rohrau, and inspected it without my prior knowledge.

I used a part of my garden rather thickly overgrown with various leaf-bearing trees, and a place where the Leitha is quite broad and deep and makes a sudden bend. I had a navigable canal dug in a backward direction, and in this way created an island of perhaps a quarter of a yoke of land.

This island I then had cleared of brush and set out entirely in Lombardy poplars. The near bank, however, I planted with weeping willows, plane trees, tulip trees, and similar exotic species.

On one bank the monument now stands on three stone steps, and consists of a pedestal some ten feet high, on which are arranged musical trophies.

Two sides of the monument are provided with inscriptions,* because they are in sight. The well-known Abbé Denis furnished the text for the two larger tablets, and the first tablet reads as follows: †

TO THE MEMORY
OF JOSEPH HAYDN
THE DEATHLESS MASTER
OF MUSIC,
TO WHOM EAR AND HEART
CONTENDING DO HOMAGE,
DEDICATED,
BY
KARL LEONHARD COUNT VON HARRACH.
IN THE YEAR 1793.

The second tablet bears the short inscription:

* I don't know now on which visit I saw at Haydn's a little plaster-of-Paris model of this monument. The two blank tablets intrigued me and gave rise to the following epigram:

> Dem Nahmen Haydn giebt kein todter Marmor Leben;
> Unsterblichkeit muss Er vielmehr dem Marmor geben.
> [Dead marble does not make the name of Haydn live;
> He rather immortality must to the marble give.]

Haydn modestly sought to decline the praise. "That is too much; I do not deserve so much!" he said.

† In the *Leipzig Musikalische Zeitung* is a picture of the monument along with a description.

ROHRAU
GAVE HIM LIFE
IN THE YEAR 1732 THE 1ST APRIL *
EUROPE
UNDIVIDED APPROVAL,
THE 31ST MAY 1809.
THE ENTRANCE TO THE ETERNAL
HARMONIES.

There are also arranged above with the musical insignia, musical quotations of several motives from Haydn's compositions. In addition to these the well known Fräulein Gabriela von Baumberg has furnished several little verses, namely on one side:

> Thou gracious Philomel
> enliven now this shore,
> A thousand throats let swell
> this song forever more.

On the other side:

> A stone to Haydn's fame designed
> Consecrates this place enshrined,
> And Harmony mourns in dismay
> That this hand finally shall decay.

That Haydn was not indifferent to the honor shown him by Count von Harrach, he proved by the care he expressed even in illness for the future maintenance of the monument. During this illness (1804) he sent for the Count and informed him that he intended to make binding upon his future heirs in his will the perpetual maintenance of the monument at Rohrau.

"On this occasion (so writes Count von Harrach) I now offered a legal endowment in government bonds of 5 to 600 florins with the interest from which the monument might be perpetually cared for. But Haydn turned down my offer. There arose between us a sort of contest, but about the matter itself nothing at all has been done; meanwhile I am daily prepared to devote such an amount to the maintenance of the said monument."

* April 1 is incorrectly given as Haydn's birthday, and March 30 is to be understood instead.[98]

From what Haydn says, it cannot be certainly stated whether he continued to contest the right of Count von Harrach, as founder of the monument, to provide for its future maintenance. The thought occurred to him instead to establish in his will a fund for the benefit of several children of Rohrau, but of what this may consist, and whether the thought has been realized, I cannot now state. [See p. 195.]

Twenty-fifth Visit

December 11, 1806

I FOUND Haydn in a lively humor; his whole being was lifted. With astonishment I remarked on the great difference to be seen in Haydn since my previous visit. I could read the deepest joy in his features over my astonishment. "I'm not doing badly for this time of year, am I?" said he. I wished him well in the change for the better, and inquired for the cause.

"Don't think me a flatterer if I must attribute the cause to my beneficent Prince or to the Princess Maria, or to both princely people at once."

"You make me curious."

"A short time ago the Princess Maria honored me with a visit. Every visit is a new proof of her charity, and she always knows how to direct the conversation toward the discovery of a new opportunity for her beneficence.

"In this conversation the Princess coaxed from me the admission that on account of my great age and the frequent indispositions that go with it, I needed more caring for. I could not pass by in silence the increasing expense of this, and observed that I had numerous relations to be thought of after my death, but that I must surely be prevented from doing so if I lived very long, because in several years I had had to sacrifice more than 2,000 florins of my savings.

"The Princess interrupted me to ask how much I thought I needed to satisfy all my wishes.—I named the sum, and received in reply: 'Leave the matter to me.'

"Already the very next day the Princess herself delivered from his Serene Highness her consort, the reigning prince, a letter in his own hand."

Haydn took the letter out of his writing case, handed it to me to read, and added that the Prince had not allowed himself to be deprived of the opportunity of bestowing favor, even by his wife.

I hope for forgiveness from the princely persons if I make bold to give my readers the letter, which surely must have a more beneficent influence on Haydn's health than all the medicine in the world.*

Dear Kapellmeister Haydn!

My wife, the Princess Maria, has brought me your wish to receive six hundred gulden yearly from me besides the present emoluments, adding that its fulfilment would greatly quiet and content you. I hasten with pleasure to meet this opportunity to convey to you my esteem and friendship, impart to you herewith the assurance by which you will receive from my court treasury, which is being so notified at once, three hundred gulden half-yearly.

I wish you continuing good health, and am most readily yours,
Vienna, November 26, 1806   PRINCE ESTERHÁZY

Haydn told me that his noble patronness, the Princess Esterházy, some time before had added yet another to so many signal proofs of her favor, and had presented him with a writing case that included also an album (all of very great value). I wished to see the album, but Haydn said that there were so many noble persons who wished to honor him with a sentiment that he could not be sure when it would return to his hands again.

For several years now Haydn had been unable, for want of

* The word medicine reminds me that Haydn often receives by the Prince's kindness presents of Malaga wine, and that he attributes to this wine especially the preservation of his life. The Prince wished several years ago now to see to Haydn's comfort, and to provide him a coach. Haydn asked the Prince to alter this favor somewhat and transform the coach into wine. Since then Haydn has received as much princely wine as he can use.

strength, to bring to an end a quartet he had begun. His friend
G[riesinger] persuaded him (with my assistance) to publish it uncompleted. It occurred to Haydn to substitute for the wanting last
movement his already mentioned [page 144] calling card. Thus he
ended his great career with the confession of his weakness: *Hin ist
alle meine Kraft!*

Härtel, in Leipzig, was the publisher of this last of Haydn's musical output, and sent him an honorarium of fifty ducats for it.
Haydn dedicated it to Count von Fries and received from him also
a present of fifty ducats.

I now led the conversation to Haydn's second journey to London.
He complained of his weak memory and admitted to me that he was
in doubt whether he had not mixed up some incidents of the first
and second journeys and related many to me in the wrong place. If
that should indeed be the case, it is of no importance.[99]

When Haydn asked Prince Anton (father of the present Prince)
for permission to undertake a second journey to London, he found
great difficulties to overcome. The Prince, to be sure, required no
services of Haydn, but took pleasure in his presence, and was of the
opinion that Haydn had acquired for himself fame enough. He
should therefore be content, and at the age of one-and-sixty no longer
expose himself unprotected to the dangers of a journey and the consequences of jealousy stirred up in London. Haydn recognized, to
be sure, that all these expressions of Prince Anton's were proofs of
his noble disposition; nevertheless, since he felt keenly his own
strength and preferred an active life to the quiet in which the Prince
had placed him, it was natural that the wishes of the Prince did not
coincide with his own. There was the added fact that Haydn on his
first stay in London had cleared 12,000 gulden, and in addition knew
that the English public still greatly favored his muse. Also he had
contracted with Salomon, who was now no longer under contract to
Gallini, to write six more symphonies; he had besides made very
profitable contracts with various publishers. All these and other
points were compelling reasons for his going against the wishes of

the Prince, who ended by giving up his own will to Haydn's profit and granting him the permission for the journey, which ensued on January 19, 1794.

Twenty-sixth Visit

February 23, 1807

BY THIS time our Haydn had gone through another illness. Although his growing strength had permitted him to be out of bed only a few days before, he still denied himself all comfort in dress, and I found him, as usual, fully clothed. He told me the troubles he had been having, and I saw in his features again the joyous vitality which I had thought missing for quite a while. Haydn joked about not yet having died this time. I replied to this: *"Die Dichter irrten nicht, die Dich unsterblich nannten"* [The poets did not err who thee immortal named].

Haydn with the utmost lack of affectation gave this compliment a twist of his own, applying the words to himself in a purely physical sense, and said, "My aching bones remind me only too often that I am still alive."

I turned the talk to the journey, and learned that it proceeded at top speed, so that Haydn had no time to halt along the way and strike up acquaintance with any celebrities.

In Wiesbaden he met with an occurrence which, unimportant in itself, nevertheless gave him pleasure. In the inn where Haydn had stopped he heard next his room the beloved Andante with the Drum Stroke [Symphony No. 94] being played on a pianoforte. Counting the player a friend, he stepped politely into the room where he heard the music. He found several Prussian officers, all great admirers of his music, who, when he finally made himself known, would not take his word for it that he was Haydn. "Impossible! Impossible! You Haydn?—Already such an old man!—That doesn't rhyme with the fire in your music!—No! We shall never believe it!"

In this doubting vein the men persisted so long that Haydn produced a letter received from their King which he had fortunately brought along in his trunk. Then the officers overwhelmed him with their fondness, and he had to stay in their company till long past midnight. Haydn was loath to leave his new-found friends. He traveled on, and his arrival in London ensued on February 4, 1794.

A short time after Haydn's arrival came the sad news of the death of Prince Anton [January 22, 1794]. Thus Haydn had by now served with distinction as Kapellmeister to three reigning Prince Esterházys. Prince Nikolaus, son of the deceased Prince Anton, succeeded him, and nothing was clearer from his conduct than that in him humanity, arts, and sciences would find a great protector.

I saw today at Haydn's various silver pieces. My glance fixed especially on a plaque something like a shoe in cross-section and with feet, on which is engraved an inscription that reads as follows [in English]:

Dr. Haydn, Dr. Arnold, Mr. John Stafford Smith, and Mr. Atterbury declared their readiness to cooperate with Dr. Cooke, Dr. Hayes, Dr. Dupuis, Dr. Parson, Mr. Calcott, the Rev. Osbome Wight, Mr. Webber, Mr. Shield and Mr. Stevens in their Exertions towards perfecting a Work for the Improvement of Parochial Psalmody; as a smal Token of estem, for his abilities and of gratitude for his services, this Pice of Plate is presented to Dr. Haydn by W. D. Tattersall.

All the doctors of music named in this inscription had taken part in the composition of church songs, and each of them received as a memento such a plaque.[100]

Today's talk having once turned to gifts, Haydn showed me a cup made of a coconut but tastefully trimmed in silver. The worth of this cup was raised in Haydn's eyes because it reminded him of Clementi, from whom he received this present.

Twenty-seventh Visit

June 4, 1807

HARDLY HAD Haydn (whom I found in good health) seen me when he began to talk about his beloved pupil Herr Neukomm. He had received from him some time before a letter whose contents had given him such extraordinary pleasure that the effect of it was still to be seen in his countenance. Haydn bade me make the letter known in my account. I promised, and hope, since Herr Neukomm is one of my honored friends, to receive his forgiveness.

St. Petersburg, April 5/17, 1807

Dearest Papa!

I gave a concert here yesterday and enclose the *affiche.* Your splendid choruses from *Tobias* were received with the complete enthusiasm,[101] which, with deepest joy, I have always noted here at the performance of your matchless masterworks. I chose for No. 2 the chorus *Ah gran Dio! sol tu sei, etc.;* for No. 4, *Odi le nostre voci, etc.;* and for No. 6, *Svanisce in un momento,* in which already at the end of the first part they began to applaud quite extraordinarily. I directed, and the excellent court chorus, joined by a hand-picked, well-filled orchestra, worked with so much love that you would surely have been perfectly satisfied with the performance if we had had the good fortune to enjoy your presence.

I spared nothing to get good performers for my concert, so I had expenses above 1,100 rubles, despite which I have still, after subtracting all costs, over 1,200 rubles clear profit. And what endlessly increases my pleasure is that everyone left the hall satisfied.

I write you all this because I can in no other way prove to you my gratitude except by assuring you that everything pleasing which ever falls to my lot is your work alone.—You are my father and the author of my good fortune.

How much I envy Vienna the fortune to keep you within its walls! How often I long to see you, dearest Papa, if only for an hour! Shall not this happiness, then, soon fall to my lot?

Let me know something of your well-being from time to time, and no one will be happier than

your
ever grateful pupil,
NEUKOMM

Herr Neukomm several years ago traveled from here to St. Petersburg, and was engaged immediately upon his arrival as Kapellmeister at the theater. Haydn took the opportunity to send some music to the widowed Empress Maria, writing at the same time a recommendation of his latest pupil. The Empress replied by her own hand, and sent to Haydn a ring as proof of her pleasure. Herr Neukomm had to play before the Empress; his composition and his playing had the good fortune to be highly approved by the Empress. [See p. 43.]

The conversation came to *Tobias*, Haydn's oldest oratorio. He was of the opinion that Herr Neukomm was obliged to adapt the much-too-long choruses to the present age and shorten them. "When I wrote the oratorio," he said, "long notes were still worth something; now everything swarms with sixty-fourth notes. It's the same with this as with money. There used to be nothing about but heavy gold and silver; now you see only copper kreutzers and pennies."

Haydn had already during earlier visits told me of an incident that finds a suitable place here. He was closely acquainted in London with a German musical amateur who had acquired a skill on the violin bordering on virtuosity, but who had the bad habit of always playing too close to the bridge in the highest tones. Haydn decided to try if possible to break the dilettante of his habit and give him a feeling for a solid manner of playing.

The dilettante often visited a Miss J[ansen] who played the pianoforte with great skill while he usually accompanied. Haydn wrote in perfect secrecy a sonata for the pianoforte with a violin accompaniment, entitled the sonata "Jacob's Dream," and sent it, sealed and unsigned, by a trusty hand to Miss J[ansen], who likewise did not delay to try over the sonata, which appeared easy, in company with the dilettante. What Haydn had foreseen duly came to pass. The dilettante remained stuck in the highest registers, where most of his passages lay. Soon Miss J[ansen] suspected that the unknown composer intended to depict the ladder to heaven that Jacob saw in his dream and then noticed how the dilettante now ponderously, uncertainly, stumbling, now reeling, skipping, climbed up and down this ladder. The thing seemed so funny to her that she could not hide her laughter, while the dilettante abused the unknown composer, and boldly maintained that he did not know how to write for the violin.

Only after five or six months did it come out that the sonata's author was Haydn, who then received for it a present from Miss J[ansen].[102]

About half a year after Haydn's arrival in London, a letter was sent him from Naples from the then-reigning Prince Nikolaus Esterházy (who was at the time traveling in Italy) which contained the news that the Prince had named Haydn as his Kapellmeister and wished to re-establish the entire chapel.[103] Haydn received this news with greatest pleasure. He had always had a hearty affection for the Esterházy princes, who had assured his daily bread, and (what he especially liked) given him great opportunity to develop his musical talents. Of course, Haydn saw that his income in England was large and far surpassed that in his fatherland. Besides it had become easy for him there to command an imposing salary anywhere. He had been since the death of Prince Anton a fully free person. Nothing bound him to the princely house except his love and his gratitude. It was these that met every objection and moved him to accept the proposal of Prince Nikolaus with joy and, as soon as his contract in London was ended, to return to his fatherland.

Twenty-eighth Visit

November 21, 1807

HAYDN WAS indeed lively, but he complained of his usual infirmities, among which forgetfulness dealt these accounts the hardest blow. He put me off till the next spring, when he hoped to be invigorated by the returning warmth.

I did succeed, though, in rendering this visit not entirely fruitless. I asked all sorts of questions and thus set his slumbering memory to work. Haydn recalled his youth much more easily than subsequent later incidents. He chanced upon the time when he was still a choirboy, and told me several tales of a low comic order to which my readers will not begrudge the space allotted them.

Concerning Haydn's second journey, I find in his notebooks only the following few incidents, sketched in a few words, that I can make use of.

When Haydn left Bath, a crown of laurel was sent him the same day by a French emigrant. Enclosed with the crown were four verses which, though expressing nothing except good will, are still too bad to be passed on.

Haydn in the company of several friends saw the wild animals in the Tower. The keeper had carelessly left open the trap door to the tiger's cage. Madame Donelli was so fortunate as to discover it in time, although the keeper hurried up just at the moment when the tiger reached the trap door.[104]

On February 1, 1795, Haydn was invited by the Prince of Wales to his brother, the Duke of York's, to an evening of music. The King, the Queen together with the whole royal family, and several great persons were present. Haydn was especially honored in that none but his own compositions was played. He directed at the pianoforte and in the end had to sing. Among others he sang also his German song *Ich bin der verliebteste, etc.* [See note, p. 225.] The King was very attentive, approached him at the end of the concert, spoke about musical matters, and even showed him the honor, afterwards, of presenting to him the Queen.

Several days after the marriage of the Prince of Wales, to a princess of Brunswick, the Prince invited Haydn to an evening of music [on April 10, 1795; see p. 30]. The concert was opened with an old symphony, which Haydn directed at the pianoforte. Afterwards there was a quartet. Haydn had to sing German and English songs.

The fifteenth, the seventeenth, the nineteenth of April, a concert at the Prince of Wales'—the twenty-first, at the Queen's.

Haydn told me that he had set fifty Scotch songs to music for the publisher L——. The man was so impoverished that he could not pay Haydn, who, because he knew the publisher to be a good man, gave him the music. L—— published them, and was so unbelievably fortunate that he saw his previous wretched situation suddenly transformed.[105]

On March 4 [properly May; see p. 31], 1795, Haydn gave his benefit concert in the Haymarket Theater, and produced on this occasion the twelfth symphony from the celebrated collection. I found in Haydn's diary the following note about this benefit: "The whole company was extremely pleased, and I too. I made this evening 4,000 florins—one can do this only in England."

One can see that Haydn at that time was far removed from the idea that he might in the future in Vienna on the occasion of the performance of *The Creation* have a much richer harvest and take in around 9,000 florins.

Haydn's present stay in London increased his fortune by 12,000 florins. It came thus to 24,000 florins in all that he earned in the space of three years.

The talk turned to *The Creation*. The first suggestion for this work came from Salomon in London. Since he had been fortunate in so many musical undertakings up to then, and Haydn had contributed no little to this fortune, his courage for new undertakings was always greater. Salomon resolved to have a great oratorio written by Haydn, and delivered to him for that purpose an already old text, in the English language. Haydn had doubts about his knowledge of the English language, did not undertake it, and finally left London on August 15, 1795.

Haydn this time traveled back by way of Hamburg expressly to make the personal acquaintance of C. P. E. Bach. He came too late; Bach was dead, and of the family he found only one daughter living.[106] In Dresden he visited Naumann, but did not find him at home. A female domestic was busy at the moment cleaning the room. Haydn asked whether a picture of Naumann were not at hand, and being told Yes, asked to be shown it so that he might at least be acquainted with Naumann's picture.[107]

Haydn did not remember the English text again until, shortly after his arrival in Vienna, Baron van Swieten said to him, "Haydn, we have still to hear an oratorio of yours!" He informed the Baron of the state of affairs and showed him the English text. Swieten offered to make an abridged free translation of it into German. Once this was done, he also knew how to push Haydn so that he had no choice and earnestly resolved to compose the German text. From this it is seen that all those who said Haydn had originally written this work for London were in error.

Baron van Swieten was a great admirer of Haydn and Mozart. His knowledge heightened his birth, and both supported his inclination to elevate music as much as possible. He was the power by which the high aristocracy was often spurred on to ally itself with great undertakings and to produce things that without Swieten would perhaps never have been realized. Industry was also a great merit of Swieten's that no one could deny him. He showed it particularly this time, and through him was brought about a union of twelve persons of the highest nobility who got together an honorarium of 500 ducats for Haydn's composition of *The Creation*. These noble persons were the Princes N. Esterházy, Trauttmannsdorf, Lobkowitz, Schwarzenberg, Kinsky, Auersperg, L. Lichtenstein, Lichnowksy, the Counts Marschall, Harrach, Fries, Barons von Spielmann and Swieten.

Under these circumstances *The Creation* came into being and was performed to unbelievable applause in the hall of Prince Schwarzenberg.[108] Haydn had exceeded all expectations. The nobility were so greatly charmed by it that the persons already named united a second time, and so originated under similar conditions *The Seasons* as well. Both were presented in the theater for Haydn's benefit. The receipts were large. *The Creation* alone yielded around 9,000 florins; *The Seasons* was not so lucrative.

The German text of *The Creation* was received with approval at that time, but this approval decreased in the future, and criticism at last ventured to find the text unworthy of Haydn's music and wished aloud to fit a better to it. *The Seasons* suffered the same fate. Haydn was too much obliged by both texts to quit the sphere of music and to wander around in the region of painting. And the aestheticians would grant no permission to this offense, as they labeled it; for, they say, "One may not require of a thing something which, by virtue of its nature, it does not possess and consequently cannot give. The painter shall not above all try to *speak,* nor the musician to *paint.* Both arts have, within their limits, sufficient means for working on the sensibilities."

Though this is truly said, it still admits some exceptions. A significant exception might occur when the poet's material is taken supernaturally, or from a world of magic where everything is produced in a wonderful way. When, for example, the poet conjures us off to the gardens of Armida or to a fairyland, allowing beasts and trees to talk, why then should it not also be allowed to the musician to elevate his art to the truly wonderful, and in doing so to take many liberties? Let him every time, though, consider with care whether his material is serious or comic, for otherwise how easily may he not run the risk with the serious of provoking laughter instead of moving the heart? And that will always happen if he uses the serious and the playful in the wrong place. Telemann lets us hear the cock crow at Peter's denial, and the audience has to laugh. Why? Because the comical does not belong there; one must otherwise assume that Telemann intends to make fun of the text.

Every imitation in art shall strive for nobility. Nobility excludes all superfluity, it admits only what is necessary. But imitation without nobility is nothing more than a low, comic aping.

The critic usually deals very severely with the composer. The latter is not seldom blamed if he has the misfortune to be shipwrecked on a bad text. But why? When the poet does not understand his own art, and in all seriousness, instead of wooing the composer's sensibilities, forces him to scenes that require painting and mimicking? The words of the poet often outrage all nature. Storm, waves, lightning and thunder cross one another; a ship is wrecked—really! a pretty scene, in which the picture of a storm is necessary; but surely also laughable where one expected simply the interior struggle of the soul, the play of excited, struggling, bursting passions. In this case, the poet should at most call to mind with a few words the picture of outraged nature, thus powerfully to set off the words of his hero; but instead of this, he tells of thunder and lightning, and works himself through a detailed portrayal of a storm, in which he himself and the composer as well go to ruin. Now if we put the same scene in a comic piece, the hero is a *buffo,* and the applause will not be wanting.

I have already said that after the demise of his father the then-reigning Prince Nikolaus Esterházy advanced Haydn to the post of Kapellmeister. Besides the usual extra allowances, he now enjoyed 2,300 florins yearly, part pension, part salary.

I asked Haydn how he had possibly managed at that age to fulfil his service to the Prince and besides to write two large oratorios, etc.? He gave me the answer that my readers have already read in the dedicatory letter at the head of these accounts.

Twenty-ninth Visit

April 5, 1808

ON MARCH 27 [1808] was one of the greatest honors Haydn had till then experienced. The old man had always loved the fatherland, and he valued inexpressibly any honor enjoyed in the fatherland.

The Society of Amateur Concerts gave, under the sponsorship of the Supreme Steward, Prince von Trauttmannsdorf, on March 27 the last concert of the year in the University Hall, and thought to conclude most fittingly with Haydn's *Creation*. Carpani had supplied a masterly Italian translation of the text.[109] Haydn was ceremoniously invited to the celebration, at which he was to be the foremost guest, and his health as well as the bright weather permitted him by good fortune to appear at the performance. Prince Esterházy was at court on the day, but sent a carriage to Haydn's house in which Haydn drove slowly to the hall. On his arrival here, he was received by some of the great members of the nobility. The crowd was very large, so that a military guard had to see that order was kept. Now Haydn, sitting on an armchair, was borne along aloft, and at his entrance into the hall, to the sound of trumpets and timpani, was received by the numerous assemblage and greeted with the joyful cry, "Long live Haydn!" He had to take his place next the Princess Esterházy. Next him on the other side sat Fräulein von Kurzbeck. The greatest nobility of that place and from afar had chosen their places in Haydn's vicinity. It was much feared lest the weak old man catch cold, so he was obliged to keep his hat on.[110]

The French Ambassador, Count Andreossy, appeared to notice with pleasure that Haydn was wearing on a ribbon in his buttonhole the gold medal presented to him, in consideration of *The Creation,* by the *Concert des Amateurs* in Paris, and said to him, "You should receive not this medal alone but all medals awarded in the whole of France."

Haydn thought he felt a little draft, which the persons sitting near
him noticed. Princess Esterházy took her shawl and put it about
him. Several ladies followed this example, and Haydn in a few moments was smothered in shawls.

This festive ceremony was celebrated by Herr von Collin in German and by Carpani in Italian verse. The songs of the two poets were
presented to the much-moved old gentleman by the Baroness von
Spielmann and Fräulein Kurzbeck. He could no longer control his
feelings; his sore-pressed heart sought and found relief in an outburst of tears.

He had to take a bracer of wine to restore his fainting spirits.
Despite this Haydn remained in such melancholy humor that he
had to go away at the end of the first part. His departure overpowered him altogether: he could barely speak and could express only
with intermittent, weak words and gestures his deepest thanks, and
his warmest wishes for the well-being of the assembly of musicians
and of their art in general. Deep emotion was to be read in every
face, and tearful eyes accompanied him as he was borne off all the
way to the carriage.

Prince Esterházy, as I have already said, could not be present at
the celebration; but as soon as circumstances permitted he sent by
messenger to find out whether it were not too late to appear there. It
was too late; Haydn had already gone away.

I append here the two poems I spoke of:

To
Joseph Haydn
at the
Performance of *The Creation* in the University Hall
in Vienna
March 27, 1808 [111]

Thou hast borne the world in thine own breast.
The gloomy gates of Hell thou hast put down;
   Free in thy flight e'en Heaven's realms to test,
One hears thee in the mighty wings of sound.
   Thou shouldst not sorrow then, now old and blessed,
To find the years thy powers now ring round:

Time's gloomy force will overcome the flesh;
What thou hast wrought will evermore be fresh.

As to the Muse's temple in this hall
Expectant happy multitudes now throng;
  So will the future's sons come at the call
Of thy Creation's high and heavenly song;
  So will be heard the joyous cries of all
At hallelujahs by thine angels sung.
    That which a man sings pure from his pure heart,
    Will from the heart of men not soon depart.

O listen long charmed by thy music's style,
In circling throng of ever-loving friends,
  So shalt thou wean thyself from earth awhile,
So make thee ready for the journey hence.
    Ever the earth with Heaven to reconcile
Of thy life and thine art has been the sense.
    From deepest earth thanks still to thee arise,
    Receive thee Hallelujah in the skies.

by Collin

All' immortale Haydn
per la sua
Creazione del Mondo

Sonetto [112]

A un muover sol di sue possenti ciglia
  Trar dal nulla i viventi e l'Universo,
  E spinger Soli per cammin diverso,
  E immensa attorno a lor d'astri famiglia;
E Natura sì ordir, che, di sè figlia,
  Si rinnovi ogni istante, e il dente avverso
  Le avventi invan lo Struggitor perverso,
  Se Dio lo volle e il fe', qual meraviglia?
Ma ch' uom l'opra di Dio stupenda e rara
  Eguagliar tenti con pittrici note,
  E la renda al pensier presente e chiara,
Non possibil cimento a ognun parea.
  Haydn, tu il festi. In te chi tutto puote
  Tanto versò di sua divina idea.

de Carpani

Today it was as if an electric current were flowing in Haydn's veins, so greatly had the events of the foregoing days stimulated his spirits. He urged me once again in these accounts to assure all the musicians who took part in the performance of *The Creation* of his warmest thanks. In praise of Mademoiselle Fischer, he said, "She had sung her part with the utmost grace and so truly that she allowed herself not the least unsuitable addition." [113]

"I fortunately survived the day of *The Creation*," he said. "I doubted whether I could summon that much strength."

He now showed me a gold medal [see p. 68] and said, "There's something new." "When?" I asked. "Recently." He promised to show me shortly the accompanying letter, along with his answer, which was being taken care of by some friends; and this he did.

Société académique des enfans d'Appollon.[114]

Paris le 30. Decembre 1807

Monsieur!

Les Français s'honorent des immortelles productions de Votre Génie, puisqu'il en est plusieurs que Vous avés composées pour Eux. Un grand Concert, à Paris, ne paraitrait pas bon, si l'on n'y entendait une ou deux de Vos symphonies. Aussi peut on dire, avec verité, que les artistes se font un devoir religieux de donner tous leurs soins à leur éxécution, bien assurés du goût et de la sensibilité des auditeurs, qui partagent constamment leur juste enthousiasme.

Notre société réunit dans son sein Vos plus zélés admirateurs. Elle jouit de quelque estime. Mais elle a jugé que la célébrité serait mieux méritée, et qu'elle serait plus digne du culte d'Apollon en s'enrichissant de Votre association, et en inscrivant Votre nom sur la liste de ses membres.

Daignés, Monsieur, agréer son hommage. Elle fait consister sa gloire et son bonheur dans Votre assentiment.

Veuillés également recevoir avec bonté l'exemplaire cy joint de ses statuts et reglemens suivi du tableau de la société, ainsi qu'une médaille d'or frappée au type du jeton d'argent que chaque membre reçoit pour son droit de présence à chacune de ses séances.

Nous avons l'honneur d'être avec la plus haute considération

Monsieur etc.

Haydn's Answer [115]

Vienne le 7. Avril 1808

Messieurs!

Le choix que la société académique des enfans d'Apollon a daigné faire, en inscrivant mon nom sur la liste de ses membres m'est aussi flatteur, qu'il me penêtre de la plus vive sensibilité.

En l'assurant par Votre organe, qu'elle ne pouvoit honorer personne, plus fait pour apprécier son estime, et plus propre à sentir le prix de l'honneur qui en est la suite, je Vous prie Messieurs, de souffrir que mes sentimens s'expliquent aprés les Votres, et d'être en même tems les interpretes de ma réconnoissance des marques distinctives que Vous m'avés transmises, pour l'envoi d'un exemplaire des statuts et reglemens, accompagnés d'une medaille d'or.

Vous avés jetté, Messieurs, quelques fleurs sur le chemin de la vie, qui me reste encore à parcourir. J'en suis profondement touché, et je sens vivement, que la vieillesse peut bien affoiblir les facultés, mais qu'elle n'ote rien à la sensibilité, car c'est elle qui me fait regretter que mon grand age m'interdit de nourrir l'espoire de me voir parmi Vous, de partager Vos traveaux, de cooperer à la culture d'un art qui fait le charme de la société, et de participer à la célébrité dont l'Académie jouit à des titres si chers et si precieux.

C'est une consolation, à la quelle mes infirmités me forcent de rinoncer; et mes regrêts sont aussi vifs, que ma réconnoissance est profondement sentie; daignés en recevoir l'assurance, accompagnée de l'expression des sentimens de l'estime la plus sincère, et de la consideration la plus distinguée avec les quels j'ai l'honneur d'étre

Messieurs etc.

Thirtieth Visit

August 8, 1808

THE WHOLE world of culture in Europe is in tireless rivalry to offer our Haydn proofs of its great esteem. The name of Haydn sparkles like a star—a great triumph for the art!

Haydn received the following letter from his beloved pupil Herr Neukomm:

St. Petersburg, June 4/16, 1808

Dearest Papa!

This is the last letter that I shall be writing to you from here; the day after tomorrow I set out and hope to arrive in Vienna in September. I am going by a very roundabout way, traveling through a great part of Germany in a north-west-east course. My trip to Germany will be interesting to me only because I shall be so happy to see you again.

The Philharmonic Society of St. Petersburg has had a medal struck in your honor and dispatched to you through the present Russian ambassador in Vienna. The directors of the Society wished to give it to me, but I refused because I shall not reach Vienna for three months and because it is more to your honor if it be delivered by the Ambassador. The Directors also bade me point out to you that the year 1802 is the year of the founding of the Society, and because your generally admired masterwork *The Creation* formed the cornerstone of their edifice, the Society thus thought best to maintain this year, so remarkable for you, in the memory of posterity. The medal weighs forty-two and a half ducats.

Your diploma of honorary membership in this Society is not yet drawn up. I shall soon be so fortunate as to see you again. Keep well, my dearest Papa, and preserve me in your love, the one thing that makes my lot enviable and myself the most fortunate on earth,

ever

your grateful son,
NEUKOMM

Vienna, July 25, 1808

The Philharmonic Society of St. Petersburg wishes to transmit the enclosed medal to the Doctor of Music, the father of harmony, the immortal Haydn. With the greatest pleasure I undertook this charge, which presented me with so splendid an opportunity to attest to the author of *The Creation,* of *The Seasons,* and of so many great works, my sense of constant admiration as well as of unlimited esteem.

A. PRINCE KURAKIN

Well born Sir!

Most highly respected Herr Kapellmeister.

The Directors of the Philharmonic Society of this city, etc. [Here Dies gives the letter already quoted by Griesinger on p. 46.]

In the fall Herr Neukomm arrived here again. His stay in Vienna was to last only a few months; during this time he gave his teacher pleasure by having performed the Haydn oratorio *Tobias,* which he adapted to our times. [See pp. 169–170.]

Not long before the outbreak of open war Herr Neukomm left here for France, and received from Haydn as an eternal keepsake the original score of one of his masses. "This gift," said Herr Neukomm, "I would not sell for all the world." [116]

Above (Twenty-eighth Visit) I have told by what circumstances both Haydn's *Creation* and *The Seasons* came into being. I will here pick up again the broken thread of narrative and report what else I have learned of the two works of art. One of the first public performances of *The Creation* was brought about, as already mentioned, in the Imperial National Theater [the Burg Theater], for Haydn's benefit. I do not know whether on this occasion or on that of an earlier performance the well known poetess, Gabriele Batsányi, published the following verses: [117]

> Refreshing, like all beauty, soft,
> And fiery like a real wine,
>   Streams thy music's magic oft
> Through th'ear into this heart of mine.
>
> Lately thy creative Word
> Made thunder through the kettle drums
>   With heaven, sun and moon and earth,
> A new creation thus become.
>
> Astonished, moved, ecstatic-drunk,
> As Adam once in Paradise,
>   Into the arms of Eva sunk,
> All speechless praised his Maker wise.
>
> So we now hear encharmed these tones
> The art-work of thy fantasy—
>   And pledge with tearful eyes again,
> To thee Creator of Harmony.

Copies of *The Creation* soon spread throughout Europe. In Paris, in view of this interest, they sought to outdo other cities, and the first [foreign] performance in fact took place there, although with some alterations; so great was the approval that the participating musicians grew splendidly enthusiastic, and, to attest their respect for Haydn, decided [to commemorate] this performance with a great gold medal that boasts on one side Haydn's likeness, but that is decorated on the other side with a lyre erect, above which a burning flame in the midst of a crown of stars is blazing. At the base of the lyre the artist N. Gatteaux placed a most significant allegory of barely visible figures that, if I saw correctly, represented Apollo and Pan, or Nature and Art. The circumscription is: Hommage à *Haydn,* par les Musiciens qui ont éxécuté l'oratorio de la création du monde, au théatre des arts l'an IX de la République française ou MDCCC [Homage to *Haydn* from the musicians who performed the oratorio The Creation of the World, at the Arts Theater in the year IX of the French Republic or 1800].

My readers will find a picture of this medal in the *Leipzig Musikalische Zeitung* in Volume 4, Number 5 [p. 79].

The company of musicians had placed their letter together with the medal in the hands of the imperial ambassador in Paris, Count L. von Cobenzl, who added a letter to Haydn and forwarded it to the state minister, Prince von Colloredo, in Vienna. The latter also added a letter to Haydn and had the medal delivered to him.

Here follows the letter of the French musicians

"Les artistes français réunie au *theatre des arts,* etc." [Here Dies gives the letter already quoted by Griesinger on p. 41.]

Signed by 127 musicians

Haydn's Answer

[August 10, 1801]

My dear sirs! It is for great musicians especially to bestow glory, and who may lay greater claim to this fine privilege than you; you, who unite the most thorough and judicious theory with the most skilful and perfect execution to cast a veil over the shortcomings of composers, and often to uncover beauties in them that they themselves had not suspected? In such manner have you, by your enhancement of *The Creation,* won the right to share in the approval that this composition has received. This prerogative, which I must accord you, the public accords you as well. The respect of the latter for your talents is so great that your approval determines theirs, and that your approval for those who receive it is in a certain measure the anticipated renown of posterity. I have often doubted that my name would outlive me, only your kindness inspires me with confidence, and the souvenir with which you have honored me entitles me perhaps to believe that I *shall not die altogether*. Indeed, my dear sirs, you have [rewarded in one day the labors of sixty years; you have] crowned my gray hair and scattered the verge of my grave with flowers. My heart cannot express all that it feels, and I cannot write you my deep gratitude and devotion. You yourselves will appreciate this; you, my dear sirs, who cultivate the arts out of enthusiasm, not self-interest, and who count fortune's gifts as nothing but renown as all.

I am, etc.[118]

Little by little copies of *The Creation* were spread through all of Europe. The masterwork was heard with amazement everywhere. Poets, aesthetes, and critics took occasion to express themselves thereon in all sorts of ways.

The following pretty sonnet, sung, by what author I do not know, to Haydn's *Creation,* may find a place here.[119]

Haydn's Creation

Lovely, strange, and magic tones now bind
Our spirit, till the world is quite forgotten,
And old Chaos is anew begotten,
Worlds anew from chaos are refined.

Shy the baser spirit must grow blind
When the new creation shall arise.
Where the soul-creator's harmonies
Are borne the higher spirit is defined.

'Tis a stranger-soul? in lofty trill
Does its plumage rushing in the wind
Strange air brush with an harmonious thrill?

Out of love it homeward now will wend;
In thyself, my soul! life-music will
Come from the soul and turn to the soul again.

Our Wieland also greeted the splendid appearance with an occasional poem, which I give here.

To Haydn

"How streams thy swelling song, etc." [Here Dies gives the poem already quoted by Griesinger on p. 39.]

It has already been said elsewhere in these accounts that Herr Zelter is the author of the review that appeared in the *Musikalische Zeitung*. Haydn called this review "an excellent piece of work" and wondered how Herr Zelter had managed to come on the right track so well. [See p. 136.]

It is interesting to hear Michael Haydn's opinion of *The Creation*. I borrow the whole passage from his biographical sketch.[120] He wrote to his friend:

You may receive this oratorio with awe and devotion!—The inserted slips of paper mark places that specially pleased me. You will find none at the arias, and so on, otherwise the score would have looked like a hedgehog. The spot *Und liebe girrt das zarte Taubenpaar* particularly seems to me to be very successful. Here and there you will be surprised; and what my brother manages in his choruses on eternity is something extraordinary, and so on.

What worlds apart is this opinion from that which he expressed concerning *The Seasons!* He wrote, "I have occupied myself with it right well for several days, and have found some places set in a manner extraordinarily difficult, others on the contrary much easier."

Since *The Seasons* followed so quickly after *The Creation,* since Haydn was still older by several years and at his age wished to see through this bold task of creating a work that should have poured forth from the power of youth, it is easy to believe, as he said (Twenty-fourth Visit), that he overworked in the attempt.

To this were added several minor annoyances that arose between him and Baron van Swieten on account of the text. Haydn was often annoyed over the many graphic representations or imitations in *The Seasons*. Above all the croaking of the frogs displeased him. He sensed something base about it and tried to keep it from being heard. Swieten took him to task on this account, produced an old piece by [Grétry] in which the croaks were set with prominent display, and tried to talk Haydn into imitating it. He, at last provoked by this, resolved to be pestered no longer and gave vent to his indignation in a letter in which he wrote, "It would be better if all this trash were left out." This letter passed through several hands and even appeared in the *Zeitung für die elegante Welt.* Swieten was very angry over the public appearance of the letter, and allowed Haydn to feel this for a long time after.[121]

Swieten criticized the [first] aria in *The Seasons,* in which the peasant walks behind the plow and whistles the melody of the Andante with the Drum Stroke [Symphony No. 94]. He tried to persuade Haydn to pick out in place of it a song from a really popular opera and named two or three operas himself. This demand was truly insulting; Haydn felt so, and answered confidently, "I will change nothing! My Andante is as good and as well-known as any song from any opera." Swieten took this ill and stopped visiting Haydn. Ten or twelve days thus went by. Then Haydn went to Swieten, but was kept waiting a good half hour in the anteroom. He finally lost patience and was just about to go away when he was called back and let in. Haydn could not immediately temper his fury, and said to the Baron, "You called me back just in time. I came close today to seeing your waiting room for the last time."

Haydn said of *The Seasons* that in order to lift it out of the eternal monotony of imitating, he hit on the notion of representing drunkenness in the final fugue. "My head," he said, "was so full of the crazy nonsense *Es lebe der Wein, es lebe das Fass!* [Long live wine and the barrel] that I let everything fly hither and yon; so I call the final fugue the tipsy fugue." [122]

The Seasons, like *The Creation,* was first performed in the hall of Prince Schwarzenberg [April 24, 1801]. Public opinion was divided over it. Some placed this work above *The Creation;* others ranked both works together; others contested both opinions. A very fine review by Zelter appeared in the *Leipzig Musikalische Zeitung.*[123]

It will not displease my readers to learn Haydn's own view in a few words. The Emperor Francis [II] asked him on the occasion of a performance of *The Seasons* to which of his works he himself gave the first place, to *The Creation* or to *The Seasons?* "To *The Creation*," Haydn replied. And why? "In *The Creation* angels speak and tell of God; but in *The Seasons* it is only Simon talking."[124]

Haydn had lent Baron van Swieten the original scores of *The Creation* and of *The Seasons* for revision. He retained them a long time, and kept them in a drawer of his desk. They were seen there a short time before the Baron's death. Afterwards Haydn asked for them, but the scores had disappeared and have still not been turned up. The thief had better keep them well hidden, for Haydn's estate is clearly entitled to them.[125]

Even before the appearance of *The Creation* or *The Seasons*, to wit, in the year 1798, Haydn was admitted as a member of the Swedish Academy of Sciences and Fine Arts in Stockholm. In 1801 the Academy of Arts in Amsterdam showed him the same honor.

When Prince Esterházy was in Paris in 1803, he was very pleasantly surprised one evening at the *Concert des amateurs*. They had made Haydn's laurel-crowned portrait an object of veneration and displayed it, richly illuminated, in a prominent position in the hall.[126]

The Paris society of musicians had already paid our Haydn a great honor, as I have told above. Now the National Institute of the Sciences and Arts followed suit, and named him to their foreign membership. I give here the relevant documents in full:[127]

Institut National des sciences et des arts a Paris le 5. Nivose an 10 de la République.

Le Président et les secrétaires de l'institut national des sciences et des arts.

a Monsieur *Haydn*, celebre compositeur de musique, à Vienne.

Monsieur!

L'institut nat. des sciences et des arts, dans sa séance générale de ce jour, vient de vous élire *associé étranger*, pour la classe de Litterature et Beaux arts[.]

Persuadés, que vous apprendrez avec plaisir vôtre nomination, nous nous hâtons de vous l'annoncer.

Veuillez, Monsieur agréer le sincêre hommage de nôtre estime la plus haute[.]

Institut National
Classe des Beaux arts.

Paris le l. Messidor an 13 de la République française.

Le secrétaire perpétuel de la classe à Mr. *Haydn,* compositeur, membre associé de l'institut national.

Monsieur!

L'institut national de France vous choisit pour associé etranger; dès son origine c'est un hommage qu'il c'est plu à rendre à votre juste célébrité. Les changemens operés depuis dans l'institut Vous y ont en quelque sorte attaché plus atroitement; on y a crée une section de musique, et ceux qui la composent sont de dignes appréciateurs de votre genie.

Comme associé etranger vous avez voix consultative dans l'institut[,] endroit d'y sieger, d'en porter le costume, enfin vous en êtes membre. En cette qualité je Vous adresse la medaille qui constate votre titre et le livret qui contient nos reglemens, ainsique les noms des membres. Vous y trouverez le Votre à l'article de la classe des beaux arts.

Je desirerais, Monsieur, que Vous prissiez assez d'intérêt à la classe des beaux arts de l'institut de France pour lui faire part de Vos savantes observations sur l'art que Vous professez avec tant de gloire en Europe. Je puis Vous assurer qu'elle recevrait avec une profonde estime ce témoignage de Votre confiance. En mon particulier, je regarderai comme un des avantages précieux de fonctions dont je suis honoré celui de corréspondre avec Vous et de pouvoir Vous assurer souvent de ma parfaite admiration.

Conservatoire de Musique.

Paris le 7. messidor an 13
de la Republique française.

Le Conservatoire de France à *Haydn.*

Les membres du conservatoire de France pénétrés des plus profonds sentiments d'estime et de vénération pour l'immortel talent d'*Haydn* ont le plus vif dèsir d'inserire le nom de cet artiste célèbre dans les fastes de l'etablissement.

L'expression de ce voeu porté à l'illustre *Haydn* par *Chérubini* ne peut être que bien accueilli; les membres du conservatoire pleins de cette confiance chargent leur collegue de remettre, au grand homme qu'ils

considèrent comme un des pères de l'art musical l'empreinte du monument que le conservatoire espère voir elever dans son sein et dont le type a
été choisi pour consacrer l'heureuse époque de la fondation de cet etablissement.

Puisse ce légitime hommage d'admiration pour l'un des plus grands
génies qui ont illustré la Republique des arts être agrée par *Haydn;* il
deviendra pour le conservatoire de France un Trophée dont il s'honorera
à jamais[.]

Almost every year Haydn received medals from Paris, among
them some of silver, which, however, I never laid eyes on; for every
time I asked about them, none of them was in Haydn's possession,
but they were in the hands of persons who looked after his interests.
So I can tell nothing about them.

In 1803 Haydn again received a gold medal from Paris, which the
ingenious Gatteaux had engraved. The obverse shows a star (symbol
of immortality) under which the words *à Haydn* are to be read. A
laurel wreath surrounds the medal on whose circumference is set the
inscription: *Concert des Amateurs de Paris.* The reverse exhibits a
column-shaped tripod on which blazes the holy flame. On either side
of the tripod stands a lyre; a luxuriant laurel branch winds around
both lyres and unites them with the tripod, or rather with the flame
burning thereon, as the circumscription clearly sets forth: *Le même
feu les anime* [The same fire animates them].* The thoughtful artist
has quite without ostentation decorated each lyre with a miniature
allegorical figure. Namely, on one lyre is seen an owl, on the other a
butterfly; this probably stands for the Serious and the Playful.

While Haydn was receiving from so many sides the proofs of
unfeigned esteem, it is all the more striking to learn that the great
approbation that Haydn had received for so many years in London
was degenerating into strong reproof. This sudden alteration was
brought about by the well-known member of Parliament, theater
director, orator, and poet, Mr. Sheridan. Now Sheridan took it very
ill that the French National Institute had elected Haydn to foreign
membership but not himself. He sought revenge. The public was
flooded through newspapers with rhymed and unrhymed lampoons

---

* Perhaps I ought to have said "Torch of Prometheus." [See p. 2.]

of Haydn.[128] Naturally, there were two parties, but it was deemed difficult to decide, in view of the platitudes that each uttered against the other, which of them was the wiser. After the wrangling in the newspapers had gone on for a while, a respected critic rose up and decided the quarrel in the following way: "The French National Institute has acted stupidly in its choice of a foreign member for the class of the fine arts in preferring Haydn to Mr. Sheridan. Haydn is to be sure a great musician, but music is still only an accompaniment to poetry and is meant merely to exalt the latter. To place a musician at the head of the fine arts is almost the same as if one were to award to the weaver who had made the canvas or to the joiner who had made the frame for a painting the prize that belongs alone to the great painter."

This oracular pronouncement soothed the passionately heated tempers![129] My readers will smile at this grotesque business and be convinced that the wise part of the population of London took no part in it.

The following letter from the Municipal Council of the city of Vienna my readers will have more pleasure in reading: "After the many proofs of philanthropy with which, etc." [Here Dies gives the letter already quoted by Griesinger on p. 44.]

Haydn's Answer
[drawn up by the Abbé Hofstätter]

When I strove to contribute through my knowledge of music to the relief of the aged impoverished citizens, I counted myself fortunate in having fulfilled one of my pleasantest duties, and could not flatter myself that the worshipful Municipal Council of the imperial and royal capital and court city would honor my slight effort with such marked attention.

It is not so much the gift, honored sirs, which I shall deeply honor as a monument to your kindness throughout my remaining allotted days, but it is much more your kind letter, the complete proof of your noble minds, which stirs me to the heart and leaves me uncertain whether I admire more your kind behavior toward me or the charitable care that you bring to the impoverished citizens. While I here solemnly declare my deepest gratitude for both, in my own and in the name of the impoverished citizens, permit me, honored sirs, to add the warm wish that Providence may long maintain to the benefit of this imperial city so philanthropic a Municipal Council.

I remain, etc.

The above letter from the Municipal Council was followed by the large municipal Diploma of Honor.

The content of the Council letter tells my readers that Haydn's oratorios were turned to charitable purposes. He spoke with visible joy of the profit that for several years flowed into so many cashboxes from the performance of his works. He showed me an extract of the accounts of the musical society whose *Assessor perpetuus* he was for over eight and a quarter years (until 1805) which showed that the net balance at that time amounted already to 3,369 florins. The first performance of *The Creation* brought to the benefit of this society, after expenses, 4,162 florins; that of *The Seasons* 3,209 florins.

Were it possible for me to appear in person at this moment, through some magic power or other, before my readers, they would recognize both from the expression of quiet grief spread upon my countenance and from my whole presence that I have sorrowful news to impart to them. My readers will easily guess that this news concerns Haydn's death, and will allow me to relate briefly to them the circumstances through which it came to pass.

For a long time now Haydn's accumulating indispositions had been keeping me from my customary visits. Fortunately I had previously collected all the materials necessary to this account, otherwise very little would have come of it, because Haydn's extraordinary exhaustion kept him from thinking of the past. Even the present was not clear to him. His memory was completely dulled, but things had not gone so far that one could call him childish. Probably he would have reached this point only at a still greater age had not that moment in the war when French troops entered the suburbs of Vienna, with all its attendant circumstances, passed sentence on the life of this unforgettable man. Those events made him ripe for nearing death. Haydn's dwelling lay near the outer limits of the suburb

Gumpendorf. On May 10 [1809] in the morning at about seven
o'clock a cannon shot fell on the boundary, the unexpected loud
thunder of which startled Haydn so greatly that he would have
fallen to the floor without the quick support of his people. Haydn
was seized with a violent trembling. Unfortunately three more shots
resounded one right after the other, increasing Haydn's convulsive
trembling and generally aggravating the state of alarm. Nevertheless,
the old man summoned all his powers and, straining his voice un-
naturally, called out in fearful tones, "Don't be afraid, children!
Where Haydn is, nothing can happen." [See p. 232, note 70.]

The servants then put him to bed and took care to call the doctor,
who tried by appropriate means to counteract the ill effect, with such
success that Haydn was able to get up the same day and resume his
accustomed routine. Even in the fearful night of May 11/12, in
which the city was bombarded with howitzer fire, he remained fairly
calm, but there was about him a certain melancholy that never left
him in the following days. He seemed to wish to forget his sorrows
at the pianoforte. Every day towards midday he sat down to the
instrument and played his favorite piece, *Gott erhalte Franz den
Kaiser!*

He received visits from several French officers. On May 26 a captain of hussars in the French service named Sulimi visited him while
he was taking his midday rest. Haydn received him, contrary to his
habit, in bed. The Captain, a great admirer of Haydn, admitted that
he sang himself, and to give Haydn proof of it, he sang the tenor
aria from the second act of *The Seasons*. Haydn admired the stir-
ringly beautiful voice but still more the virtuosity of the singer, who
opened the way to Haydn's heart by the true expression of the song,
and moved him so much that he wept. Hardly had the Captain
finished singing the aria and approached the bed when Haydn,
desiring to embrace him, drew him down and covered him with
countless kisses. Both men became so emotional that they were
seized with a violent trembling, which kept the Captain at his departure from writing his name legibly.[130]

The following day, the very day indeed on which Haydn took to his bed, he had his servants gather around him and played to them in exaltation the Emperor Hymn. I might make use of a poetical expression and say that it was the last time he felt the presence of the Muse, who was seen to take eternal leave of her darling. Haydn left the pianoforte, sat down at table, ate a light meal, but afterwards felt so tired out that he had to go to bed.

I should surely give my readers no pleasure if I undertook to depict the sufferings of a dying man who is so dear to us.—I draw a curtain before the scene of sorrow. Three and a half days—and Haydn was no more! On May 31, shortly after midnight, he departed this life. He had attained the age of seventy-seven years and two months. Chance placed his tomb very close to that of the celebrated actress Rose.*

As soon as the war in progress was ended and peace returned to the Austrian Empire, the illustrious Prince Esterházy made the splendid decision, which will shortly become reality, to exhume Haydn's remains, bury them in the Capuchin monastery in Eisenstadt, and raise a monument to the memory of the great man.[131]

About six weeks before Haydn's death, he had his will read over to his servants, in the presence of the witnesses, and then asked them whether they were satisfied with its provisions or not. The good people were surprised by their master's kindness. They saw their futures secured, and thanked him for it with tears in their eyes.

Since I once saw Haydn's will,[132] I shall give here the paragraphs that might interest my readers:

In the 4. and 5. ¶ Haydn allots a very insignificant sum, in all only some 30 florins, to masses for the departed.

In the 9. ¶ he reveals his charitableness, and bequeaths to the poor citizens of St. Marx 1,000 florins to be divided among them.

In the 10. ¶ to the Brothers of Mercy as well as to the Franciscans at Eisenstadt, 50 florins to each monastery.

In the 25. ¶ to the hospital foundation for the poor there, 50 florins.

30. ¶. I bequeath to Philipp Schimpel, choirmaster at Hainburg, and

* It will not be uninteresting to the physiognomist that on my advice Haydn's death mask was taken.

to his wife, 100 florins together, as well as the portrait (to be found on the first floor of my house) of her father, named Franck, who was my first music teacher.

33. ¶. I bequeath to Mad. Aloisia Pulcelli [Luigia Polzelli], former singer to His Highness Prince Esterházy, during her lifetime, 150 florins yearly, wherefore 3,000 florins from my estate at death will be invested in 5 per cent government bonds, to assure Mad. Pulcelli the lifelong interest bequeathed her; after her death, however, I wish

34. ¶. that half of these 150 florins, to wit 75 florins, shall be diverted in equal shares to the education of the two poorest orphans of my birthplace Rohrau till they come of age, at which time two others of the poorest orphans of Rohrau shall share in this sum; the other half, of 75 florins, however, shall

35. ¶. remain with the domain of Rohrau, to keep in good condition the monument set up by it in my honor, and the image that my late father placed near the sacristy in the church there.

38. ¶. to my sister-in-law Magd[alena] Haydn in Salzburg, I bequeath 1,000 florins.

41. ¶. I leave to my faithful and honest cook, Anna Kremnitzer, 6,000 florins, as well as the bedding that she uses in her room; also two linen sheets, four armchairs, a hardwood table, also hardwood chest of drawers, the repeater-clock, the mirror, the statue of the Virgin, a splinter of the Cross,[133] the flatiron, the kitchen crockery together with all the little items of kitchen equipment; besides this I bequeath to her that 200 florins cash that she lent to me.

42. ¶. I bequeath to my faithful and honest servant Joh. Estler [*for* Elssler] 6,000 florins, also a plain suit including waistcoat and trousers, a coat, a hat, and I decree that my executor shall pay all the necessary fees, mortuary duties, etc. without reducing the legacies decreed in the 41. and 42. ¶s.

48. ¶. I bequeath the great gold commemorative medal from Paris, together with the accompanying letter from the Paris musicians [see p. 184], to His Highness Prince Esterházy, and pray him to accord this memento a place in his treasure chamber at Forchtenau.[134]

49. ¶. I bequeath to Count von Harrach, Lord of the Rohrau domain, the little gold medal from Paris, with the accompanying letter from the *Amateurs* of music [see p. 180]; also the large bust *à l'antique* (Haydn's bust by A. Grassi).

In the fiftieth and last paragraph Herr Mathias Fröhlich, blacksmith in Fischamend and the son of a deceased sister of Haydn's, is designated residuary heir to all that remains in the estate after all legacies are paid.

After the death of his sister, Haydn took Mathias Fröhlich, then eleven years old, into his house and brought him up to be a black-smith, since that was the boy's own desire.[135] The present war caused him such deep misfortune that he would have lost all and fallen into great need if the inheritance had not saved him. The paragraphs omitted here contain legacies to relatives, friends, and poor. The total sum taken from the residuary heir amounted to around 24,000 florins.

On June 15 Haydn's memorial celebration was observed in the Schottenkirche. Between him and Mozart had always existed, while both lived, the noblest and most respectful friendship. One pictures the blessed spirits of these two great men surrounded by denizens of Heaven come down with them, listening to Mozart's *Requiem,* which with lofty splendor the assembled musicians of Vienna performed on this day, and at which the highest members of the French general staff appeared.

Haydn trained the following students whose names he gave to me. He charged those who could afford to pay 100 ducats for the course, one half payable in advance, the other at the end. The names follow: Hoffmann, a Livonian; Kranz in Stuttgart; Anton Wranizky; Lessel; Fuchs, in the service of Prince Esterházy; Tomisch; Graf; Specht; Pleyel; Hänsel; *Destouches;* Struck; two brothers Pulcelli, of whom one died; the living one is in the service of Prince Ester-házy; Neukomm.[136]

The *Neuwieder Blatt* (*Reich der Todten* No. 54) carried a little piece in which Haydn's early years were portrayed in brief. It is not worth the trouble to speak of the insignificant differences which may turn up between that account and my own. When, however, Herr V. writes, "Haydn never went to Italy. Had this fortune befallen him, then he would without doubt have made for himself a great name as an opera composer, through sound fundamentals in singing and in instrumental accompaniment," then I confess that I doubt whether this journey would have had a particular influence on Haydn's genius. For since all good Italian operas are performed also in Vienna, since we compose for the most celebrated singers from Italy, and so on, it is superfluous for our native composer to visit that land. He becomes acquainted with Italy in Vienna, and if he had received from Nature the gift and the will for a flowing melody, easy for every ear to grasp, gently charming, and if he knows how to stir the heart, so above all will he reach people and compose operas that are applauded.

From as many of Haydn's works as I know, I cannot pick an example in which he has ever sought to imitate a foreign style. He was always driven by extraordinary powers of genius to blaze new trails, a fact to be seen especially in his instrumental music.

We come here imperceptibly to matters of criticism. I can spare myself the need to say something about Haydn's music as a whole since a critique has already appeared in the *Leipzig Musikalische Zeitung,* twenty-fourth issue, that leaves little to be desired. The author (Herr Triest) may ascribe it to the excellence of his article that I make use of an excerpt appropriate here. The excerpt follows: [137]

All who have written either symphonies or quartets remain behind the man who for almost a half century now has worked with ever new, inexhaustible, astounding power, and become the greatest benefactor of German instrumental music in the third period of the previous century. All Germany has long cherished the exceptional spirit of our great J. Haydn; the hoarse voices * of pedantic fuddy-duddies, who feel called upon to carp at an entire work, distinguished by a thousand beauties, as

* In matters of taste one finds the most copycats. It is not always the pedantic fuddy-duddies, but even so-called great men, who copy one another's ideas and express opinions often grotesque. My readers will permit me to cite an example. Franklin copies J. J. Rousseau when he says in his little letters on music: "Most tunes of late composition, not having this natural harmony [of ancient Scotch tunes] united with their melody, have recourse to the artificial harmony of a bass and other accompanying parts."—[Benjamin Franklin, Letter of June 2, 1765, to Lord Kames at Edinburgh, *On the Harmony and Melody of the old Scotch Tunes.*] In a note J. J. Rousseau's *Dictionnaire de*

soon as they are met by a set of forbidden, or even concealed, fifths and octaves, and who even provoked Haydn on this account, have long been stilled, since it has been seen that even in depth of knowledge of musical grammar Haydn is superior to many a self-vaunted contrapuntist. And who does not rejoice that now at the end of the century the name of Haydn is spoken abroad with veneration, that London and Paris are eager to praise one of his last works, one for which we are no longer waiting before placing him on the highest rung of the ladder of musical fame?

Still, why should I pour one drop into the sea by mere declamations over his immortal worth, admitting the temptation?—Instead I will try to make clearer to myself (and perhaps to many who have not yet pondered

---

Musique is quoted to show that R. did not think at all favorably of the harmony of recent composers. He cites various reasons, tries to back them up, and says in the end: "When one has seen all that, it is quite difficult not to suspect that all our harmony is only a gothic and barbarous invention, which we should never have thought of if we had been more sensitive to the true beauties of the art, and to a music truly natural."

We must nevertheless allow the Europeans unique among all earth-dwellers in having harmony and chords and in finding this mixture beautiful. We have many other things unknown to the oriental lands and which even the Greeks did not dream of. The northern mind has expanded and diversified its sphere of activity; if unity is not missed in doing so, the results must be beautiful. Granted that a straight way is always the shortest; yet it in no way follows that it is also the best and most beautiful. Nothing repels more easily than the eternal sameness of a dead straight course, and the traveler sometimes gladly goes for a pleasant change by the winding and even the rough byway. In the fine arts, which must strive after variety, probably nothing is more necessary and useful than to avoid dishing up only sweet fare. Satiety and even nausea must necessarily soon arise from this. But let the sweet dishes alternate in all sorts of combinations with bitter and sour fare, and the appetite will increase. Why is this? For no other reason than the contrast that must necessarily exist in nature, because it can produce a given thing only once, with the result that two things of the same kind must contrast with one another. Hence arise the great scales from the good to the bad; the great; the small; the beautiful; the repulsive, and so on.

To harmonic consonance, dissonance must be opposed; and since everything has its opposite, so also to homophony polyphony must be opposed. Rousseau asserts that man could not have learned chords from the singing of the birds, but this assertion is false. If several hundred birds in the wood sing simultaneously, the most beautiful chords, and surprising dissonances, are bound to be heard. With a strong wind I have often heard in the stillness of night the wind whistling through door and window in splendid chords, now strong, now weak, *crescendo* and *decrescendo*. Is this not nature?—Shall genius have no ear for it? [This note is by Dies.]

the matter) on what Haydn's greatness really rests.

Everything unites in him to place him in the forefront of instrumental composers. In his youth he was (like Graun, Hasse, Schulz, *et al.*) a very well-liked singer. He studied the great Italian masters, and who will now be surprised that he gave us such masterful melodies; that everything in his works, even in the most complicated places, sings so splendidly; that his principal themes in serious or comic style have such a meaningful, powerful simplicity that carries away the connoisseur and the amateur alike? With this he combined the most penetrating study of harmony (in the works of Bach and others), the fruit of which is the boldest, most astonishing, and nothing less than baroque modulations with which he enraptures us. Now one may add to this the knowledge of the individual character of the instruments and their working, and all this combined with the rarest originality of a brain that even in the huge number of his works copies neither others nor itself, although he has his own unmistakable manner (as everyone who once knows something of Haydn hears in a forged work). Thus it is that our great master stands before us wonderful to behold but not inexplicable.—Still the causes of his greatness are not all presented here. The quintessence thereof seems to me to lie in the exceptionally light handling of rhythm, in which no other equals him, and in that which the English call humor and for which the German word *Laune* will not do at all. By this last characteristic his bent for the comic turn, and the even greater success of it than of the serious, may be accounted for.—If, moreover, one wished to hunt up a parallel with other celebrated men, Haydn may be compared with regard to the fertility of his imagination perhaps to our own Jean Paul (discounting, of course, the chaotic arrangement; for lucid arrangement, *lucidus ordo,* is not the least of Haydn's excellences), and with regard to his humor, his original wit (*vis comica* [comic vigor]) with Lor. Sterne.—If one wished further to suggest the character of Haydn's composition with two words, it would be, I think, artistic popularity or popular (intelligible, penetrating) artistry. But in what sort of pieces is Haydn probably greatest and most exemplary? One must ask this question of almost any significant composer of the third period, for he is expected to write not merely much but multifariously as well. Now it is of course true that a genuine composer stirs up interest in every branch of his art that he cultivates; but it is also agreed that even the greatest original genius, especially in a time when the art has grown up from a little plant to a tree of many branches, can work with distinguished success only in one or a few divisions thereof. And so then I am not afraid of running counter to the opinion of most connoisseurs and critics when I draw up the following classification of Haydn's works. His symphonies and quartets unquestionably take the first rank, and no one has yet surpassed him in this. His compositions for clavier come second, but only in fullness of feeling, delicacy, and understandable superiority in every ingenuity, for in other respects many new clavier composers (besides Mozart) might contest the place with him, especially Muzio Clementi with his fire and spirit (even perhaps in the future, if his wild rioting subsides, Beethoven). Next come his church compositions, and last his theater works, so far, that is, as these have become known. The proof of this statement is provided among others by the work that has caused so extraordinary a sensation (almost as much as Mozart's *Zauberflöte*), namely *The Creation*. Of this work I venture to assert that it can neither subtract from nor add anything to Haydn's true artistic fame, not that fame, I mean, which the great multitude accords.* Respect for the great man must not make us blind to the aesthetic requirements in such a work. And what can these well say to a natural history or geogony set to music, where the objects pass before us as in a magic lantern; what to the perpetual pictorializing, to the mixture of church and theater style (which shows to what a pass we have already come in those regions), in a word to the tendency of the whole? Must it not pain every admirer of Haydn to see the great power of the man wasted, to the detriment of the art (for such examples are often dangerous), on a text that is not worthy of him? Truly, the author of the old Mosaic story of the seven days of creation probably did not dream that it would make such a great hit again at the end of the eighteenth century, decked out in all the display of modern music!—The exceptionally beautiful, masterly choruses may compensate us for the aesthetic mistakes of most of the other sections only if we wish away the text of the latter (as many perhaps did when they heard it).—Enough, it is my conviction (which if need be I will defend in detail) that this work as a whole cannot increase Haydn's fame. It can also, however, take little or nothing away from him. For the text was certainly not his own, and it was thus not his fault that it forced him to perpetual representation of objects instead of subjects. Besides (and this fact, for the sake of the man's great worth one will not fail to take into account), he wrote this oratorio solely for the English,† who are still accustomed to Handel's rain and snow paintings, and who, if they remain true to their taste, must find in this *Creation* one of the greatest masterpieces that they have ever heard. Thus no composer of the previous cen-

---

* All respect to the public; but I know in matters of art no worse judge than mass public opinion. The Author [i.e. Triest].

† This is wrong: Haydn, as I have already told, was to have written *The Creation* for Salomon; but Swieten altered the project. [Dies.]

tury has done so much for the development of instrumental music as our father J. Haydn. None has made such use of its outward and inward power; none was in a position like his to place it in its rightful balance with vocal music, and even to require it to summon all its powers, toward the beginning of the new century, in order not to be left behind the other.

I take pen again here to say that Haydn has been generally recognized as creator of modern instrumental music. He always set the fashion for masterworks of a new sort, and found many imitators, who often fell into excess. Haydn was, for example, one of the first of those who made use of melody in unison octaves (*de Luca* in *das gelehrte Oesterreich* wrongly cites him as the inventor of octave-writing), and soon there was a fashionable epidemic of octave-reinforced melody.[138]

Haydn is the inventor of the so-called Haydn minuets, which are stamped with the mark of the rarest originality.

Concerning Haydn's Outward Appearance, Character, Habits

I said, earlier, in the introduction that I draw no character sketch of Haydn because I do not presume to have so explored his character in the course of five years that I could produce a strictly accurate picture of him. I wished to do Haydn no injustice, so I went carefully to work, observed, tested, and still I dare not assert that I correctly noted the difference between character trait and habit every time; where I remained in doubt, I preferred to omit my entire observation. Hence the small number of them.

Haydn's exterior figure was something under medium size. The lower half of his body was too short for the upper, something commonly to be seen in small persons of either sex, but very noticeable in Haydn because he kept to the old fashion of having his trousers reach only to the hips and not above the waist. His features were fairly regular; his look was eloquent, fiery, but still moderate, kind, attractive. The features joined with the look to express dignity if Haydn was inclined to be serious; otherwise in conversation he easily assumed a cheerful, smiling countenance. I never heard him laugh aloud. Haydn had a moderately strong bone structure; the muscles were slight. His hawk's nose (he suffered much from a nasal polyp, which had doubtless enlarged this part) and other features as well were heavily pock-marked, the nose even seamed so that the nostrils each had a different shape.

Haydn considered himself ugly, and told me of a prince and his consort who could not bear his face, "because," said he, "I was too ugly for them." This supposed ugliness, however, was not at all basic, but simply a matter of deeply pocked skin and brown complexion.[139]

Haydn already in early youth wore for the sake of cleanliness a wig with a pigtail and several side curls. Fashion had no effect on the form of his wig. He remained true to it till death, and wore it only two fingers above the eyebrows, so that his forehead seemed proportionately very low.

Love of order seemed as inborn in him as industry. The former was to be observed, as also his love of cleanliness, in his person and in his entire household. He never received visits, for instance, if he were not first fully clothed. If he were surprised by a friend, he tried to get at least enough time to put on his wig.

Loving order, Haydn had his study and business hours tightly scheduled, and he took it amiss if compelled to alter them. Still he was by no means ruled by the clock. At the end I will give Haydn's daily schedule, from which my readers can see his time distribution. He was sensibly economical. Various times I heard people who did not know him well accuse him of avarice.* I had occasion enough to investigate this accustion and found it false. Avarice has no feeling for the need of others, and does not even support its closest kin; it is so unfortunate as not to know gratitude. If Haydn had need of money, he was very industrious in earning it, but once it was earned

---

* The Kapellmeister Reichard in his Letters on Vienna accuses Haydn of avarice, and will not soil his recital with touches thereof.

Reichard must really have been drawing from a dirty well; for many persons hold that he has placed himself in a muddied light, while he copies without further proof the current gossip of the city. [See p. 234.]

and in his hands, he felt the inclination to share it. So he often called his household together with the words, "Children! there is money," and gave to each according to his service five, ten, fifteen, or twenty florins.

Had Haydn been avaricious, he could never have made the sacrifice necessary in a certain delicate matter. Swieten once asked him to have one of his oratorios copied for him, regardless of cost. The copy was completed. Swieten asked the copyist (he was a servant of Haydn's) the price, and received the answer sixty-two or sixty-three florins. "Good," said Swieten, and set the day for payment. The man went on the day set, but because Swieten had noted the price incorrectly, he received for this enormous task only six florins and a few kreutzers. When Haydn learned this, he wanted nothing said about it, but made good the loss.—

In his character there was much cheerfulness, jest, and musical wit both popular and refined, but original to the highest degree. It has often been called humor, from which is rightly derived Haydn's bent for musical teasing.—

He was grateful and paid back good turns done him in his youth as soon as he could do so *in secret,* without forgetting his numerous relatives.

Honor and fame were the two powerful motives that ruled him, but I know of no instance where they degenerated into ambition. His natural modesty prevented that.—

He never found fault with other musicians.

In younger years he is said to have been very susceptible to love. I would have been silent about it here, but I noticed that he was still very attentive to ladies in his old age, and even kissed their hands.

Haydn's Daily Schedule.

The distribution of hours and the resultant order might seem machine-like to some of my readers; but if you think of the many creative works that flowed from Haydn's pen, you will admit that Haydn was merely employing his time wisely. He had observed his own body and knew what he could expect of it. He could not be idle.

Variety was pleasant to him, and order came naturally to him. So arose his daily schedule.[140]

Haydn rose in the warmer season at half-past six, and shaved at once; up to his seventy-third year, he allowed no strange hand to do this for him. Then he dressed completely. Were a student present while he dressed, he had to play the lesson assigned him on the clavier. Mistakes were noted, a grammar lesson based on them was delivered, and then a new problem set for the next lesson.

At eight Haydn had his breakfast. Immediately afterwards Haydn sat down at the clavier and improvised until he found some idea to suit his purpose, which he immediately set down on paper. Thus originated the first sketches of his compositions.

At half-past eleven he received visits, or he went for a walk and paid visits himself.

The hour from two to three was devoted to the midday meal.

After dinner he always took up some small domestic business or went into his library and took a book to read.

About four o'clock he returned to musical tasks. He then took the morning's sketches and scored them, spending three to four hours thus.

At eight in the evening he usually went out, but came back to the house around nine and either set himself to score-writing, or else took a book and read till ten o'clock. The hour of ten in the evening was set for supper. Haydn had made it a rule to have nothing in the evening but wine and bread. This rule he only now and then violated if he were invited somewhere to supper.

He liked jocularity at table and cheerful conversation in general.

At half-past eleven he went to bed, in old age even later.

Winter time made no difference in his daily schedule on the whole, except that Haydn rose a half hour later in the morning. Everything else remained as in summer.

In advanced age, especially in the last five or six years of his life, bodily weakness and ills upset the schedule outlined above. The active man could at last no longer keep busy. Also he had grown used in this period to a half hour's rest in the afternoon.

Reader hark! The Muse still tells of the bold one,[141]
Hark! she speaks of the enterprising man,
Who, resembling Prometheus, through the immeasurable ether
That from earthly earth separates high Olympus,
Dared on powerful pinions relying (by kindly Omnipotence
Given to him as a gift at the first pulse beat) to soar,
And, obeying the mighty, the inner on-spurring drive,
To penetrate the holy realm of harmony,
And, O glorious deed! at holy fire to light
The torch. He himself becomes a creator. In tonal realms
He gives to tone—even to silence spiritual life; and rejoicing
The chords ascend on high in thundering symphonies,
Shattering now, and so they threaten the worlds with collapse;
Now in melting grace, just as the Graces appear
To the sight of poets great. With such omnipotence armed,
The tones mount on, and reach the dwelling of the Muses
On the heights of Parnassus by the Castalian fountain.
Harkening the Muses learn, sunk in silent astonishment,
Harmony's shape and form. Yet long they sit and harken,
Till the last whisper of eloquent tone fades away.
See, there Phoebus Apollo opens his mouth to inquire:
Muses! is Haydn not the creator of magical tones
That bewitch us gods? In truth! I think we accord
To him in our midst the place that is rightfully his;
For, as a mortal he knew how to win for himself
Immortality's crown, to become like the gods!—

Verzeichniss [Catalogue

der J. Haydn'schen Werke vom of those works of J. Haydn from
achtzehnten bis zum dreyundsie- the ages of eighteen to seventy-
benzigsten Jahre seines Alters, de- three that he recalled]
ren er sich erinnerte [142]

---

118 *Simfonie*
125 *Divertimenti a tre, per il Bariton, Viola e Violoncello*
Baritonstücke für das Lieblingsin- [Baryton pieces for the favorite
strument des verstorbenen Fürsten instrument of the late Prince Nico-
Nicolaus Esterhazy laus Esterházy]
  6 *Duetti*
 12 *Sonate per il Bariton col Violon-*
    cello
  6 Cassationsstücke [6 Cassation pieces]
  5 *detto a 8 Voci*
  3   "   " 5   "
  1   "   " 3   "
  1   "   " 4   "
  1   "   " 6   "
  3 *Concerti con 2 Violini e Basso*
In allem 163 Baritonstücke [In all 163 Baryton pieces]

Divertimenti per diversi stromenti
 a 5, 6, 7, 8, 9 *Voci*
 5 *a cinque Voci*
 1 " *quattro*   "
 9 " *sei*   "
 1 " *otto*   "
 2 " *nove*   "
 2 *in dubio*
 2 *Marcie*

---

21 *Trii per 2 Violini e Violoncello*

---

6 *Sonate, a Violino solo, coll' accompagnamento d'una Viola*

Concerti

3 *per Violino*
3 *per Violoncello*
1 *per il Contra basso*
1 *per il Corno* in *d*
2 *a due Corni*
1 *per il Clarino*
1 *per Flauto*

Missae, Offertoria, Te Deum, Salve Regina, Chori

1 *Missa Celensis*
2 *Missae sunt bona mixta malis*
2 *Missae brevi*
1 *Missa St. Josephi*
8 *Missa in tempore belli*

---

4 *Offertoria*
1 *Salve Regina a 4 Voci*
1 *Salve, Organo solo*
1 *Cantilera pro Advento* [*sic*]
1 *Respons. de Vener. Lauda Syon salvatorem*
1 *Te Deum*
2 *Chori*
1 *The Strom Hatck*

---

82 *Quartetti*

---

1 *Concerto per l'Organo*
3 *detto per Clavicembalo*
1 *Divertimento per Cembalo, col Violino, 2 Corni e Basso*
11 *detto a 4 mani*
1 " *Con Bariton e 2 Violini*
4 " *Con 2 Violini e Basso*
1 " *20 Variazioni*

---

15 *Sonate per il Pianoforte*
1 *Fantasia*
1 *Capriccio*

1 *Thema con Var.* in *C*
1 *Thema con Var.* in *Es*

---

29 *Sonate per il* Pianoforte *con*
   Violino e Violoncello
42 Deutsche und einige italieni-   [42 German and several Italian
   sche Lieder und Duetten   Songs and Duets
39 Mehrstimmige Canons   39 Canons for several parts]

    Deutsche Opern   [German Operas]
1 Der krumme Teufel.
2 Philemon und Baucis. Marionettenoperette 1773
3 Hexenschabbas. Marionettenfest 1773
4 Genovefa. Marionettenoperette 1777
5 Dido, eine parodirte Marionettenoperette 1778

---

14 *Opere ital. La Canterina. L'incontro improviso. Lo Speciale. La Pes-*
   catrice. Il mondo della Luna. L'Isola disabitata. L'Infedeltà fedele.
   La Fedeltà premiata. La vera costanza. Orlando Paladino. Armida.
   Acide e Galatea. L'Infedeltà delusa. Orfeo.[143]

    Oratorien   [Oratorios]
1 *Ritorno di Tobia*
1 *Stabat mater*
1 Die Worte des Heilandes am   [The Words of the Saviour on the
   Kreuze   Cross
1 Die Schöpfung   The Creation
1 Die Jahrszeiten   The Seasons
13 3 und 4 stimmige Gesänge   13 3- and 4-part Choruses]

---

150 *A Selection of original scoth* [*sic*] *songs*
216 *Scoth songs with symphonies et accompaniments*

Verzeichniss[144]
sämmtlicher, von J. Haydn in London geschriebener Werke (aus Haydn's Taschenbuch)

[Catalogue of the complete works written by J. Haydn in London (from Haydn's Notebook)]

Orfeo, opera seria
  6 Symphonies
Concertant Symphonie
The Storm. Chor.
  3 Symphonies
Aria for Davide
Maccone for Gallini
  6 Quartettes
  3 Sonates for Broderip
  3 Sonates for P——
  3 Sonates for Ms. Janson
  1 Sonate in F minore
  1 Sonate in g
The Dream
Dr. Harringtons Compliment
  6 English songs
100 *Scotch songs*
 50 *Scotch songs*
  2 Flüte divert.
  3 Symphonies
  4 Song for S——
  2 Marches

  1 *Aria for Mss. P——*
  1 *God save the King*
  1 *Aria con Orchestra*
Invocation of Neptun
 10 *Commandments (Canons)*
March—Prince of Wales
  2 *Divertimenti a più voci*
 24 *Minuets and german dances*
 12 *Ballads for Lord A——*
Different songs
Canons
  1 *Song with the whole orchest.*
Of Lord A.
  4 *Contrydances*
  6 *Songs*
Overtura Coventgarden
Aria per la Banti
  4 *Scotch songs*
  2 *Songs*
  2 *Contrydances*
  3 *Sonates for Broderip*

REFERENCE MATTER

TABLE OF MONEY
USED BY HAYDN

Half-groschen, pfennigs, kreutzers	varied according to coin and locality
3 kreutzers (in general)	= 1 groschen
20 groschen	= 1 gulden (or florin)
2 gulden (or florins)	= 1 taler
10 talers	= 1 silver mark
4 florins, 10 to 30 kreutzers	= 1 (gold) ducat

Viennese very approximately equals	*English*
Kreutzer	$\frac{6}{15}$ d. (something less than a half-penny)
Groschen	$1\frac{1}{5}$ d.
Gulden (C.M.)	2 shillings (10 gulden = 1 pound)
Taler	4 shillings
Ducat	9 to 10 shillings (2 ducats = 1 pound to 1 guinea)

NOTES

Griesinger, *Biographical Notes*

1   Two equally unreliable biographical pamphlets appeared in Paris in 1810, N. E. Framery's *Notice sur Joseph Haydn. . . . Contenant quelques Particularités de sa Vie privée, relatives à sa Personne ou à ses Ouvrages* and J. Le Breton's *Notice historique sur la vie et les ouvrages de Joseph Haydn.* Griesinger's judgment of Framery is applied equally to Le Breton by Fétis (in the *Biographie Universelle*) and C. F. Pohl (in the preface to *Joseph Haydn*). Framery names Pleyel as his main source of information. Le Breton, who had read Griesinger's Notes in the *Allgemeine Musikalische Zeitung* (and who is the author of the letter on p. 261), added anecdotes from Pleyel and Neukomm. The case of the Ox Minuet is discussed at length in Hoboken, *Joseph Haydn,* p. 577.

2   This catalogue, compiled by Haydn and his valet-copyist, Johann Elssler, at the request of Gottfried Härtel (see p. 65), is now known as the *Haydn Verzeichnis (HV)*. It was published in facsimile by Jens Peter Larsen in *Drei Haydn Kataloge* (Copenhagen, 1941). Dies (p. 206) prints a lengthier summary of this same list. The figure 118 Symphonies includes 104 symphonies, 11 overtures, one sinfonia *concertante,* one partita, and the original version of the *Seven Words.*

3   Haydn's mother was born Anna Maria Koller (d. 1754), and his stepmother was born Maria Anna Seeder (m. Mathias Haydn, 1755). (Haydn's wife was born Maria Anna Keller!) Father Haydn had twelve children by his first wife and five by his second (according to Pohl). Joseph was not the eldest; he had an elder sister Franziska (1730–81).

4   Johann Mathias Franck (1708–83) was the husband of Mathias
     Haydn's stepsister. In his will, Haydn left Franck's portrait, even
     then hanging in his house, and 100 gulden to Franck's daughter and
     her husband, Philipp Schimpel, who was also choirmaster at Hain-
     burg.

5   Georg Reutter (1708–72), after 1740 "von Reutter," was a Viennese
     court composer who in 1738 succeeded his father in the additional
     post of Kapellmeister at St. Stephen's. Dr. Burney described
     Reutter as "an old German composer without taste or invention"
     and a *Te Deum* that he heard under Gassmann's direction at
     St. Stephen's in 1772 as "dull, dry stuff" performed with "great
     noise and little meaning" (*The Present State of Music in Germany,*
     I, 356–57). Prince Nikolaus Esterházy II, Haydn's last employer,
     nevertheless preferred Reutter's church music to Haydn's masses.
        Burney's description of St. Stephen's in 1772 probably pretty well
     represents what Haydn knew there in the 1740's: "The church is a
     dark, dirty, and dismal old Gothic building, though richly orna-
     mented; in it are hung all the trophies of war, taken from the Turks
     and other enemies of the house of Austria, for more than a century
     past, which gives it very much the appearance of an old wardrobe"
     (*The Present State of Music in Germany,* I, 239–40). It is a pity
     that Haydn was "out of town" during Burney's visit, for we are thus
     deprived of a valuable firsthand account.

6   Among the titles held after 1731 at St. Stephen's and at court by
     Adam Gegenbauer (d. 1754) were second violinist, subcantor,
     assistant first violinist, "concert-dispensator" (manager), and
     copyist. Ignaz Finsterbusch (d. 1753) was a better teacher than
     singer, according to Pohl (*Joseph Haydn,* I, 64–65), and
     Griesinger's "elegant" refers to his dress, not to his voice.

7   One cannot help agreeing with Fétis (*Biog. Univ.,* art. "Haydn"),
     who says that despite the testimony of Pleyel, Le Breton, and
     Framery, this anecdote is still dubious, and finds it unlikely "that in
     a country where castration has never been practiced, a Kapellmeister
     such as Reutter should have risked the grave consequences of such
     an act in the sole interest of preserving a beautiful voice for the
     choir."

8   Mariazell, in the mountains sixty miles southwest of Vienna, is the
     site of an ancient shrine of the Virgin. Haydn's pilgrimage and
     adventures in the Gnaden-Kirche there occurred in the spring of
     1750.

9   The dismissal occurred late in 1749, so Haydn was nearly eighteen.

10 The church and square of St. Michael's are in the Inner City not far from St. Stephen's Cathedral.

11 Dies quotes this compliment (p. 96). Haydn also said of these sonatas to Rochlitz, "I played them over for my own pleasure countless times, especially when I felt weighed down by cares or discouraged, and I was always cheered by them and went away from the instrument in a good mood." Pohl sensibly points out that if Haydn first got the 1742 *Sei Sonate per Cembalo* (dedicated to Frederick the Great), as Griesinger implies, he undoubtedly soon got hold of the 1744 *Sei Sonate per Cembalo* (dedicated to the young Duke of Württemberg) as well. Both sets were published in Nuremberg (Pohl, *Joseph Haydn*, I, 132).

12 Marianne Martinez (1744–1812) was not much over six when Haydn moved into the Michaelerhaus. It seems quite probable that he gave her voice as well as clavier lessons, but she soon studied singing with Porpora (who was close to seventy at the time) and composition with Hasse. She was still living in Metastasio's house when Dr. Burney visited them in 1772. Burney praised her playing, asked for copies of her compositions, but especially lauded her singing, and referred to her as "St. Cecilia Martinetz at the harpsichord" (*The Present State of Music in Germany*, I, 357). Michael Kelly, who met her about 1785, says, "She was reckoned a deep blue, and very well versed in all the arts and sciences. . . . Mozart was an almost constant attendant at her parties, and I have heard him play duets on the piano-forte with her, of his own composition. She was a great favourite of his" (*Reminiscences*, I, 252).

13 The identity of Griesinger's "very reliable source" is suggested by the following comments of Carpani: "I shall never forget when 30 years ago Mislivicek was in Milan at an *accademia,* and hearing there some old symphonies by Sammartini, about whose music this able Bohemian had not the first notion, he blurted out, I being present,—I have found the father of Haydn's style!—To tell the truth, Mislivicek went too far. Haydn's style, considered in its totality, is completely his own, completely new, and, so to speak, inspired. Maestro Venceslao Pichl was also inclined to the opinion of his compatriot, but he did not carry it to such an extreme. Haydn could easily pick up the flavor of Sammartini and imitate the movement, the fire, the brilliance, and certain beautiful extravagances which dominated this music full of ideas and invention. . . . but Haydn was too good a contrapuntist and loved too well that orderliness of controlled advance found in a pure and rational style to

imitate deliberately this most whimsical Milanese, who in his work
gave little thought to texture but pursued madly the impetus of his
eager imagination, and hence produced here and there the most
beautiful brightness next to disordered masses of indefinite color"
(*Le Haydine*, pp. 62–63). For the translation of Carpani's book from
the Italian I am indebted to my colleague Professor Philip Keppler.
Sammartini (1698/1701–75) was seventy years old in 1768/71;
Carpani dates this event ten years later, about 1779, the year that
Mysliveczek (Misliweczek) produced his *Armida* in Milan. This
story dies hard: see R. Sondheimer, *Haydn, A Historical and Psychological Study Based on his Quartets* (London, 1951), esp.
pp. 10 and 23.

14 Pohl says that Griesinger is mistaken; the Albrechtsberger who was
Beethoven's teacher had no brother, though this may possibly be a
relative of his (*Joseph Haydn*, I, 184 n.) or the man himself
(Hughes, *Haydn*, p. 27). But see Bartha, *Briefe*, p. 202.

15 This paragraph is tantalizing because it is largely unverifiable. The
Seilerstätte is a quarter mile from St. Stephen's, in the opposite
direction from the Michaelerplatz, Haydn's earlier address. Concerning his losses, Pohl remarks that "Haydn was already too old to
fall back on his parents and his father neither so poor nor so hard
hearted as to be unable or unwilling to stand by his son" (*Joseph
Haydn*, I, 188, n.12). The Hospital of the Barmherzige Brüder is a
little over half a mile from St. Stephen's and the palace of Count
Haugwitz about a mile and a half in another direction, so Haydn
could have met all these engagements in one morning; but Pohl
turned up no evidence of his appointment to them. The quintet is
not otherwise identified.

16 The music for *Der krumme Teufel*, composed in 1751 or 1752,
was also used in a 1758 revision, *Der neue krumme Teufel*, but is
no longer extant. Griesinger gives Kurz's words in dialect that
cannot be rendered in English: "*Sehts nit, wie i schwimm!*"

17 Carpani mentions Count Morzin in the following way: "Count
Harrach was the governor of Austrian Lombardy. He was the first
to bring the music of Sammartini to Vienna, where it quickly won
applause and became the vogue in that great capital so enamored of
this kind of diversion. Count Pálffy, grand chancellor of Hungary,
Count Schönborn, and Count Morzin vied with one another in
procuring novelties for display in their almost daily concerts.
Haydn, young and studious, could and must have heard them.
. . ." (*Le Haydine*, p. 66).

18 Griesinger is in error. It was the younger sister who entered the convent, and it was the elder whom Haydn married on Nov. 26, 1760 (Pohl, *Joseph Haydn,* I, 195–96; cf. p. 99).

19 Haydn's wife died on March 20, 1800. Griesinger was doubtless referring to the following incident reported by Hermann von Hase in *Joseph Haydn und Breitkopf & Härtel* (Leipzig, 1909), p. 19: "Breitkopf & Härtel, wanting to express their gratitude to the aged master, even if his work [for them] consisted of nothing much more than looking over proposed publications, intended to give his wife a present. But when Griesinger let something of this be known, Father Haydn answered him, 'I make formal protest against this, I love my wife, she wants for nothing; but she has done nothing to deserve a reward.'" In the end, the firm gave Haydn, and he happily accepted, a diamond ring, saying, "I am like a child. Presents of this sort please me more than great sums of money."

20 Actually to Prince Paul Anton Esterházy, who died on March 18, 1762, and was succeeded by Nikolaus. The contract of Haydn's appointment, dated May 1, 1761, is translated in Geiringer, *Haydn* (N.Y., 1946), pp. 52–54. The "other emoluments" were board at the officers' table or a half gulden a day in lieu of board.

21 This is a complete list for the period 1761–90 except for the four festival works (or arias?) of 1762 and the lost *Hexenschabbas* mentioned by Dies alone (pp. 116 and 208). Dies like Griesinger writes *La Pescatrice* on p. 208, but he gives it correctly *Le Pescatrici* on p. 107. Griesinger's list and those of Dies on pp. 107, 116, and 208 are all printed with original spellings. Both biographers (Griesinger here, Dies p. 208) list *L'Infedeltà fedele,* a riddle whose solution is reported in Bartha and Somfai, *Haydn als Opernkapellmeister,* pp. 95–96. The libretto of *L'Infedeltà fedele* is by Lorenzi, and was first composed by Cimarosa. "Haydn had to write a new opera in great haste for the new opening of the opera house (autumn 1780 or beginning of 1781). Where to find a libretto?—Haydn had the idea of looking through the libretti of the operas lying unused in the music archives. Here he stumbled across the Cimarosa opera *L'Infedeltà fedele,* which did not at all suit him musically but whose text appeared usable. Quickly deciding, he took the score home. . . . and, relying heavily on its text, composed his own opera *La Fedeltà premiata!*—The new title variant was probably invented by Haydn expressly to conceal somewhat the connection with the Cimarosa model. . . ." In other words, *L'Infedeltà fedele* and *La Fedeltà premiata* are the same opera. A copyist's error is re-

sponsible for the appearance of the original title in the *Entwurf-Katalog* and thence in the *Haydn-Verzeichnis,* in Griesinger, in Dies, etc.

22 Eisenstadt (Kismarton) is about twenty-five miles southeast of Vienna, on the Leitha River. Bartha and Somfai (*Haydn,* pp. 15–18) have recently shown how mistaken is Griesinger's bland statement. "As we know for certain from theater records and letters, Haydn must have spent the nine to ten months a year in princely service not in Eisenstadt but (at least from 1767 on) regularly in Esterháza. Eisenstadt on the other hand was for Nikolaus the Magnificent and his Kapellmeister nothing but a winter abode for the months of December and January, whence Haydn only exceptionally (with express permission of the Prince) might travel to Vienna." And at Esterháza Haydn prepared, rehearsed, and conducted between 1776 and 1790 some 100 operas (88 premières), extensively editing and adding to the works of others, in addition to his own composing. "In these 15 years Esterháza under Haydn's direction figured as one of the most important centers of Italian opera in Europe (outside Italy)," far surpassing even Vienna (Bartha and Somfai, *Haydn,* pp. 25–26). In the banner year 1786, "125 opera performances were held (together with many rehearsals) including 8 premières, one newly rehearsed, and 8 repeated operas; the repertoire thus included 17 works!" (p. 130).

23 In August, 1768, a fire that burned for two days destroyed everything but nineteen houses and the Stadt-Pfarrkirche. In July, 1776, one hundred and four of the new houses again burned (Pohl, *Joseph Haydn,* II, 82).

24 "I know from certain of the musicians who lived with him at Esterháza," Carpani wrote (*Le Haydine,* pp. 56–57), "that frequently he interrupted his work, left his chamber, gathered the orchestra together, tried out one passage or another on different instruments, and, having made the experiment, dismissed them, returned to his worktable, and continued his composition with assurance."

25 Haydn's angry letter of Feb. 4, 1779, dealing with this piece of discrimination is printed by Landon, *Col Cor,* pp. 22–23.

26 Cf. Dies's reports of *Tobias* on pp. 169 and 170.

27 Perhaps the "Divertimento per il Cembalo" (Hoboken, *Joseph Haydn,* Group XVI 2c, p. 735).

28 C. M. Brand, in *Die Messen von J. H.* (Würzburg, 1941),

pp. 373–74, skeptically cites this passage as an example of Haydn's powers of wit, irony, and satire: "To understand the sting in Haydn's wit, and how finely he developed it, it suffices to show that Griesinger, learning that Haydn in younger days occasionally went out shooting, and wanting to know more about this point, let Haydn pass off on him the most improbable hunters' tales as true adventures, and did not notice even years later when he put his notes together, that he was spinning huntsmen's yarns for his readers." *Caveat lector!*

29 *"Ach, das ist ja erbärmliches Zeug!"* When Haydn told this story to Dies, his words were even stronger. Cf. p. 93. Karl Ditters von Dittersdorf (1739–99) was a native Viennese. He was a protégé of the same Prince Hildburghausen at whose house Haydn played in Mannersdorf. In his autobiography he said, "During the rest of the summer [1763?] and the following winter, when I was off duty, I often came into contact with the amiable Joseph Haydn. What lover of music does not know the name and the beautiful works of this distinguished writer? When we heard any new music by other composers, we criticised it between ourselves, praising, or the reverse, as we thought just. . . . Haydn and I did this in a spirit of inquiry, and if all prejudices are laid aside, I maintain that nothing so materially assists a young musician's progress as mutual and friendly criticism of this kind" (*The Autobiography of Karl von Dittersdorf,* tr. by A. D. Coleridge [London, 1896; original edition, 1801], pp. 127–28).

30 The music together with the twenty stanzas of the poem is in the Breitkopf and Härtel *Joseph Haydns Werke,* Serie XX, Vol. I, p. 107.

31 See note p. 242 for details of this work.

32 Sir John Gallini (1728–1805) was an Italian dancer who became a concert and opera impresario in London, owned the Hanover Square Rooms, and built the new King's Theater. Johann Peter Salomon (1745–1815), a noted violinist, had become a concert manager and musical director in London. Giacomo Davide (1750–1830) was generally known in London as Signor David. Pohl (*Haydn in London,* p. 123, n. 2) says that the strength, range, and agility of his tenor voice were matched by a thoroughly grounded musicianship (see note p. 245).

33 The commissioned works are the 8 Notturni for 2 *Lire organizzate* and orchestra (Hoboken, *Joseph Haydn,* Group II, 25–32; see also H. R. Edwall, "Ferdinand IV and Haydn's Concertos for the *Lira*

organizzata," Musical Quarterly, XLVIII, 1962, pp. 190–203). One of the first visits Haydn paid in London was to Prince Castelcicala, who at once returned the visit and invited Haydn to dinner. This was the beginning of a social life which, though gratifying, constantly threatened Haydn's health and musical output during his stay in England.

34 There were four of these little notebooks in the days when Griesinger and Dies were visiting Haydn. Their history may be recapitulated in outline:

1791–92: 2 notebooks in Vienna National-bibliothek	Translated (with minor omissions) in H. E. Krehbiel, *Music and Manners in the Classical Period* (New York, 1898).

1794–95: 1 Notebook is lost (extracts preserved only by Griesinger and Dies).

1 notebook in Salzburg Mozarteum	Transcribed (unsatisfactorily) in J. E. Engl, *Joseph Haydns handschr. Tagebuch aus der Zeit seines 2. Aufenthaltes in London* (Leipzig, 1909).

All of this material without omission is available in English translation in Landon, *Col Cor.*

35 *The Woodman* was a comic opera with music by William Shield (1748–1829). The tenors in this performance have only recently been identified as Charles Incledon and Mr. Johnstone, but Elizabeth Billington (*née* Weichsel) is very well known indeed. She and her brother had been *Wunderkinder* in London in the 1770's. Haydn made the following entry in his diary on January 14, 1792: "Today. . . . the life of Madam Bilingthon was published in print. Her life is exposed in the most shameless detail. The publisher is said to have got hold of her own letters, and to have offered to return them to her for 10 guineas; otherwise he intended to print them publicly. But she didn't want to spend the 10 guineas, and demanded her letters through the courts. She was refused, whereupon she appealed, but in vain; for even though her opponent offered her £500, he nevertheless issued this treasure of hers today, and you couldn't get a single copy after 3 o'clock in the afternoon.

"It is said that her character is the worst sort, but that she is a great genius, and all the women hate her because she is so beautiful.

N.B. She is said, however, to have written the most scandalous letters, containing accounts of her amours, to her mother. She is said to be an illegitimate child, and it is even believed that her own supposed father is involved in this affair.

"Such stories are common in London. The husband provides opportunities for his wife so that he can profit from it, whereby he relieves his "brother-in-law" of £1000 Sterling and more" (Cf. Landon, *Col Cor*, p. 255).

Carpani (*Le Haydine*, pp. 234–35) tells another story about Mrs. Billington. Someone painted her portrait as St. Cecelia. When she showed it to Haydn, he said there was an error in it. "He has pictured you listening to the angels. He should have pictured the angels listening to you." Mrs. Billington rewarded him with a kiss!

36 Actually May 22, 1792, according to Pohl, *Mozart und Haydn in London*, p. 197. See also Griesinger, note 53.

37 Pohl identified this music as a chant by the Cathedral organist, John Jones, and printed a harmonized version in *Haydn in London*, p. 214.

The next sentence provides an excellent example of Griesinger's procedure with Haydn's diaries. The full entry follows: "Today, 4th June 1792, I was in Vauxhall where the King's birthday is celebrated. Over 30,000 lamps were burning, but because of the severe cold there were very few people present. The grounds and its variety are perhaps unique in the world. There are 155 little dining booths in various places, most charmingly situated, each comfortably seating 6 persons. There are very large alleys of trees, which form a wonderful roof above, and are magnificently illuminated. Tea, coffee and milk with almonds all cost nothing. The entrance fee is half a crown per person. The music is fairly good. A stone statue of Handel has been erected. On the 2nd inst. there was a masked ball, and on this evening they took in 3000 guineas" (Landon, *Col Cor*, p. 262).

38 These lists are thoroughly annotated by Landon, *Col Cor*, pp. 262–66. They appear here exactly as Griesinger printed them except for minor alterations in punctuation. Griesinger apparently asked Haydn for additions, because these names do not appear in the diary: the singers Mad. de Sisley and Miss Nield, the pianist Hässler, and the flautist Mr. Ashe. Mad. de Sisley was a French refugee who in happier days had studied singing under Piozzi, Piccini, and Sacchini. "Miss Nield" is presumably Haydn's failing memory of the tenor J. Nield, who appeared frequently in Salomon's

concerts. J. W. Haesler (1747–1822), a composer as well as a pianist, shared Haydn's programs in both capacities. Andrew Ashe (*ca.* 1759–1838), an Irishman, made his successful London debut at the concert of Feb. 24, 1792, at which Haydn's chorus *The Storm* was also first performed, and his benefit concert of June 8, 1795, may well have been the last London concert in which Haydn participated.

39   This entry and Pohl's subsequent confusion over it were only deciphered by Oliver Strunk. Cf. Hughes, *Haydn*, p. 71, and Landon's documentary account, *Sym*, pp. 473–80. The entry refers to the second season:

     1st concert, Feb. 17, 1792, Symphony #93 in D.
     2nd concert, Feb. 24, 1792, Chorus: *The Storm*.
     3rd concert, Mar. 2, 1792, Symphony #98 in B flat.

40   Mme. Mara (*née* Gertrud Elisabeth Schmeling, 1749–1833) was as successful a singer as she was unfortunate in her personal life. Her name appears repeatedly in Haydn's diaries, he accompanied her in public several times, and he also noted down his private opinion of her public carryings on (see Landon, *Col Cor,* p. 288).

41   This touching account refers to Symphony #75 in D, performed at the singer Miss Corri's benefit concert rather than at the violinist Barthelemon's, which took place on May 28 (Pohl, *Haydn in London*, p. 193). The correct theme:

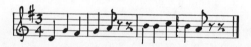

42   The opera was *The Banditti,* written for Covent Garden in 1781 by Samuel Arnold (1740–1802), organist at Westminster Abbey and a friend of Haydn (see Landon, *Col Cor,* p. 308). Arnold issued an incomplete but important edition of Handel's works in the 1790's.

43   This entry refers to Joah Bates, who in addition to the Concerts of Ancient Music also conducted the first and subsequent Handel festivals in Westminster Abbey. His wife (*née* Harrop) was an oratorio singer, here compared to the *castrato* Gasparo Pacchierotti, the perfection of whose voice, Dr. Burney wrote, "is as superior to the generality of vocal sweetness, as that of the pine apple is, not only to other fruits, but to sugar or treacle" (*General History*, Bk. IV, ch. vi).

44   The anthem was "Sing unto God" (*The Wedding Anthem*), which Handel had composed in 1736 for the marriage of an earlier Prince

of Wales. In the end, Parsons conducted the band, Arnold the singers, and Dupuis accompanied on the organ, as Haydn had suggested (Pohl, *Haydn in London,* p. 299).

45 "I am the most in love." This song, overlooked by Max Friedlaender in Serie 20, Vol. I, of the Breitkopf and Härtel edition of *Joseph Haydns Werke* (1932), is the original setting of the English song "Content" and appears in Paul Mies's edition for the *Werke* (Joseph Haydn-Institut, Köln) of the Lieder (München-Duisburg, 1960), as No. 36a, pp. 70–71. The poem, by J. N. Götz, is conventional pastoral verse ending, *ich bin der verliebteste von allen Sterblichen auf Erden.*

46 Pohl corrects this date to July 28 (*Haydn in London,* p. 270) and identifies the music as *The Mountaineers* and *Auld Robin Gray,* both composed by Dr. Arnold.

47 In this programme, typical of the London Haydn knew, he had the assistance of the basso Carlo Rovedino, of the oboist Giuseppe Ferlendis, who was making his London debut and whom Haydn described as "mediocre" in his diary, of Madame Anna Morichelli and Signor Giovanni Morelli (also a basso) from the Italian opera, of the noted violinist G. B. Viotti, and of the dramatic soprano Mme. Brigida Banti-Giorgi. The new symphony was #104; the duet *Quel tuo visetto amabile* from *Orlando Paladino* (see Landon, *Col Cor,* p. 306 n); the new *scena, Scena di Berenice.*

48 Pohl points out that this index does not include those earlier works that Haydn reworked for London, not to mention a march for the Royal Society of Musicians (which was, however, simply an orchestral version of the March for the Prince of Wales), a seven-part Italian catch, and the fragment of an uncompleted English oratorio (*Haydn in London,* pp. 311–12). Doubtless there are other minor omissions. The catalogue is given here in German just as Griesinger transmits it because Dies's version (p. 209) preserves Haydn's original English. While the numbers of sheets included by Griesinger lend a touch of authenticity not overlooked by Larsen (*Die Haydn-Überlieferung,* p. 249), it is worth noting that not only do these figures not total correctly, but, as Strunk points out ("Notes on a Haydn Autograph," *Musical Quarterly,* XX [1934], p. 201, n. 21), "where it is possible to verify these 'exact' figures, there are always discrepancies between them and the actual specifications of the autographs." The two lists are in agreement except that Dies lists *three* sonatas for Miss Jansen and adds one item at the end: three [additional] sonatas for Broderip. Concerning these dis-

crepancies, Strunk (p. 202) has demonstrated how a better case can be made for Dies, "yet Pohl and Botstiber reprint the Griesinger text without even mentioning the existence of another."

49 Haydn's folksong arrangements include:

For William Napier	100 Scots published	1792
	50 Scots	1794
For George Thomson	187 Scots, Welsh, Irish	1802 ff.
For William Whyte	40 Scots	1804
	25 Scots	1807
(Mostly unprinted	43)	
	402 (445)	

For a detailed account of this fascinating area of Haydn's activity (surprisingly neglected by Griesinger and Dies, and romanticized by Carpani), see Geiringer, "Haydn and the Folksong of the British Isles," *Musical Quarterly,* XXXV, 1949, pp. 179–208.

50 Pohl thinks this refers not to the Concerts of Ancient Music, at which no music of Haydn was performed until 1832 (p. 14), but rather to the concerts of sacred music given on Friday evenings in Lent in the King's Theater (*Haydn in London,* pp. 289–90).

51 Handel's youthful *St. John Passion* also sets a German text. The Passion in question here sets the text by Barthold Heinrich Brockes: *Der für die Sünden der Welt gemarterte und sterbende Jesus aus den vier Evangelisten in gebundener Rede vorgestellet* (*ca.* 1716).

52 This is the same song, and very likely the same occasion, mentioned on p. 30. Carpani (*Le Haydine,* p. 237) remarks that the King "throughout his whole life loved only a single woman and a single music—that is, the Queen and the works of Handel (an extremely rare instance of constancy in both genres)."

53 See p. 25 for Haydn's opinion. Felice de' Giardini, b. Turin, 1716, d. Moscow, 1796. A composer as well as violin virtuoso, he lived in London from 1750–83, and again after 1790. When Haydn heard him, the 76-year-old violinist was giving concerts to recoup financial losses suffered as manager of Italian opera in London. Dies describes a composition by Giardini on p. 143.

54 Michael Denis, S.J. (1729–1800), a popular and prolific Viennese poet and bibliographer, was the author of the prose texts only, according to Dies (see p. 162). The verses were by Gabriele von Baumberg (1775–1839), a Viennese poetess who in 1805 married a Hungarian poet named Johann Bacsányi. The first verses are fitted to the Andante of Symphony #53 in D (The Imperial) and the sec-

ond to the Adagio of the String Quartet Opus 50 No. 1 in B flat.
The German texts follow:

> Ihr holden Philomelen,
> belebet diesen Hayn,
> und lasst durch tausend Kehlen
> dies Lied verewigt seyn.

> Dem Andenken
> Joseph Haydns
> des unsterblichen Meisters
> der Tonkunst,
> dem Ohr und Herz
> wetteifernd huldigen,
> gewidmet
> > von
> Karl Leonhard Graf von Harrach
> Im Jahr 1793.

Griesinger omits the fourth line of the second stanza, and according
to Grasberger (*Biographische Notizen*, p. 70) two lines that Dies
also omits belong in the complete poem:

Ein Denkmalstein zu Haydns Ruhm	(A stone to Haydn's fame designed
weiht diesen Platz zum Heiligthum,	consecrates this place enshrined,
und Harmonie klagt wehmuthsvoll	and Harmony mourns in dismay
dass dieses grossen Meisters Hand,	*that now this mighty master's hand*
die stets Gefühl mit Kraft verband,	*which force with feeling ever spanned—*
dass diese Hand einst modern soll.	that this hand finally shall decay.)

> Rohrau
> gab ihm das Leben
> Im Jahr 1732. den 1sten Apr.
> Europa
> ungetheilten Beyfall.
> Der Tod
> Im Jahr 1809. Den 31sten May
> den Zutritt
> zu den ewigen Harmonien.

The monument remained on its island from 1794 to 1887. It then stood in the castle park until 1951, when the Harrach family presented it to the town of Rohrau. There it may be seen today standing in a lane near the parish church. The tablet quoted above actually reads: "Dem Andenken Josephs Haydens . . . im Jahr 1794."

Concerning Haydn's birth date, see p. 239, n. 6. The German text of the Denis poem quoted next by Griesinger reads:

> Ihr staunt, dass Orpheus himmlischer Gesang
> Einst Thränen aus den Augen roher Menschen zwang.
> Bewundert euren Zeitgenossen,
> Durch den so oft der Edlen Thränen flossen.

55 Haydn in fact bought this house in August, 1793, between the two London journeys. The term "suburb" is misleading to the modern reader: the house lay scarcely two miles' walk southwest from St. Stephen's Cathedral. The Steingasse has long since been renamed Haydngasse, and the house is now a museum. Carpani, one of the friends who visited Haydn there, described the house as follows: "When you leave Vienna in the direction of the Imperial Villa of Schönbrunn, you come upon a little road on the left, near the Mariahülf gates, which leads towards the suburb of Gumpendorf. Midway down this road rises a solitary, neat, and modest cottage surrounded by silence. . . . If you enter this peaceful refuge and, having greeted the smiling, aged housekeeper, mount the tiny staircase, you will see in the middle of the second room only a calm old man, seated at a little table. . . ." (*Le Haydine,* pp. 1–2).

56 Joseph Starzer (1726–87) was a violinist and composer (especially of ballet music) active in Vienna and, for ten years, in St. Petersburg. Karl von Kohaut, probably Bohemian by birth and possibly elder brother of the opera composer Joseph Kohaut, was a court secretary in Vienna and an outstanding performer on the lute. He composed for that instrument and wrote symphonies and trios as well.

57 This is Zelter's review, discussed at length on p. 248. For an account of the first performance of *The Creation,* see p. 175.

58 The original German text follows:

> Wie strömt dein wogender Gesang
> In unsre Herzen ein! wir sehen
> Der Schöpfung mächtgen Gang,

Den Hauch des Herrn auf dem Gewässer wehen,
Jetzt durch ein blitzend Wort das erste Licht entstehen,
Und die Gestirne sich durch ihre Bahnen drehen;
Wie Baum und Pflanze wird, wie sich der Berg erhebt,
Und froh des Lebens sich die jungen Thiere regen.
Der Donner rollet uns entgegen;
Der Regen säuselt, jedes Wesen strebt
Ins Daseyn; und bestimmt, des Schöpfers Werk zu krönen,
Sehn wir das erste Paar geführt von deinen Tönen.
O jedes Hochgefühl, das in dem Herzen schlief,
Ist wach! wer rufet nicht: wie schön ist diese Erde!
Und schöner, nun ihr Herr auch Dich ins Daseyn rief,
Auf dass sein Werk vollendet werde.

59 August von Kotzebue (1761–1819) brought out *Die Hussiten vor Naumburg im Jahr 1432, Ein vaterländisches Schauspiel mit Chören* in 1803. The chorus that Haydn unfortunately could not undertake to compose follows:

Allmächtiger, der du mit einem Winke
Den fallenden Blitz zurück in die Wolken wendest,
Der tobenden Flut den Sturm entgegen sendest!
Mit Angst und Jammer stehen wir im Staube:
Nicht der Verzweiflung gib dein Volk zum Raube!

(Omnipotent, thou who with but a gesture,
The lightning descending back to the heavens turnest,
The raging and flooding storm as well adjournest!
In fear and anguish here in dust we're kneeling:
Give not thy folk a prey to hopeless feeling!)

60 Dies (p. 134 note) also mentions this exchange. The terminology is not unmistakable. Griesinger says that Haydn replaced his old *Fortepiano* with *ein ganz leicht zu behandelndes Klavier*. Dies has him replace his customary *Flügel* (*Clavecin*) with *ein Clavier* to avoid the *scharfe Flügelton*. Whether Haydn composed at the piano or harpsichord (he owned and therefore probably used both), it seems clear that in old age his weakened fingers and sensitive ears required the gentler clavichord (see also p. 47).

61 A recent biography of John Hunter (1728–93) is *The Reluctant Surgeon* by John Kobler (New York, 1960). For information about Haydn Kobler unfortunately relied entirely on the unsatisfactory

biography by H. E. Jacob, translated by Richard and Clara Winston, *Joseph Haydn, His Art, Times, and Glory* (New York and Toronto, 1950).

62 This sonata for clavier and violin was a reworking of the 1795 trio in E flat minor for clavier, violin, and violoncello (Hoboken, *Joseph Haydn*, Group XV, No. 31). Moreau was exiled by Napoleon, but the sonata was published in Paris and London *ca.* 1821.

63 It was Griesinger, of course, who arranged for the publication of the songs (Vol. VIII and IX of the *Oeuvres complettes,* June, 1803), and Neukomm who carried the copy to the Dowager Empress, whose letter dated Feb. 15, 1805, is printed in Landon, *Col Cor,* p. 236.

64 The song (No. X in Vol. IX) is by J. W. L. Gleim (1718–1803), and the text:

Der Greis	The Old Man
Hin ist alle meine Kraft!	(Gone is all of my own strength!
Alt und schwach bin ich,	Old and weak am I,
Wenig nur erquicket mich	Little now enlivens me
Scherz und Rebensaft!	Save for jokes and wine.
Hin ist alle meine Zier!	Gone are all my old good looks!
Meiner Wangen Roth	And my rosy cheeks
Ist hinweg geflohn! Der Tod	Drained away! And meanwhile Death
Klopft an meine Thür!	Knocks now at my door!
Unerschrocken mach' ich auf;	Unafraid I open it;
Himmel, habe Dank!	Heaven, thanks to thee!
Ein harmonischer Gesang	An harmonious song
War mein Lebenslauf!	Has been my life long!)

65 "A highly flattering and highly ungrammatical letter whose clumsiness even Griesinger made fun of when he sent a copy to Leipzig," says Botstiber (*Joseph Haydn,* p. 216). St. Marx is a suburb of Vienna. The original German text follows:

> "Wohlgeborner,
>   Hochzuverehrender Herr!

Nach den vielen Beweisen der Menschenfreundlichkeit, mit welcher Ew. Wohlgeb. die bemitleidenswerthe Lage der verarmten alten Bürger und Bürgerinnen zu St. Marx zu erleichtern mitge-

wirkt haben, fand sich die von höchsten Orten aufgestellte Bür-
gerspitals-Wirthschaftskommission veranlasst, hierorts dieses edel-
müthige Benehmen vorstellig zu machen, und den Wunsch zu
äussern, dass diese wohlthätigen Bemühungen nicht unbemerkt
bleiben möchten.

In Erwägung nun, dass Sie, verehrungswürdigster Herr Doktor
der Tonkunst, zu der Bewunderung für die Meisterwerke Ihres
Genies, zu wiederholten malen unentgeldlich und in eigener Person
die Direktion jener Kantaten übernahmen, durch welche so viele
Herzen zum Wohlthun gestimmt, und den armen Bürgern zu St.
Marx so ansehnliche Beyträge bewirkt wurden, ergreift der Magistrat dieser k. k. Haupt- und Residenz-Stadt Wien, der schon
lange einer Gelegenheit entgegen sah, einem durch sein Talent un-
sterblichen, und bereits von allen gebildeten Nationen mit besonde-
ren Ehren ausgezeichneten Mann, welcher die Vorzüge des Kün-
stlers mit den Tugenden des Bürgers in thätige Verbindung setzt,
diese Veranlassung, auf irgend eine Weise seine Achtung zu be-
zeugen.

Um aber auch in Ansehung dieses bleibenden Verdienstes nur
den entferntesten Beweis zu geben, hat der Magistrat einstimmig
beschlossen, Ew. Wohlgeb. gegenwärtige zwölffache goldne Bür-
ger-Medaille als ein geringes Merkmal des Dankgefühles der er-
quickten armen Bürger und Bürgerinnen zu St. Marx, deren
Organ wir hiermit vorstellen, anzuschliessen.

Möge sie so lange an Ihrer Brust glänzen, als die Segenswünsche
für Ihre Edelthat dankbaren Herzen entströmen werden; mögen
Sie uns Gelegenheit an die Hand geben, die Beweise der ausgezeichneten Hochachtung zu vernehmen, womit wir verharren.

Ew. Wohlgeboren
bereitwilligste
Joseph Georg Hörl, k. k. N. Oester. Reg. Rath und Bürger-
meister.

Stephan Edler von Wohlleben, k. k. Rath und Stadtoberkäm-
merer in Wien.

Joh. Bapt. Franz, der Bürgerspitals-Wirthschafts-Commission
Präses.

Wien am 10ten May 1803."

66 Actually May, 1761. Cf. Griesinger, note 20. Also Haydn's Oxford
degree dated from July, 1791, and the membership in the Institut
National from Dec., 1801 (see p. 261). Concerning the Modena
honor, see also p. 116.

67 Heinrich Josef von Collin (1771–1811) was a Viennese dramatist.
His verses (as well as Carpani's sonnet) appear on pp. 178–79.
Antonio Salieri (1750–1825), the opera composer and teacher of
Beethoven, among others, spent most of his life in Vienna, where
he had been taken by Gassmann at the age of sixteen. He set Car-
pani's sonnet to music.

68 Gerber says that Beethoven was among those present, that there
were a "considerable number" in the chorus and at least 80 instrumentalists, and that the soloists included Mlle. Fischer (see p. 180)
and Messrs. Carl Weinmüller and Radichi. Under Salieri's direction were Konradin Kreutzer at the keyboard and Franz Clement
as first violin (Art. "Haydn," *Neues Lexikon,* col. 556–57).

69 The original German text follows:

> Laut hörte man des Lebewohles Toben,
> Geklatsch und Mitleidsruf zum Himmel dringen:
> Er aber wandte seinen Blick nach oben,
> Und dachte so sein volles Herz zu zwingen;
> Doch aufgeregt will sich der Sturm nicht legen,
> Und reisst ihn fort. Umsonst ist all sein Ringen.
> Rasch sieht man vorwärts sich den Greis bewegen;
> Und als er nun der Pforte nah gekommen—
> Aus streckt er seine Hand zum Vatersegen!
> Und alles weint!—Wol wird er nie mehr kommen!

70 Griesinger is referring to the letters from Haydn's factotum, Johann
Elssler, dated June 30, 1809, and from the piano manufacturer, An-
dreas Streicher, dated July 2, 1809, with a postscript on July 12.
These letters are printed in Botstiber, *Joseph Haydn,* pp. 385–90,
and are the main source of the next six paragraphs of Griesinger's
account. Haydn's words according to Elssler were, *"Kinder, fürch-
tet euch nicht, denn wo Haydn ist kann nichts geschehen."* Griesinger and Dies both alter this quotation slightly. Streicher describes Haydn's visitor as *Sulimy, Capitain des Hussards* and dates
his visit "three days before Haydn's death, the 24th May," a palpable
error. He says that Sulemy sang the aria in Italian.

71 The Church of the Scots, which belonged to a Benedictine Monastery with the same name. Dies gives the date as June 15 (p. 196).

72 These words had already been used below an engraving of Haydn
by J. E. Mansfeld made in 1781. Anton Grassi was born in Vienna,
1755, and died there on December 31, 1807.

73 Griesinger's timetable differs somewhat from Dies's (p. 203).

74 Cf., however, p. 263.

75 This fabulous bird deserves at least one note. See Dies's description on p. 134. Carpani says, "Many tall tales are told about this feathered American; namely, that when he was younger, he could sing, and speak in many languages, and one might say that he was his master's pupil. The fact remains that today his only claim to fame is his good luck in having passed from the hands of the world's greatest symphonist into those of one of the most valiant warriors in Austria, and a most distinguished gentleman. The amazement of the blacksmith-heir upon seeing that this old bird brought 1,400 florins when he would gladly have exchanged him for a Styrian capon amused all the bidders at the auction" (*Le Haydine,* p. 269).

76 Haydn's swollen legs immediately claimed the attention of Dies at his first visit in April, 1805. The feast of St. Peregrine Laziosi (1260–1345) occurs on May 1. He was himself a Servite monk of whom it is said that for 30 years he never sat down! He was miraculously cured of a repulsive foot cancer, presumably the product of his guiding principle "that one must never rest in the way of virtue." The Servite Order had a church and monastery in the Viennese suburb of Rossau, not far from Gumpendorf, where Haydn lived (cf. Dies, pp. 91 and 244).

77 Actually this is the postscript to the first will, dated Vienna, Dec. 6, 1801 (cf. Dies, p. 194).

78 Haydn gave Cherubini the autograph of Symphony #103, the "Drumroll." The manuscript, now in the British Museum, still bears Haydn's inscription, *"Padre del celebre Cherubini ai 24to di Febr. 1806."* The Museum acquired it from Julian Marshall, who had bought it from Cherubini's grandson in 1879 (Hoboken, *Joseph Haydn,* pp. 217–18). Cherubini had brought Haydn the letter from the *Conservatoire* that appears on p. 189.

79 K. means Leopold Koželuch, to whom Mozart is also reputed to have said, "Sir! even if you and I were melted together, the result would be a far cry from Haydn" (Pohl, *Joseph Haydn,* II, 212–13). Koželuch, like Haydn, Pleyel, and Beethoven, arranged Scotch songs for the Edinburgh publisher Thomson.

80 Either Griesinger, like Dies, had read Triest's article of 1801 (see p. 199), or else he and Triest had the same idea (or a common source).

81 Giustino Ferdinando Tenducci, "an Italian deservedly of the greatest reputation for cantabile singing of any *castrato* that has appeared in this country," gave his last benefit concert in London in

May, 1786 (Pohl, *Mozart in London,* p. 180). Grove's Dictionary
(art. "Tenducci") says, "He sang at Drury Lane Theatre as late as
1790. He also sang at the Handel Commemorative Festivals at Westminster Abbey in 1784 and 1791." Pohl, however, does not list him
for 1791, and it seems unlikely that Haydn heard him sing in England. He may have heard him in Vienna about 1756 (Pohl, *Joseph
Haydn,* I, 90).

82 Haydn probably had several. Breitkopf and Härtel (p. 219 n. 19),
the dowager Empress of Russia (p. 43), and the King of Prussia
(p. 117) each made him the present of a ring, and Dies no doubt
saw them all (p. 133).

83 Michael Haydn died on August 10, 1806. Dies describes the effect of
this death on Hadyn on p. 160.

84 The niece is probably Anna Katharina Fröhlich, sister of Mathias
(their mother was Haydn's sister Anna Maria, not Therese as Griesinger says below). She was married first to J. A. Luegmayr, then to
Loder, who was a shoemaker. Pohl reports only one child from the
first marriage and three from the second, "among them Ernestine,
who in the last years lived with Haydn" (*Joseph Haydn,* I, *Anhang*). In his final will, Haydn left this niece a legacy of 30 kreutzers
a day (and to Ernestine the furniture from her room in his house,
as well as a cash legacy) but specifically renounced any further
claims in view of the debts he had paid off for Luegmayr, as Griesinger presently relates.

85 J. F. Reichardt, reporting in his *Vertraute Briefe geschr. auf eine
Reise nach Wien* (Amsterdam, 1810) a visit to Haydn on Nov. 30,
1808, says, "I shall not soil this recital with the little anxious touches
of avarice he betrayed, in the midst of treasures he could no longer
even use—but they went straight to my heart" (see O. Strunk,
Source Readings in Music History [New York, 1950] p. 732).
Reichardt wrote in February, 1809, that he had been able to see
Haydn only once. He sought another appointment several times,
but was always told that Haydn was very weak and could see no
one. Clementi, he said, received the same answer. Reichardt (1751–
1814) was Royal Prussian Kapelldirektor in Berlin, violinist, composer, and author of articles and books on music. Gerber, in the
1790–92 edition of the *Lexicon,* says that in some of his clavier and
vocal pieces "the Haydn manner is cleverly and successfully imitated to the point where only the title of the work can reassure us as
to the author, unattainable and unique though Haydn's manner
may otherwise be." Although Dies, like Griesinger, protests Rei-

chardt's remark, he himself on p. 164 reports an incident that shows clearly how Haydn suffered from those money worries common to the old, however well off.

86 This refers to the Austrian monetary standard established by the Vienna Convention of Sept. 21, 1753. See V. Gotwals, "Joseph Haydn's Last Will and Testament," *Musical Quarterly,* XLVII (1961), pp. 331–53, for a discussion of this matter.

87 Johann Georg Albrechtsberger (1736–1809), an exact contemporary of Haydn, passed his whole life in or near Vienna. A prolific composer and author of various theoretical treatises, he like Haydn gave Beethoven unsatisfactory lessons in counterpoint.

88 Concerning Handel and Haydn, Carpani reports: "There was another great man to whom Haydn did not disdain to turn for study. This was Handel, whose music Haydn did not really know until at the age of almost sixty he went for the first time to England, although he could have heard it much earlier in Vienna, where it was known and esteemed. But the fact is that Haydn, living mostly in Hungary, had not given it due attention or study. He did so later in London, where he heard it more often. I dare say that without this final schooling Haydn would not have composed his prodigious work *The Creation* in which is heard Handel's great eloquence instilled in Haydn's mind and wonderfully allied to his own richness of instrumentation. And I know that I happened to be near Haydn in the Schwarzenberg palace when Handel's *Messiah* was being performed, and when I expressed admiration for one of those magnificent choruses, Haydn told me, 'He is the father of us all [*Questi è il papà di tutti*]' " (*Le Haydine,* pp. 70–71). And on p. 167: "Haydn confessed to me that when he heard Handel's music in London, he was so struck by it that he began his studies all over again as if he had known nothing until that time. He mused over every note and extracted from these learned scores the essence of real musical magnificence."

89 C. M. Brand (*Die Messen von J. H.,* p. 321) thinks this refers to the *Nelsonmesse,* whose autograph is dated at the beginning July 10, 1798, Eisenstadt, and at the end August 31.

90 The *Paukenmesse,* C major (Novello 2). Brand does not take this anecdote very seriously: "It is easy to imagine what a fictionalizing author can make of this passage. If Haydn had really *wanted* to be so 'pictorial' as the anecdote makes out (a gentle caricature to charm the public), then he would never have been satisfied with this very vague hint" (*Die Messen von J. H.,* p. 255).

91   Referring to the *Schöpfungsmesse* in B flat major (Novello 4), not only Griesinger and Dies (cf. p. 139) but also Botstiber (*Joseph Haydn*, p. 353) missed the point that it was in the Gloria, not in the Agnus Dei, that Haydn quoted Adam's melody from the last duet in Part III of *The Creation*. Brand straightened out this confusion (*Die Messen von J. H.*, pp. 407–8): "Dies clearly misunderstood most of what Haydn told him about this and later spun his own tale out of his notes on the visit with Haydn. . . . The over-all effect will not be greatly disturbed at all by this profane thought—as Griesinger puts it. This identification will be made only by prejudiced readers to whom the musically similar (not identical) place in the text of *The Creation* is familiar. Otherwise this place makes a particularly holy and devoted impression, so that it would never occur to the unprejudiced to object to this passage in particular." Brand later (pp. 426–28) points out how Haydn changed the accompaniment and dynamic indication and augmented his theme; thus it is no longer "trifling" but "if not profound, still full of churchly gravity and hence quite transformed." The whole passage is a matter of eight measures, and at most thirteen measures had to be omitted for the younger Maria Theresa, second wife of Francis II, who sang, according to Haydn, "with much taste and expression, but a small voice."

92   Ignaz Pleyel and Sigismund Neukomm turn up repeatedly in this volume. Franz Lessel (1780–1838) was a Polish composer who, while in Vienna between 1797 and 1810, "became Haydn's favorite pupil and repaid that master with the ardent devotion of a son." His three piano sonatas Opus 2 were dedicated to Haydn, and his estate contained some autographs given him by Haydn (*Grove's Dictionary*, art. "Lessel." See also p. 196).

93   The letter, according to Pohl (*Joseph Haydn*, II, 225) was directed to a Ministry of Food official named Roth who arranged symphonic concerts at his house (see also Landon, *Col Cor*, pp. 73–74). Franz Niemetschek's *Life of Mozart* (1798; English translation by Helen Mautner, London, 1956) was dedicated as follows: "This little memorial to immortal Mozart is dedicated by the author with deepest homage to Joseph Haydn (Kapellmeister to Duke Esterhazy) Father of the noble art of music and the favourite of the Muses" (p. 10). "Haydn never missed hearing the music of Mozart whenever he knew of its being played, and he told me he always learned something every time he heard the compositions of that prodigious talent" (Carpani, *Le Haydine*, p. 208).

94 Härtel has shortened and piously edited Haydn's letter. The original is translated in Landon, *Col Cor*, p. 154. The passages here italicized apparently do not appear in the autograph.

95 Actually Haydn had the copyist, Joseph Elssler, begin a thematic catalogue around 1765. This important document, part of which was unfortunately lost during Haydn's life time, is known as the *Entwurf-Katalog* (*EK*). It was published by Jens Peter Larsen in *Drei Haydn Kataloge*, as was the *Haydn-Verzeichnis* that Gottfried Härtel is talking about here.

Dies, *Biographical Accounts*

1   Solely to thy genius, prodigious Haydn,
                             The Muses yield this grace,
                             Always to be new.

Don Tomas de Yriarte (1750–91), composer and poet, first published *La Música* in Madrid in 1779. It is a book-length poem treating many aspects of music. The last canto (V), dealing with chamber music, devotes some twenty lines to Haydn. The poem was widely circulated and translated into French, German, Italian, and English. The English translation, though far from literal, is an interesting curiosity. Published in London in 1807 by John Belfour, Esq., it renders thus the lines about Haydn:

>   But chiefest thine—the pride of modern song,
>   To whom the powers of harmony belong,
>   All powerful Haydn, favoured by the nine,
>   (Vast in conception, and in thought divine)
>   Thine whose symphonious strains delight inspire,
>   For ever new, nor though repeated tire.
>   Sooner insensible shall mortals seem
>   To voices rich, and melody supreme;
>   Than fail to praise the force, expression, grace,
>   Mellifluous chords and dignity we trace,
>   And modulation sweet, by taste arrayed,
>   And wondrous science in thy works displayed.
>   And though thy steps beside, thy haunts among,
>   Numbers with skill their golden harps have strung,
>   And with those plaudits fired thy merits claim,
>   Have haply trod the path that leads to fame,

Thou midst the throng, in Music who engage,
Or in the present, or a future age,
Shalt stand pre-eminent, of powers sublime,
And cast distinction on Germania's clime.
Long in Madrid thy works, with beauties fraught,
Of censors grave have so engrossed the thought,
Prizes have been bestowed,—so great their zeal,
Of those who best thy labours, study, feel.—
While, where the Manzanares winds her stream,
So much art thou her honor [*sic*] glory, theme,
Her nymphs with fadeless wreaths thy brows entwine,
As tho' Spain birth had given to worth like thine.

To this passage Yriarte appended the following note (Belfour's translation): "If the eulogium of Haydn were to be measured by the esteem in which his works are held at this moment in Madrid, it would appear exaggerated and partial in the extreme. The author of this poem, without entering into any odious comparisons, or wishing his readers to be as partial to Dr. Haydn as he is himself, has contented himself with pointing out some prominent excellencies in the compositions of that great composer, which no one can dispute; and, in particular, his fecundity. This eulogium, however, will be found inferior to his deserts by those who have heard his numerous symphonies, concertante and quartetted; his quintetts, quartetts, trios, and sonatas. His oratorio, entitled, Il ritorno de [*sic*] Tobia, for five voices; his Stabat Mater, for four, &c. &c."

2 This remark can be applied literally only to Prince Nikolaus I, who died on Sept. 28, 1790. His son and successor, Prince Anton, first freed Haydn from perpetual service at Eisenstadt. Anton in turn died on Jan. 22, 1794, and was succeeded by his son, Nikolaus II, to whom Dies dedicated his book. Haydn's relationship with Nikolaus I was warm and friendly. He was in London during most of Anton's brief reign, and his relationship with Nikolaus II varied from cordial to strained. This letter of dedication should, then, refer to all the princes collectively. In view of Dies's remarks on p. 176, however, it must be taken as one more example of undue flattery of titled persons.

3 Grassi, who made several busts of Haydn, died on Dec. 31, 1807 (cf. Griesinger, p. 51). One bust, life-size, of plaster, and in the classical manner, was made in 1799 (see p. 195). A miniature porcelain bust in contemporary costume was made in 1801/2. Whether

a third larger porcelain bust was made in 1799 (Jos. Muller, "Haydn Portraits," *Musical Quarterly,* XVIII, 1932, pp. 282–98) or in 1801 (Botstiber, *Joseph Haydn,* p. 195) is not clear, but Muller's estimate is interesting: "It strikes one at once as true and life-like; a study of it shows that it is also a great artist's creation. I should say that among all of Haydn's portraits it ranks first as a work of art."

4 Balthasar Denner (1685–1749) was nicknamed "the pore-painter" because of the exaggerated realism of his portraits. (Handel bequeathed to Charles Jennens, librettist of *Messiah,* "two pictures the Old Man's head and the Old Woman's head done by Denner.")

5 Including Griesinger's; cf. his Preface (p. 5).

6 It has never been incontrovertibly settled whether Haydn was born on March 31, 1732, or on the day of his baptism, April 1. Why Dies should report yet a third date is unexplained.

7 *Marktrichter,* "a magistrate supervising peace and propriety of the market" (Geiringer, *Haydn,* p. 17).

8 The distance is thus about four English miles.

9 Haydn's parents had twelve children, including a set of twins, all born between 1730 and 1745. Three of the five girls grew up and married. Of the seven boys, three died before they were a year old and a fourth was born and died on the same day (May 2, 1742) and thus possibly was entirely unknown to Joseph, who was then in Vienna.

10 This quotation is from a Trio, *Betrachtung des Todes,* No. VIII in Cahier VIII of the Breitkopf and Härtel *Oeuvres complettes* whose publication Griesinger negotiated with Haydn. The text, second stanza of Gellert's 14 stanza poem, reads:

Der Jüngling hofft des Greises Ziel,	(The youngster hopes to reach old age,
Der Mann noch seiner Jahre viel,	For more years yet hopes middle age,
Der Greis zu vielen noch ein Jahr,	The old man hopes for yet one year,
Und keiner nimmt den Irrthum wahr.	And not one sees his error clear.)

(Man's error is the supposition that life is anything more than falling leaves, Gellert explains.)

11 F. J. Schinn and G. Otter, *Biographische Skizze von Michael Haydn* (Salzburg, 1808). This 62 page volume, issued anonymously, is de-

scribed on the title page as "drawn up by the friends of the late composer, and published for the benefit of his widow."

12   Pohl points out (*Joseph Haydn,* I, 71) that since Johann Haydn was born only in 1743, he could not have been old enough to enter St. Stephen's before Haydn's departure in November, 1749. Actually he never went to St. Stephen's at all. (Michael Haydn was born on Sept. 14, 1737.)

13   The threat was a *Schillingstrafe,* and Haydn received a *Schilling.*

14   The original German text follows:

> Beharrlichkeit im Fleiss führt zu der Weisen Ziel,
> Wo endlich wir uns selbst erkennen müssen.
> O! herrlich ist der Lohn. Glaubt, wir erlernten Viel,
> Wenn wir bemerken: dass wir gar Nichts wissen.

15   Haydn's attachment to the Servites among others, however, lasted all his life. It was in their church or monastery that the score of his first mass turned up again in 1805 (see p. 244, n. 49) and thither he had himself carried in 1807 and 1808 in search of a cure (see p. 54).

16   Pohl describes the *Tiefer-Graben* as "a low lying not at all friendly Vienna street" crossed by the much higher Wipplingerstrasse on a high bridge (*Joseph Haydn,* I, 129). This is in the northwest part of the Inner City, not far from the Schottenkirche (where Haydn's memorial service was to take place in June, 1809).

17   *"Das ist ein rechter Sau-Menuett!"* Cf. this account with Griesinger's, p. 20 and note 29.

18   Cf. Griesinger, p. 12. Metastasio lived in the Michaelerhaus, where Haydn's attic lodgings were, and was thus Haydn's link with Porpora. The girl was Marianne Martinez.

19   This presumably refers to the Buchholz family mentioned by Griesinger on p. 59 (see Pohl, *Joseph Haydn,* I, 122 ff.).

20   *Versuch über die wahre Art das Clavier zu spielen, mit Exempeln und achtzehn Probestücken in sechs Sonaten erläutert* (first part), 1753. (Essay on the True Art of Playing the Clavier, with Examples and Eighteen Sample Pieces in the form of Six Sonatas.) The second part appeared in 1762. Dies is wrong in saying Haydn already showed Bach's influence in his nineteenth year. He was twenty-one when the first part appeared.

21   J. P. Kirnberger's first important treatises began to appear only in the 1770's, too late to have harmed Haydn.

22 Haydn owned the *Gradus ad Parnassum* (1725) in both German and Latin (cf. Griesinger, p. 10).

23 Haydn, however, composed a good many operas before using a libretto by Metastasio for *L'Isola disabitata* of 1779.

24 There is a touch of dramatic irony in the following narrative when we realize that Haydn's brother Johann had died the day before and that the impending visit was for the express purpose of delivering this sad news to the old man. Presumably Dies's diaristic method prevented him from exploiting this situation, though it did not prevent him from using high-flown prose, as we have just seen.

25 Horst Seeger, in his edition of Dies, suggests Dittersdorf as a possibility (*Biographische Nachrichten,* p. 222), but it is not certainly known whom Dies refers to.

26 Griesinger (p. 15) reports the salary as 200 gulden, room and board, a more reasonable figure. Haydn's mother had died on Feb. 23, 1754, aged forty-six. His father, on July 19, 1755, married Maria Anna Seeder, who was nineteen at the time and who, surviving her husband (d. 1763), also married a second time. None of Haydn's five half-brothers and sisters lived long after birth (Pohl, *Joseph Haydn,* I, *Anhang*).

27 The younger daughter was Therese Keller, and she became a nun. Haydn remembered her as "the ex-nun" in his will but struck out the legacy after her death. Haydn's wife was born Maria Anna Keller on Feb. 9, 1729, and died on March 20, 1800. The marriage took place on Nov. 26, 1760 when she was thirty-one and Haydn twenty-eight.

28 Gregor Joseph Werner (1695–1766) was Kapellmeister to the Esterházy princes from 1728 until his death. He wrote many masses, oratorios, and so on. Regardless of the inevitable strain between him and Haydn, the following announcement appeared in a Vienna newspaper of November 10, 1804: "VI Fugues in quartet for two violins, viola, and violoncello, by G. J. Werner, sometime Kapellmeister to His Highness N. Esterházy &c. &c. Now published out of especial regard for this celebrated master by his successor, J. Haydn. Respectfully dedicated to His Highness the reigning Prince N. Esterházy, Captain of the Royal Hungarian Noble Bodyguard &c., by his most obedient servants Artaria et Comp. To be had in Vienna from Artaria & Comp. 2 florins" (Hoboken, *Joseph Haydn,* p. 462).

29 Concerning this remark, Landon (*Sym,* p. 230) writes, "The first symphonies which he composed for his new patron appear to have been a trilogy entitled *Le Matin, Le Midi* and *Le Soir* (Nos. 6–8),

the idea of which, according to Haydn's biographer, Dies, was suggested by the Prince himself. Haydn's failing memory could only dimly recall the circumstances of their composition forty-odd years before, and it is therefore not particularly surprising to find Dies referring to the symphonies as 'quartets,' based on the four (*sic!*) 'Tageszeiten'; . . . . That it is nevertheless *Le Matin, Le Midi* and *Le Soir* to which Dies was referring seems clear."

30   That version reports that Prince Esterházy had determined to disband his orchestra for reasons of economy but was dissuaded from doing so by Haydn's Farewell Symphony.

31   *Hodie mecum eris in paradiso.* Today shalt thou be with me in paradise (Luke 23:43. The Second Word).

32   Johann Haydn died on May 10, 1805; see, however, Brand, p. 356.

33   *The Seven Words* was composed in 1785. Though Haydn himself believed that the rather gothic presentation described here by Dies took place in the cathedral at Cadiz, the true site appears to have been the Grotto Santa Cueva (Hoboken, *Joseph Haydn*, p. 845). The arrangement for string quartet was made by Haydn himself. The piano arrangement was made by someone else, but Haydn approved it as being "very good and. . . . prepared with the greatest care" (Landon, *Col Cor*, p. 65). Both appeared in 1787. The first vocal setting was the work of Joseph Friebert (or Friberth) of Passau. When Haydn heard it in 1794, he decided he could do better. Baron van Swieten (in his first collaboration with Haydn) revised the text, and Haydn added the vocal parts to his original score, making some alterations and additions in orchestration. This version was performed in 1796 and published by Breitkopf and Härtel in 1801 (see Sandberger, "Zur Entstehungsgeschichte von Haydns 'Sieben Worten. . . .'," *Jahrbuch der Musikbibliothek Peters*, 1903, pp. 47–59).

34   *Pater, dimitte illis, quia nesciunt, quid faciunt.* Father, forgive them, for they know not what they do (Luke 23:34. The First Word).

35   It seems likely that the argument developed in these paragraphs was Haydn's own, not Dies's. Haydn had taken pains to see that the text of each of the Seven Words preceded the music in all three instrumental versions. He was well aware of the aesthetic difficulties. Thus in 1787 he wrote to Forster, "Each setting of the text is expressed only by instrumental music, but in such a way that it creates the most profound impression even on the most inexperienced listener"

(Landon, *Col Cor,* p. 60). And by 1801 he felt impelled to remark in the preface to the vocal score, "My composition had to be adapted to this [just described] representation. The task of stringing out seven Adagios, each perforce ten minutes long, without tiring the hearers was not the easiest, and I soon found that I could not keep myself down to the prescribed time limit."

36 In the *Allg. Mus. Ztg.* V, No. 14 (Dec. 29, 1802) appeared an "Attempt at a Norm for Reviewers in the Mus. Ztg." by Hans Georg Nägeli. The remark to which Dies refers says, "We have never been told or shown why this or that key, scale, harmony, modulation, etc. awakens, and must awaken, this or that feeling or type of feeling. We have neither models nor examples. Haydn's work *The Seven Words of the Redeemer*—the original instrumental composition, that is—is no less an unfortunate experiment than Vogler's *Brouillerie entre mari et femme* or any other musical character piece."

37 This instrument is described in detail by Oliver Strunk in "Haydn's Divertimenti for Baryton, Viola, and Bass," *Musical Quarterly,* XVIII (1932), pp. 216–51. Despite the story Dies is about to tell, the baryton, says Strunk, "was limited in practice to D major and related tonalities. Of the 125 divertimenti *a tre,* 47 are in D, 38 in A, 27 in G, 8 in C, and 3 in F" (p. 221, n. 5). A minor, B minor, and B major each appear once.

38 Concerning Haydn's operas, see p. 219, n. 21. Dies is in error, of course, in placing *Il Mondo della Luna* before *La vera Costanza.*

39 Pohl says (*Joseph Haydn,* II, 87, n. 1) that it not only cannot be proven that the Emperor was present but it also appears that he never visited Esterháza, although he was a faithful friend of the dowager Princess Esterházy in Vienna.

40 Perhaps this refers to Haydn's difficulties over membership in the *Tonkünstler-Societät* (see p. 18).

41 The Latin lines are 50–51 and 55–56 of Horace's *Ars Poetica;* Dies's notes give lines 48–51 and 55–56 in Wieland's German translation. Schiller's words are quoted from section one, "Über das Naive," of the essay *Über naive und sentimentalische Dichtung* (1795–96).

42 Dies has 1808, an obvious misprint.

43 The servant throughout this encounter addresses Haydn in the third person form used only to inferiors.

44 See pp. 23 and 120. If this sum of 2,000 gulden is compared to the 700 gulden tuition paid for a choirboy at St. Stephen's in Haydn's

youth (p. 85), it will be concluded that Haydn was the victim not only of a spendthrift wife but also of a salary meager in the extreme by today's standards.

45   Haydn composed *L'Isola disabitata* (Metastasio) for Prince Ester-házy's name-day, Dec. 6, 1779. He termed the work *azione teatrale,* and it has only four roles. Haydn valued it and did indeed send a copy to Modena, but Dies's 1785 performance is probably the one of that year in the Vienna Hoftheater.

46   Haydn composed *Il Ritorno di Tobia* in 1774 (first performed April, 1775) for the Society for Musicians' Widows and Orphans (see p. 18). He revised it and added two choruses for the performance in the Hoftheater in March, 1784. Concerning the operas, see p. 219, n. 21.

47   This letter presumably must refer to the six quartets Opus 33, which were completed by 1781 (see, however, Hoboken, *Joseph Haydn,* p. 401).

48   Dies, apparently because the quartets Opus 50 are dedicated to the King of Prussia, substituted "quartets" for "symphonies," an error first corrected by Hoboken, *Joseph Haydn,* p. 408, where the correct text, as it appeared in the *Wiener Zeitung,* is printed. The Opus 50 quartets were not completed until Sept., 1787. The symphonies referred to constitute the "Paris" group, No. 82–87, of 1785–86. The ring that accompanied this letter was treasured by Haydn, but he was teasing Carpani when he "confessed many times that if he forgot to put this jewel on his finger, not one idea came to him" (*Le Haydine,* p. 75).

49   Composed around 1750, Haydn's first Mass in F called for two solo sopranos, four-part chorus, two violins, contrabass, and organ. The score was found in the Servite monastery in the suburb of Rossau, north of the Schottenring (cf. p. 240). When he reworked it in 1805, Haydn kept all youthful lapses and simply added flutes, two clarinets, two bassoons, two trumpets, and timpani. Breitkopf did not publish it, and it first appeared in London as Novello No. 11, with clavier accompaniment (see Pohl, *Joseph Haydn,* I, 123–25).

50   The shadowy Maret and Soult whom Griesinger also mentioned (p. 57). See Botstiber, *Joseph Haydn,* p. 244, where they are called Marat and Soulte.

51   Prince Nikolaus, born Dec. 18, 1714, died on Sept. 28, 1790. His son and successor Prince Anton was fifty-two years old at the time.

52   "I desire nothing more at present than the pleasure of knowing you personally, as I have hitherto by reputation, and look forward to

putting my modest talents at your disposal," Haydn wrote to Gallini on July 19, 1787 (Landon, *Col Cor,* pp. 66–67).

53 Haydn was fifty-eight at the time. Dies was a year off in his dating of the journey (see below).

54 Munich; cf. Griesinger, p. 23. The Electoral Court to which Christian Cannabich (1731–98) was attached as Concertmaster moved from Mannheim to Munich in 1778, so Haydn's error is understandable.

55 "Probably one of the two last composed, the *Caecilienmesse* [*ca.* 1769–73] or *Mariazellermesse* [1782]," according to Brand (*Die Messen von J. H.,* p. 216); but this is only a guess.

56 Lisson Grove, on the northwest border of London between the present Regent's Park and Edgware Road, was "within walking distance, for an active person, of the principal concert halls and theatres." The site is described in even more detail by M. M. Scott, "Haydn in England," *Musical Quarterly,* XVIII (1932), p. 265.

57 The première of *Iphigénie en Aulide* took place in Paris on April 19, 1774, that of *Iphigénie en Tauride* in Paris on May 18, 1779. Both were successes, but the earlier work occasioned much critical polemic and presumably is the one Dies is talking about.

58 Presumably the "Oxford" Symphony, No. 92 in G, rather than No. 93.

59 It is not surprising that Dies's following account of the Haydn-Salomon arrangement is confused. (Compare Haydn's confession of weak memory on p. 166.) Salomon had had various connections with the Professional Concerts in the 1780's, but he contracted with Haydn for Gallini, not for the Professional Concerts. According to the agreement, Haydn was to compose an opera, six (not twelve) symphonies, and twenty other new pieces; and the Gallini-Salomon-Haydn concerts were planned in competition to the Professional Concerts before Haydn ever set foot in London. Both sets were presented in the Hanover Square Rooms; it was Gallini's ill-starred production of Haydn's opera that was to have taken place in the new King's Theater in the Haymarket. Haydn's personal relations with William Cramer, with Muzio Clementi, and with his own pupil Pleyel appear to have remained friendly despite intense public rivalry. It is impossible to determine which of the many concerts Haydn was thinking of in the anecdote about the Clementi symphony. Pleyel's arrival in London did not take place until Dec. 23, 1791; he and Haydn dined together on Christmas Eve. The most complete discussion of this aspect of Haydn's life is in Landon,

Sym, chap. xii, "The First Performances of Haydn's 'Salomon' Symphonies: A Documentary Account."

60 Ignaz Pleyel (1757–1831), composer and publisher, of an "exceptionally beautiful edition of the Quartets" of Haydn among other things (Landon, *Col Cor,* p. 212), studied with Haydn for about five years during the 1770's.

61 Printed in Pohl, *Haydn in London,* pp. 361–62, these couplets read in part:

> At length great Haydn's new and varied strains
>   Of habit and indiff'rence broke the chains;
> Rous'd to attention the long torpid sense,
>   With all that pleasing wonder could dispense.
>
> Welcome, great master! to our favour'd isle,
>   Already partial to thy name and style;
> Long may thy fountain of invention run
>   In streams as rapid as it first begun; . . . .
> Blest in thyself, with rectitude of mind,
>   And blessing, with thy talents, all mankind!

The "musical journey" refers to *The Present State of Music in France and Italy* (1771) and . . . *in Germany, the Netherlands,* etc. (1773).

62 Landon, *Sym,* p. 490, adds: "Neukomm (*Bemerkungen zu den Biographischen Nachrichten von Dies*) has this to say about Dies' version: 'This long and rather silly story is really restricted to the fact that H[aydn] had noticed an old man, who occupied the same seat at every concert and who regularly went to sleep at the very beginning. H[aydn] allowed himself the joke of awakening the sleeper by a single drum beat [musical example]—everything else is silly nonsense and not worthy of repetition.' A page earlier Neukomm says: 'I should like to remark that all the information I [have] from Haydn, for the most part at our tête à tête conversation over meals, is from an earlier time than that of the visits of my friend Dies; at a time when H[aydn] was strong enough to write that huge work "Die Jahreszeiten."'" (The present editor has not had access to Neukomm's commentary on Dies's book.) Griesinger's account is on p. 33. Dies also errs in speaking of mutes, which do not occur anywhere in the symphony. Carpani (*Le Haydine,* p. 124), reporting this same tale, adds: "I should say here in all truth

that many times when this andante was discussed, Haydn did not agree that he had thought it up to conquer the somnolence of the English, but rather for the sole object of doing something new to surprise the listener. Sig. Dies supports the first of the given reasons. In dealing with Haydn versus Haydn, I leave it to each to choose the reading he prefers."

63 Symphony #96 in D (1791) is called "The Miracle," but "the chandelier fell in the last movement of No. 102 [1794/5]. . . .; thus another Haydn legend is proved false. . . . Neukomm. . . . in his *Bemerkungen*. . . . is also sceptical. 'I never heard anything of this anecdote,' he says, 'either from Haydn, or later, in England' " (Landon, *Sym*, pp. 534–35).

64 It is interesting to compare this account with Haydn's letter to Marianne von Genzinger (March 2, 1792, Landon, *Col Cor*, p. 132): "[Pleyel] arrived here with a lot of new compositions, but they had been composed long ago; he therefore promised to present a new work every evening. As soon as I saw this. . . . I announced publicly that I would likewise produce 12 different new pieces. In order to keep my word, and to support poor Salomon, I must be the victim and work the whole time. But I really do feel it. My eyes suffer the most, and I have many sleepless nights, though with God's help I shall overcome it all." It would be very unlike Haydn not to have capitalized on his former industry; but he undoubtedly worked very hard in London despite his proneness to play on the sympathies of his gracious friend.

65 Haydn bought the house in August, 1793, for 1,370 gulden. Cf. Griesinger, n. 55.

66 Cf. Griesinger, p. 42, note. Dies's three German terms here are *Flügel, clavecin,* and *clavier.*

67 Dies has already made an oblique reference at the beginning of this section to Laurence Sterne's *A Sentimental Journey through France and Italy* (1768). Here he refers to Yorick's encounter in the episode called "The Passport" with a starling hung in a little cage. "To every person who came through the passage it ran fluttering to the side towards which they approached it, with the same lamentation of its captivity—'I can't get out,' said the starling."

68 Karl Friedrich Zelter (1758–1832) succeeded K. F. Fasch in 1800 as conductor of the Berlin Singakademie, composed and conducted scores of men's choruses. He and Goethe were mutual admirers and carried on a voluminous correspondence. Mendelssohn was a youthful pupil of Zelter and member of the Singakademie.

69   Breitkopf and Härtel #4 was the Schöpfungsmesse in B flat major (1801).

70   In this letter "to a friend concerning the music in Berlin," dated January 8, 1801, Zelter reviewed a benefit performance of *The Creation* conducted by Himmel before an audience of 600. He was ecstatic about the music. "Among all the new German works of art, Haydn's *Creation* is without doubt the most original, the freest. It permits comparison only with itself and is on that account not easy to judge." It is unique; Haydn has set forth "a new garden, a new Eden." There is "a new comet on the horizon of art." Zelter described the overture at length, singled out the choral fugues for special praise, and reported that Haydn was reputedly at work on Thomson's *Seasons*. He ended with an invocation to Haydn to appear again, like a deity, among his people.

71   Zelter had offered ten *Friedrich d'or* (around 100 gulden) for each chorus, the composer retaining the rights to the manuscript.

72   The songs are the four-part *Abendlied zu Gott* and *Danklied zu Gott*. Haydn had written to Zelter in the letter of Feb. 25, 1804: "I wish that my dear Zelter would go to the trouble of taking Gellert's *Abend Lied*, 'Herr, der Du mir das Leben &c.' from my score, and arrange it for his whole choir, alternating 4 soloists with the semichorus and full chorus. N.B. It is absolutely necessary, however, that the pianoforte accompaniment be included just as it stands" (Landon, *Col Cor,* p. 225).

73   Karl Friedrich Christian Fasch (1736–1800), son of Bach's admired contemporary Johann Fr. Fasch, was court cembalist to Frederick the Great, a conductor and composer of church music, and founder of the Berlin Singverein (later Singakademie).

74   This lengthy review (July, 1802) concerns the Breitkopf and Härtel edition in score of Haydn's Mass "#1" in B flat major (Heiligmesse of 1796). The reviewer concedes that Haydn's subjects are occasionally "too sparkling for the church and the words" on paper, but not if actually heard.

75   Charles Marguerite Jean Baptiste Mercier Dupaty (1746–88), French jurist and man of letters, visited Italy in 1785 and published the *Lettres sur l'Italie* in Paris in 1788. The publisher of the 1792 edition already remarks that "one will perhaps find certain places in these Letters written with too much enthusiasm," and it seems fair to suspect that Dies and Dupaty were both a bit prejudiced against the Italians of their day. Dies's first quotation is from Letter 47, at Rome: "Yesterday was the Feast of Saint Luigi Gonzaga, Jesuit;

consequently there was a grand fête at the church of Saint Ignatius. I followed the crowd and have been to hear the opera at vespers and to see the illuminations at the Benediction of the Blessed Sacrament. These expressions describe perfectly what takes place here on solemn occasions. The entire office is sung; people walk about, talk, laugh, and crowd around the orchestras."

76 This account is interesting in the light of Haydn's entry in his diary: "On 21 May [1792] was Giardini's concert in Ranelagh; he played like a pig" (cf. p. 25). Dies relates another Haydn encounter with Giardini on p. 143.

77 This refers to Griesinger and his remarks on p. 62. The note there corrects Dies's following erroneous statements.

78 The ninth letter of Carpani's *Le Haydine* is a lengthy and interesting discussion of Haydn as a church composer. At the end, Carpani mentions Dies's conversation with Haydn, but he concludes: "The masses of Haydn are of a magnificent order, new, lovely, and full of feeling. They are original, they are most beautiful; but they occasionally err in unsuitable sections" (p. 162).

79 Haydn began to write his will in May, 1801, and completed it on Dec. 6. A second will was dated Feb. 7, 1809. The lawyer is probably the man in ¶ 47 of the second will: "I name Herr Franz Klemp, licenced attorney and registrar of deeds in the chapter-domain Dornbach [on the northwest edge of Vienna], as testamentary executor, trusting in his integrity for the certain and best execution of this my last will, and I bequeath him 1,000 gulden of which he is to use 500 Fl., according to his own conscience and without bond thereto, for the purpose made known to him elsewhere." (In ¶ 40, Haydn left 100 gulden to Herr Franz Kugler, solicitor.)

80 These words are not by Gellert but by Gleim; Haydn had composed them in his part-song *Der Greis* (see p. 43).

81 Dies has March, an obvious error.

82 That Haydn followed this procedure in other instances has been pointed out by Landon in connection with Haydn's use of Neukomm for the Scotch song accompaniments (*Col Cor*, pp. 215–16).

83 Haydn's memory betrayed him again, for despite the reference to *Orfeo*, this incident deals with the two marches composed in 1794 for Sir Henry Harpur and the Derbyshire Volunteer Cavalry (Hoboken, *Joseph Haydn*, Group VIII, 1, 2). These marches "are short and virile," according to Karl Haas; "the first in E flat is most probably a march for mounted use, whilst the second in C is a slow march for dismounted troops" ("Haydn's English Military

Marches," *The Score,* 2 (1950), p. 55). Carpani, having given a somewhat different version of this tale (*Le Haydine,* pp. 230–31), implies in a footnote that Dies's version is less accurate. The surviving marches, however, discredit Carpani's version with its ship's captain in the India trade.

84 One can see here very well how Haydn (and Dies?) added details to brief entries in the diaries. On Sept. 17, 1791, Haydn wrote to Marianne von Genzinger, "During the last two months. . . . I have been living in the country, amid the loveliest scenery, with a banker's family where the atmosphere is like that of the Gennzinger family, and where I live as if I were in a monastery. . . . I work hard, and . . . in the early mornings I walk in the woods, alone, with my English grammar. . . ." (Landon, *Col Cor,* p. 118). The banker was "Mr. Bressy Nr 71 Lombard Street" (*ibid.,* p. 278) about whom Haydn also noted down (*ibid.,* p. 271): "On 4th August [1791], I went to visit Herr Brassy, the banker who lives in the country, 12 miles from London. Stayed there 5 weeks. I was very well entertained. N.B.: Herr Brassy once cursed, because he had had too easy a time in this world" (cf. p. 58).

85 Cf. p. 27. This event is dated March 26, 1792. The Symphony is #75.

86 Giovanni Alessandro Brambilla (1728–1800) was a native of Pavia who became physician and surgeon to the Emperor Joseph II in Vienna and who "profited by the imperial favor to advance the cause of Italian culture in Austria" (*Encyclopedia Italiana*).

87 This dinner took place on Dec. 14, 1791 (see p. 26).

88 Haydn wrote in his diary, "On 2nd August 1794, I left at 5 o'clock in the morning for Bath, with Mr Ashe and Mr Cimador, and arrived there at 8 o'clock in the evening. . . . I lived at the house of Herr Rauzzini" (Landon, *Col Cor,* p. 295). There is no mention of Dr. Burney. The correct words to the inscription are "Turk was a faithful dog, and not a man." The canon is printed in Pohl, *Haydn in London,* p. 276. Venanzio Rauzzini (1746–1810) was an Italian *castrato* who had first come to England in 1774 and retired to Bath in 1787. Mozart composed the motet *Exsultate, Jubilate* (K. 165) for Rauzzini.

89 One would be the more inclined to think Haydn was teasing Dies if he had not told the same tale to Griesinger (p. 62).

90 The young prince was just past his twentieth birthday at the time of this visit.

91 This debt dated from 1794. If Haydn were really so delicate in these

matters as Dies says, the loss of the Fourth London Notebook (Landon, *Col Cor*, pp. 304 ff.) may be accounted for here. If Haydn listed his debtors in one of these little diaries, he may have destroyed it himself. The First and Second London Notebooks passed to Joseph Weigl, the Third to Mozart's son Wolfgang. But, of course, it is hard to imagine that Haydn was really so eager to shield his faithless acquaintance, and the lost Fourth Notebook may simply have suffered the fate that so nearly claimed the first two when Weigl's servant was about to burn them up (Pohl, *Haydn in London*, p. vi).

92 Hoboken (*Joseph Haydn*, p. 828) thinks it not impossible that this visit was to Mälzel, in which case Haydn might have heard his own Military Symphony played on the "Panharmonicon" mechanical orchestra.

93 Johann Samuel Schroeter (*ca.* 1750–88) was the brother of the celebrated singer-actress Corona Schroeter and a composer as well as a player (see Konrad Wolff's article in the *Musical Quarterly*, XLIV [July, 1958], pp. 338–59). Mrs. Schroeter's letters to Haydn will be found in Landon, *Col Cor*, pp. 279–86. One might observe here that Haydn appears never to have mentioned Luigia Polzelli either to Dies or to Griesinger. She and her husband entered the Esterházy service in 1779 as soprano and violinist. She was then, according to Pohl, nineteen years old, much younger than her husband. She soon captured Haydn's affection and may have become his mistress. Antonio Polzelli died in Vienna in 1791 while Haydn was in London. At that time Haydn clearly expected to marry Luigia if his own wife died before him. But many considerations (including his friendship with Mrs. Schroeter?) led him, when Frau Haydn died in 1800, merely to give Signora Polzelli a written promise to marry no one but her and to leave her a pension after his death (Landon, *Col Cor*, p. 169; and see p. 195). According to Pohl (*Joseph Haydn*, II, 93), she "married even before Haydn's death the singer Luigi Franchi with whom she remained until 1815 in Bologna. In 1820 she traveled with him from Cremona to Hungary. She died in 1832 at the age of 82 [72?] in poverty in Kaschau [Kassa]." Polzelli was reputedly not much of a singer. Haydn gave her only one role in all his operas (Silvia in *L'Isola disabitata*), but his attachment for her resulted in six or seven insertion arias and five to seven reworkings of other arias, at least a dozen compositions (there may be many more) made solely for this "personable southerner" (see Bartha and Somfai, *Haydn*, pp. 50–52).

94   On Dec. 20, 1791, Haydn wrote to Marianne von Genzinger about a letter lost en route from London to Vienna, "The principal part of the letter I entrusted to Herr Diettenhofer described the conferment of the doctor's degree on me at Oxford, and all the honours I received there" (Landon, *Col Cor,* p. 123). Perhaps it was this letter Haydn was thinking of here; or perhaps there was a fifth pocket diary lost during Haydn's lifetime.

95   Haydn's departure took place on June 23, 1792, or shortly thereafter, and he arrived in Vienna on July 24.

96   Botstiber (*Joseph Haydn,* p. 63) says of Haydn's return to Vienna in 1792, "There is talk—without any proof—in several biographical works of a fête in the Augarten got up in his honor, in others of an academy in the Redoutensaal; despite the most zealous investigation, not even the slightest hint has been found that any of these supposed honors took place." Haydn's second return from London (in August, 1795) was followed by "a great musical academy in the small Redoutensaal" at which were performed "three great symphonies, not yet heard here, that the Herr Kapellmeister produced during his last stay in London" (quoted by Botstiber, p. 96, from the *Wiener Zeitung*)—a concert, however, for which the music-loving public had to wait until December 18, 1795.

97   An obsolete land-measure meaning the amount of land a yoke of oxen could plow up in one day.

98   See note 6 concerning Haydn's birth date. The German texts of these inscriptions are in Griesinger, note 54.

99   The only clearly misplaced incidents in the accounts up to this point are the commissioning of the marches (p. 149) and the visit to Rauzzini (p. 153), both of which belong to the year 1794.

100 The entry in Haydn's London catalogue which Dies gives as "4 Song for S——" and Griesinger as "Vier Gesänge für Thallersal" refers to the four shorter (there were also two longer) three-part compositions to metrical psalm texts that Haydn contributed to the Rev. William Dechair Tattersall's *Improved Psalmody* of 1794. Dies's inaccurate transcription from the original silver is reproduced here verbatim. Haydn had also copied this inscription into his diary, and it will thus be found in Landon, *Col Cor,* p. 290.

101 *Il ritorno di Tobia,* which Haydn composed in 1774–75. Neukomm apparently made minor cuts and enlarged the orchestration of the work, but even this did not make his December, 1808, performance of it in Vienna a success (see p. 18).

102 This composition has apparently not been preserved. For an account

of Therese Jansen (Mrs Gaetano Bartolozzi), see Strunk, "Notes on a Haydn Autograph," *Musical Quarterly*, XX (1934), pp. 192–205.

103 Haydn arrived in London the second time on Feb. 4, 1794, and learned soon after of the death of Prince Anton on Jan. 22, 1794. The son Nikolaus II's reestablishment of the entire chorus and orchestra was tempered by his preference for church music above all other. Nevertheless, a considerable number of musicians was again employed, as the following figures show:

Musicians at Esterháza

1762 (Pohl, I, 227)		After 1767 (Pohl, II, 8, 13)	1796 (Botstiber, 104–5)
strings	7	9–11	8
winds	7	10	(8)
singers	6	10–12 (opera)	6
organist	1		1
bassoon	–		1
	21	29–33	16 (24)

Landon (*Sym*, pp. 111–12) demonstrates, however, that Haydn could probably draft as many as 25 instrumentalists in 1762, and quotes Forkel's report of 23/24 players (including Haydn) in 1783. (This figure includes trumpets and timpani as well as singers.) The 1796 list includes Tomasini, concertmaster and assistant to Haydn at that time. The duties of the 8 winds were mainly military. Bartha and Somfai (*Haydn*, pp. 166–76) provide some new information on this subject. They say Pohl's figures must be revised because his "list (contrary to expectation) is full of wrong dates, omissions, and inaccuracies." They give employment statistics for singers and players from 1775–90. The tables are not easy to read, but taking 1780 and 1790 as representative years, one finds 21 and 22 instrumentalists (10 or 12 strings, 4 horns, 2 oboes, 2 bassoons, 1 or 2 flutes, and 2 trumpets). Cf. summary on p. 49.

104 This item and the previous one appear to have been preserved by Dies alone. Botstiber (*Joseph Haydn*, p. 82) reports the Frenchman's verses as printed in *The Bath Herald and Register*. A sample will confirm Dies's judgment of them:

> De l'immortalité Haydn, reçois la couronne,
> Tu ravis tous les coeurs, et le mien te je donne. . . .

Madame Donelli may have been the wife of that Signor Dorelli listed (Pohl, *Haydn in London,* p. 123) as a singer in the ill-starred Gallini troupe of January, 1791.

105 L——— is Dies's error for William Napier, for whom Haydn arranged altogether 150 songs, not only to Napier's profit but ultimately to his own as well (see p. 33).

106 C. P. E. Bach died at Hamburg on Dec. 15, 1788, news that must surely have reached Haydn before August, 1795!

107 Johann Gottlieb Naumann (1741–1801), court composer, Kapellmeister, Oberkapellmeister in Dresden. He was trained in Italy and produced mainly Italian operas, in Italy and in Sweden as well as in Germany. He also wrote much church music, and performed fluently on the glass harmonica. Haydn's formal letter to Naumann's widow is less indicative of his true opinion than the casual remark in another letter: "As often as you speak of our Naumann, I envy you his friendship; perhaps I shall be able to see him before I die" (Landon, *Col Cor,* pp. 169 and 210).

108 The public dress rehearsal was April 29, 1798, the first performance on April 30. Neither Dies nor Griesinger claims to have been present, but Carpani was there. "Even I, who was present, can assure you that I never saw anything like it in my life. The flower of cultivated society, both national and foreign, was gathered there. The best possible orchestra; Haydn himself at their head; the most perfect silence; and the most scrupulous attention; a favorable hall; the greatest precision on the part of the performers; an atmosphere of devotion and respect on the part of the entire assembly. . . . the audience experienced for two consecutive hours something that they had never experienced before. . . ." (*Le Haydine,* p. 170). Carpani says later (p. 191) that *The Creation* must be done with a chorus of twenty-four and an orchestra of at least sixty, proportions that today's conductor might ponder.

109 According to Carpani (*Le Haydine,* pp. 189–90), there were two Italian translations, an unsatisfactory one in the score printed in Paris, and his own, printed in the Artaria piano score and publicly approved by Haydn and van Swieten. This translation was first performed under Haydn's direction at the house of Prince Lobkowitz. The audience had the German and Italian texts before them, "and when a passage was heard that was felicitously translated, or indeed even improved by the greater sweetness and sonority of the language, Haydn called out from the orchestra to the applauding audi-

ence, pointing to the translator, 'There he is; the praise is not mine.' "

110   In addition to the immortal nobility, Salieri, Gyrowetz, Hummel, and Beethoven were supposedly present on this occasion! Magdalena von Kurzböck was a beloved Viennese pianist to whom Haydn's last sonata (Hoboken, *Joseph Haydn*, Group XVI, 52) and a trio (*ibid.*, XV, 31) are dedicated. The sonata, it should be noted, was written for Therese Jansen, and the dedication of the version published by Artaria was probably not Haydn's idea (see Strunk, "Notes on a Haydn Autograph," *Musical Quarterly*, XX [1934], pp. 192–205).

111   The original German text follows:

> Du hast die Welt in deiner Brust getragen.
> Der Hölle düstre Pforten stark bezwingen;
> Den freyen Flug in Himmelsräumen wagen,
> Hört man dich auf der Töne kräft'gen Schwingen.
> Drum sollst du, theurer Greis, nicht traurend klagen,
> Dass mit dem Alter deine Kräfte ringen:
> Zwar weicht der Leib den düstern Zeitgewalten;
> Was du gewirkt, wird ewig nie veralten.
>
> Wie nun in dieses Musentempels Hallen
> Erwartungsvoll sich frohe Schaaren drängen;
> So sieht man einst die späten Enkel wallen
> Zu deiner Schöpfung hohen Himmelsklängen;
> So hört man noch der Enkel Jubel hallen
> Bey deiner Engel Hallelujahsängen.
> Was rein der Mensch aus reiner Brust gesungen,
> Ist wohl nie leicht in Menschenbrust verklungen.
>
> O lausche lang' entzückt den eignen Tönen,
> In deiner Freunde dicht gedrängtem Kreise,
> So wirst du sanft der Erde dich entwöhnen,
> So froh dich rüsten zu der grossen Reise.
> Die Erde mit dem Himmel zu versöhnen
> War deiner Kunst erhabne Lebensweise.
> Noch schallt dir Dank tief von der Erde Klüften,
> Empfängt dich Hallelujah in den Lüften.

112   The text is from Carpani's second edition. A translation follows:

With a single movement of His powerful brow
   To draw from nothing all that lives, the Universe,
   To set the suns on ways diverse,
   With countless stars as family to endow,
And order Nature so that, child of self,
   Self may renew each instant, quite averse
   To useless ravages of Time perverse,
   If what He wished, God did, is that a marvel?
But that a man the work of God, stupendous, rare,
   Should try to equal with pictorial notes,
   And render clear and present to the aware,
This seemed impossible to human mind.
   This, Haydn, thou hast done. With thee all potent
   God has so far shared His thought divine.

113   Miss Fischer, who sang the role of Gabriel, was the daughter of
Ludwig Fischer (1745–1825), a basso whom Haydn knew in London in 1794 (and for whom Mozart had created the role of Osmin).
Gerber described her, *ca.* 1800, as "already showing great promise
as a singer."

114   Academic Society of the Sons of Apollo. Paris the 30. December
1807. Sir! The French pride themselves on the immortal products of
Your Genius, since there are several of them which You composed
for Them. A grand concert, in Paris, would not seem good, if one
did not hear one or two of Your symphonies. One might also say,
truly, that the musicians make it a religious duty to take great pains
in the execution of them, being well assured of the taste and sensitivity of their audience, which constantly shares their justifiable enthusiasm.

Our society embraces Your most zealous admirers. It enjoys a
certain esteem. But it has judged that its celebrity would be better
merited and that it would be worthier of the cult of Apollo were it
enriched by Your association and were Your name inscribed on the
list of its members.

Deign, Sir, to receive its homage. It bases its glory and its happiness on Your assent.

Be likewise so good as to receive kindly the appended copy of its
rules and regulations followed by a list of members, as well as a gold
medal struck in the form of the silver piece that each member receives to show right of attendance at each of its meetings.

We have the honor to be with the highest consideration, Sir, etc.

115 Vienna the 7. April 1808. Sirs! In the choice which the Academic
     Society of the Sons of Apollo has deigned to make in inscribing my
     name on the list of its members I am as much flattered as I am
     rendered sensible of the honor.

     In assuring it through your agent that it could honor no one more
     ready to appreciate its esteem and more suited to sense the value of
     the resultant honor, I pray You, gentlemen, to allow my sentiments
     to be made clear by your own, and at the same time to be the inter-
     preters of my gratitude for the marks of distinction that You have
     transmitted to me in the sending of a copy of the rules and regula-
     tions, accompanied by a gold medal.

     You have scattered, gentlemen, a few flowers on the road of life
     that remains to me still to travel. I am profoundly touched thereby,
     and I feel keenly that though old age may enfeeble the faculties, it
     takes nothing from sensitivity, for it is the latter which makes me
     regret that my great age forbids me to nourish the hope of finding
     myself among You, of sharing Your labors, of cooperating in the
     cultivation of an art that is the charm of society, and of partici-
     pating in the celebrity in whose titles, so dear and so precious, the
     Academy rejoices.

     It is a consolation that my infirmities force me to renounce; and
     my regrets are as lively as my gratitude is profoundly felt; deign to
     receive this assurance, accompanied by the sincerest expression of
     sentiments of esteem, and by the most distinct consideration with
     which I have the honor to be, Sirs, etc.

116 Neukomm left on Feb. 16, 1809, with the autograph of the *Har-
     moniemesse* in B flat (1802), Haydn's last mass. His note to p. 141
     is perhaps more pertinent here: "After my return from Russia, 1809,
     I stayed on the whole winter in Vienna in order to be able to see my
     dear father Haydn every day. I used to visit him in late afternoon,
     after he had risen somewhat strengthened from his afternoon nap
     and was, as Dies says, dressed again. One day I appeared somewhat
     later than usual. Haydn came to me very cheerfully and said to me
     with triumphant countenance, 'You know, today I really played
     my prayer very well, really very well' (at the end he used to refer
     this way to his song *Gott erhalte,* which he played every day). I
     could not repress my tears at this outbreak of self-satisfaction from
     the exalted creator of so many hundreds of unrivaled masterpieces,
     who hardly ten years before would not allow me to make opportune
     expression of my wonder at places from his *Creation* or *Seasons*."
     [Haydn's words: *Weisst Du wohl, dass ich heute mein Gebet recht*

brav, ja recht brav gespielt habe? Quoted from Botstiber, *Joseph Haydn*, p. 272.]

117   Botstiber (*Joseph Haydn*, p. 395) gives a corrected version of these lines in which the last stanza reads:

So huld'gen wir im Aug die Thräne	(We pledge with tearful eyes again
Dem Kunstwerk deiner Phantasie—	The art-work of thy fantasy—
Der Allmacht deiner Zaubertöne	The power of thy magic tones
Und Dir, dem Gott der Harmonie!	And Thee, the God of Harmony!)

They were written of the performance on March 19, 1799. For Gabriele Batsányi (mentioned on p. 163 by her maiden name, von Baumberg) see p. 226. Dies's German text reads:

Erquickend, sanft, wie alles Schöne,
Und feurig, wie ein ächter Wein,
Strömt oft der Zauber Deiner Töne
Durch's Ohr in unsre Herzen ein.

Jüngst schuf Dein schöpferisches Werde
Den Tonner durch den Paukenschall
Und Himmel Sonne Mond und Erde,
Die Schöpfung ganz zum zweyten Mahl.

Gefühlvoll, staunend, wonnetrunken,
Wie Adam einst im Paradies,
Am Arm der Eva hingesunken,
Zwar sprachlos den Erschaffer pries.

So hören wir entzückt die Töne
Des Kunstwerks Deiner Phantasie—
Und huldigen im Aug' die Thräne,
Dir Schöpfer hoher Harmonie.

118   Botstiber (*Joseph Haydn*, pp. 184–85) prints this letter (with minor errors but including the missing line supplied here) as it appeared in the diary of J. C. Rosenbaum, the Esterházy official and friend of Haydn who married Therese Gassmann. He says it is dated from

Vienna, although Haydn was in Eisenstadt. These circumstances
and the style of the letter suggest that someone (Rosenbaum?)
drafted it for Haydn, or at least helped him with it, although in 1801
he was certainly still perfectly able to write it himself.

119   The original German text follows:

Haydn's Schöpfung.

Holde, fremde Zaubertöne binden
Unsern Sinn, dass ihm die Welt vergeht,
Und das alte Chaos neu entsteht,
Neu dem Chaos Welten sich entwinden.

Schüchtern muss der niedre Sinn erblinden,
Wenn hervor die neue Schöpfung geht.
Wo der Schöpfergeist harmonisch weht,
Darf der höh're Sinn nur kühn empfinden.

Ist's ein fremder Geist? und streift im Schweben
Sein vorüberrauschendes Gefieder
Fremde Luft nur mit harmon'schem Beben?

Liebend lässt er sich zur Heimath nieder;
In dir selbst, mein Geist! Harmonisch Leben
Kommt vom Geiste, kehrt zum Geiste wieder.

120   This refers to the *Biogr. Skizze von Michael Haydn* (see note, p.
239) which quotes Haydn's letter, dated Salzburg, May 8, 1806, to
his friend Pastor Rettensteiner in Arnsdorf. The quotation "And
coos the tender pair of doves its love" is from the first aria in Part
II, in which Gabriel sings of the creation of the birds and the violins
and bassoons imitate cooing.

121   Haydn's remarks were written (Landon, *Col Cor,* pp. 196–97) in
connection with an alteration in the trio and chorus at the end of the
"Summer" section, made for the piano score that A. E. Müller prepared for Breitkopf and Härtel. Müller showed the remarks to the
editor of the *Ztg f. d. elegante Welt,* J. C. G. Spazier, who printed
an article on Dec. 31, 1801, ending as follows: "For all those, however, who with their textbooks bother the venerable old man with
the perpetually youthful imagination, we give here an avowal of this
great artist that he himself recently made and that redounds equally
to his honor and to the rebuttal, within the limits of modesty, of

those strict gentlemen who find it easier to judge than to improve, etc. 'This whole passage,' he writes, 'in imitation of a frog did not flow from my pen. I was forced to write down this Frenchified trash. In the full orchestra, this wretched notion disappears soon enough, but it won't do in a clavier edition.' 'The critics need not deal so strictly,' he says elsewhere; 'I am an old man and can't revise the thing all over again.' Praise and honor to a worthy Haydn!" (Botstiber, *Joseph Haydn*, p. 367).

122   This fugue ends the "Autumn" section, and the singers are too tipsy to sing it. It occurs mainly in the orchestra, with the singers echoing the subject.

123   A long and favorable review of the first performances in Vienna appears in Vol. III, col. 575–79. It is unsigned, as are all subsequent notices of *The Seasons*.

124   Carpani echoes this in *Le Haydine* (pp. 217–18): "I was present the first time this oratorio was performed, in the house of Prince Schwarzenberg. . . . I. . . . ran in search of my Haydn at the end of the concert to offer him my prompt and sincere congratulations. Hardly had I opened my mouth when Haydn's voice stayed me with the following memorable words: 'It pleases me that my music has pleased the public, but I will not accept compliments on it from you. I am sure that you understand that this is not *The Creation*. I am aware of it, and you must be aware of it too. But this is the reason: there the characters were Angels; in the *Four Seasons* they are peasants.' "

125   Swieten died on March 29, 1803. Against Dies's assertion is to be set Haydn's letter of July 3, 1801, to Griesinger, in which he says of *The Seasons*, "The autograph, like that of the *Creation* is to remain in the hands of Baron von Swieten, inasmuch as, after the Baron's death, both works, together with his own beautiful collection, will be left as mementos to the Imperial and Royal Library" (Landon, *Col Cor*, p. 184). Apparently this did not happen. "No original manuscripts of Haydn's most celebrated vocal works, the two great oratorios, have been preserved," says Larsen (*Die Haydn-Überlieferung*, pp. 57–58); "but the Elssler copy of *The Creation* (with many autograph entries) extant in Berlin was quite certainly a conductor's copy. An obvious explanation of the disappearance of the original scores lies in the fact that these two works were immediately printed in score. Dies, however, gives another explanation. . . . It can hardly be established whether he was really talking about autographs or perhaps only of authentic copies of the score—possibly of

the copy of *The Creation* just mentioned and of a similar copy of *The Seasons.*—It is not at all impossible but certainly improbable that both manuscripts should suddenly turn up." (One of Elssler's copies is mentioned again on p. 203.)

126 This idolatry spread. Gerber (*Neues Lex.,* art. "Haydn," col. 548) reports that the *Concert de la rue de Clery* "set up a bust of [Haydn] in the midst of the orchestra at its last concert and after the performance of his newest symphony crowned it to the jubilation and applause of those present. In the absence of a real bust of Haydn, they had, to be sure, made do in this ceremony with a head of Cato, on the pedestal of which sparkled in great gold letters the words 'To the immortal Haydn.' But since nobody in the audience was personally acquainted with Haydn, nobody was the worse for this innocent deception; and not one whit of sincerity was lost in the ceremony of homage." This event took place sometime after 1801.

127 National Institute of the Sciences and Arts at Paris, 5 Nivôse, Tenth year of the Republic [Dec. 26, 1801]. The President and the secretaries of the National Institute of the Sciences and Arts. To Monsieur *Haydn,* celebrated composer of music, at Vienna. Monsieur! The National Institute of the Sciences and Arts in plenary session today has just elected you *foreign associate,* class of Literature and Beaux arts. Persuaded that you will learn with pleasure of your nomination, we hasten to announce it to you. Be so kind, Monsieur, as to accept the sincere homage of our highest esteem.

N.B. This document is also translated in Landon, *Col Cor,* p. 197, and Haydn's answer, dated April 14, 1802, appears on p. 204. The following two documents will be found in *Col Cor,* pp. 236 ff.

NATIONAL INSTITUTE, CLASS OF BEAUX ARTS. Paris the 1st Messidor, 13th year of the French Republic [June 20, 1805]. The permanent secretary of the class [Joachim Le Breton] to Mr. *Haydn,* composer, associate member of the national institute. Monsieur! The national institute of France elected you an associate member, an homage that from the moment of its founding it has been pleased to render your just celebrity. Changes since effected in the institute have in a certain manner attached you to it more closely; a music section has been created and its constituents are worthy admirers of your genius. As foreign associate you have an advisory say in the institute, the right to attend meetings, to wear the uniform, in sum, you are a member of it. I address to you in that capacity the medal that verifies your title and the booklet that contains our rules as well as the names of members. You will find there your own in the section of the class of Beaux arts. May I hope, Monsieur, that you might take enough interest in the class of Beaux arts of the institute of France to inform it of your savant observations on the art that you profess with so much glory in Europe? I can assure you that this witness of your confidence would be received with profound esteem. And I personally, I shall regard it one of the precious advantages of the functions with which I am honored, to correspond with you and to be able to assure you often of my perfect admiration.

CONSERVATORY OF MUSIC. Paris, the 7th Messidor, 13th year of the French Republic [June 26, 1805]. The Conservatory of France to *Haydn*. The members of the Conservatory of France, imbued with the deepest sentiments of esteem and of veneration for the immortal talent of *Haydn,* most actively desire to inscribe the name of this celebrated artist in the annals of this establishment. The expression of this wish, carried to the illustrious *Haydn* by *Cherubini* can only be well received: the members of the conservatory, fully confident of this, commission their colleague to hand to the great man whom they consider one of the fathers of musical art the print of the monument which the conservatory hopes to see raised in its midst and the design of which has been chosen to consecrate the happy era of the founding of this establishment. May this rightful homage of admiration for one of the greatest geniuses to illuminate the Republic of the arts be received by *Haydn*. It will become for the Conservatory of France a trophy to its eternal honor.

128   In his *Memoirs of the Life of Sheridan* (chap. xviii), Thomas Moore says, "These verses show that he was not a little piqued by the decision of the Institute," and offers the following specimen:

> The wise decision all admire;
>   'Twas just, beyond dispute—
> Sound taste! which, to Apollo's lyre
>   Preferr'd—a German flute!

129   Dies got this quotation from the *Allg. Mus. Ztg.* (IV/37, June 9, 1802); see Botsiber, *Joseph Haydn,* p. 195.

130   See note 70 on p. 232. According to Griesinger, the visitor came on May 17, was named Clement Sulemy, and sang "In Native Worth and Honor Clad" from *The Creation.*

131   According to Elssler, Haydn died at twenty minutes before one in

the night of May 30/31. The "celebrated" Betty Roose, a much loved actress at the Burg Theater, died on October 8, 1808. She and Haydn shared the honor of having their graves robbed. Both skulls were stolen by Rosenbaum (see Dies, n. 118) and J. N. Peter. "After Peter's death, his widow turned over Haydn's skull as well as that of the actress Roose. . . . to Dr. Karl Haller, who gave both skulls to the renowned anatomist Rokitansky. His sons finally turned over Haydn's skull to the Society of Friends of Music, where it is kept in the museum as a costly relic. As the master shared his life and works between Vienna and Eisenstadt, so also each place henceforth secures a share of his earthly remains." Thus Botstiber ended his completion of Pohl's life of Haydn (Botstiber, Vol. III, p. 286). We are not told what became of the Roose's skull. Dies's faith in Prince Esterházy, moreover, was not justified until October, 1820, when Haydn's remains were finally transferred to the Bergkirche at Eisenstadt and the theft of the skull discovered. Not until June 5, 1954, was Haydn's skull reburied with due ceremony at Eisenstadt.

132 Haydn began to write his will in May and completed it on Dec. 6, 1801. A thorough revision is dated Feb. 7, 1809. The total estate amounting to something over 55,000 florins was soon devalued by post-war inflation. Nevertheless, Haydn at his death was a well-to-do man, and, as Dies's excerpts show, a generous and thoughtful man as well. The first will, in English translation, is printed in Lady Wallace's *Letters of Distinguished Musicians* (and reprinted with corrections in J. C. Hadden's *Haydn*). The second will which Dies excerpts, is printed, in English translation, in Gotwals, "Joseph Haydn's Last Will and Testament," *Musical Quarterly*, XLVII (1961), pp. 331–53.

133 Haydn also left a splinter of the Cross to Ernestine Loder, and his wife owned yet another splinter of the Cross, which she left to her cousin's wife! See her will, printed by R. F. Müller in *Die Musik*, XXII/2 (Nov. 1929), p. 95.

134 Forchtenau is a village about thirty-five miles southeast of Vienna, ten miles west of Eisenstadt. It is the site of a château called *Fracnó* (Forchtenstein), set upon an abrupt limestone rock, which belonged to the Esterházy family.

135 Dies is in error. Pohl says (*Joseph Haydn*, I, 16) that Fröhlich was thirty-three years old at the time of his mother's death. Haydn did, however, have Fröhlich's niece, Ernestine Loder, living with him. See Griesinger, n. 84. (Fischamend is a village about ten miles down the Danube from Vienna.)

136 Of this palpably incomplete list, Lessel (1780–1838), Neukomm
     (1778–1858), and Pleyel (1757–1831) have already been mentioned
     by Griesinger (p. 63). Pleyel went to Haydn *ca.* 1774; Neukomm
     was sent to him by Michael Haydn in 1798. Hoffman and Fuchs
     are possibly the violinists of those names in the Esterházy orchestra.
     Joh. Nepomuk Fuchs (d. 1839), who joined the group in 1788,
     became Vicekapellmeister in 1802 and in 1809 succeeded to Haydn's
     title as Kapellmeister. J. F. Kranz (1754–1807) went to Stuttgart
     from Weimar, where he was presently succeeded by Franz Seraph
     von Destouches (1772–1844), a native of Munich. Kranz must have
     known Haydn sometime in the 1780's, and Destouches studied
     briefly in 1787. Anton Wranitzky (1761–1820) studied with Haydn,
     Mozart, and Albrechtsberger before becoming Kapellmeister to
     Prince Lobkowitz in 1794. (His elder brother Paul, 1756–1808, was
     connected with the Esterházy orchestra and a pupil and friend of
     Haydn.) Tomich is probably the Francesco Tomich "who later
     arranged many of Haydn's Symphonies for piano" (Landon, *Col
     Cor*, p. 264); he published three clavier sonatas in 1794 dedicated to
     Haydn. Specht is Johann Spech (1764–1836), the Hungarian musi-
     cian for whom Haydn wrote the Certificate printed by Landon,
     Col Cor, p. 174 (dated August 28, 1800). Peter Haensel (1770–
     1831) is described by Haydn in the letter to Pleyel of Dec. 6, 1802,
     as "a good violin player. . . . in the service of the Polish Princess
     Lubomirsky" (Landon, *Col Cor*, p. 212). Paul Struck (*ca.* 1775–*ca.*
     1823) was a Swedish composer of German birth who studied with
     Haydn sometime between 1795 and 1799. The "Pulcellis" were the
     sons of Haydn's friend, Luigia Polzelli (Pietro, 1777–96, and Anton,
     1783–1855). Graf remains otherwise unidentified. Perhaps the most
     conspicuous omission here is Beethoven. Carpani, who was fully
     aware of Beethoven's importance in 1812, says, "Haydn was asked
     once by one of my friends what he thought of this young com-
     poser. The old man replied in all sincerity, 'His first works pleased
     me quite a bit, but I confess that I do not understand the latest ones.
     It seems to me that he always writes fantasias' " (*Le Haydine,*
     p. 257).

137 Dies has helped himself liberally to an installment of Triest's
     "Observations on the Development of Musical Art in Germany in
     the 18th Century" which appeared in Vol. III, pp. 405–10 (March
     11, 1801) of the *Allg. Mus. Ztg.* Triest was a Stettin clergyman
     whose articles on music Gerber considered of a superior quality.

138 So apparently does Gerber, who in 1790 wrote that it was Haydn

"who first introduced in these [early] quartets of his the manner of reinforcing the melody by octaves, which with large orchestras makes such a great effect at expressive places. People were soon used to this manner, however, despite all the outcries. Indeed, they ended up by imitating it themselves" (*Lexicon,* art. "Haydn"). Landon writes that "Gerber probably took [this idea] from the article on Haydn and other Austrian composers in the *Wiener Diarium* of 1766" (*Supplement,* p. 36).

139 This theme crops up in Carpani (*Le Haydine,* p. 93). He gives a fanciful account of Haydn's first meeting with Prince Esterházy, who called him a Moor. "Haydn was certainly not the color of lilies," adds Carpani.

140 This outline is virtually identical to the *Tagesordnung des Sel. Herrn v. Haydn* in the Salzburg Mozarteum that Botstiber supposes to have originated with Haydn's valet, Johann Elssler (*Joseph Haydn,* p. 293).

141 Probably Dies himself is the author of these lines. The original German text follows:

Horche Leser! Noch erzählt die Kamöne von dem
Kühnen, horche! sie spricht von dem unternehmenden Manne,
Der, dem Prometheus ähnlich, den unermesslichen Luftraum,
Der von irdischer Erde, den hohen Olympos entfernet,
Wagt' auf kräftige Schwingen, vertrauend (von gütiger Allmacht
Ihm zum Geschenk bey erstem Pulsschlag ertheilt) zu durch-
        schweben,
Und, dem inneren mächtig spornenden Triebe gehorchend,
In das Heiligthum der Harmonien zu dringen,
Und, o ruhmvolle That! an heiliger Flamme die Fackel
Anzuzünden. Er selbst wird Schöpfer! Im Reiche der Töne
Gibt er dem Tone—der Pause selbst, geistiges Leben; und jubelnd
Steigen Akkorde empor in rauschenden Symphonien,
Bald erschütternd, und so bedrohn sie den Einsturz der Welten;
Bald in schmelzender Anmuth, wie Charitinnen dem Blicke
Grosser Dichter erscheinen. Mit solcher Allkraft gerüstet,
Steigen die Töne hinauf, erreichen die Wohnung der Musen
Auf des Parnassos Höhen an der kastalischen Quelle.
Horchend vernehmen die Musen, in stillem Erstaunen versunken,
Die harmonischen Formen. Noch lange sitzen sie horchend,
Bis das letzte Geflüster der redenden Töne verhallt ist:
Siehe, da öffnet Phöbus Apollo den Mund zu der Frage:

Musen! ist nicht Haydn der Schöpfer der magischen Töne,
Die uns Götter bezaubern? In Wahrheit! ich denke wir räumen
Ihm in unserer Mitte den ihm gebührenden Sitz ein;
Denn, als Sterblicher wusst' er sich der Unsterblichkeit Krone
Zu erringen, und Göttern ähnlich zu werden!—

142 Cf. Griesinger's and Härtel's accounts of this Catalogue on p. 7
     and p. 65. Since the document on which Dies based his catalogue
     is readily available in Larsen's facsimile, it seems supererogatory to
     "edit" this list. It is reproduced here exactly as it appears in Dies's
     book (together with translations of the German where necessary).
143 Concerning Haydn's operas, see Griesinger, p. 219.
144 Griesinger's version of this Catalogue is given on p. 31, and its
     significance discussed in note 48 there. It is reproduced here exactly
     as it appears in Dies's book.

BIBLIOGRAPHY

A partial list of works cited in the notes. Standard reference works and some items referred to only in passing are not listed here.

Bartha, Dénes, ed. *Joseph Haydn, Gesammelte Briefe und Aufzeichnungen* (Kassel and Budapest, 1965).

——, and László Somfai. *Haydn als Opernkapellmeister* (Budapest and Mainz, 1960).

Botstiber, Hugo. *Joseph Haydn, unter Benutzung der von C. F. Pohl hinterlassenen Materialien weitgeführt von . . .* , Vol. III (Leipzig, 1927).

Brand, Carl Maria. *Die Messen von Joseph Haydn* (Würzburg, 1941).

Burney, Charles. *The Present State of Music in Germany, the Netherlands, and United Provinces,* 2 Vols. (London, 1773).

——. *A General History of Music* (London, 1776–89; ed. Frank Mercer, 1935).

Carpani, Giuseppe. *Le Haydine,* 2nd edition (Padua, 1823).

Dittersdorf, Karl von. *The Autobiography of K. v. D.,* tr. A. D. Coleridge (London, 1896; original edition, 1801).

Geiringer, Karl. *Haydn, A Creative Life in Music* (New York, 1946).

——. "Haydn and the Folksong of the British Isles," *Musical Quarterly,* XXXV (1949), pp. 179–208.

Gerber, Ernst Ludwig. *Neues historisch-biographisches Lexikon der Tonkünstler* (Leipzig, 1812–14), esp. article on Haydn, col. 535–605.

Gotwals, Vernon. "The Earliest Biographies of Haydn," *Musical Quarterly,* XLV (1959), pp. 439–59.

——. "Joseph Haydn's Last Will and Testament," *Musical Quarterly,* XLVII (1961), pp. 331–53.

Grasberger, Franz, ed. *Biographische Notizen über Joseph Haydn von Georg August Griesinger* (Vienna, 1954).

Haas, Karl. "Haydn's English Military Marches," *The Score*, No. 2 (1950), pp. 50–60.

Hadden, J. Cuthbert. *Haydn* (London and New York, 1902).

Hase, Hermann von. *Joseph Haydn und Breitkopf & Härtel* (Leipzig, 1909).

Hoboken, Anthony van. *Joseph Haydn: Thematisch-bibliographisches Werkverzeichnis*, Vol. I (Mainz, 1957).

Hughes, Rosemary. *Haydn* (London, 1950. Reprinted with corrections and additions, 1956).

Kelly, Michael. *Reminiscences* (London, 1826).

Landon, H. C. Robbins. *The Symphonies of Joseph Haydn* (London, 1955).

———. ———, *Supplement* (London, 1961).

———. *The Collected Correspondence and London Notebooks of Joseph Haydn* (London, 1959).

Larsen, Jens Peter. *Die Haydn-Überlieferung* (Copenhagen, 1939).

———. *Drei Haydn Kataloge in Faksimile* (Copenhagen, 1941).

Muller, Joseph. "Haydn Portraits," *Musical Quarterly*, XVIII (1932), pp. 282–98.

Pohl, C. F. *Mozart und Haydn in London* (Vienna, 1867).

———. *Joseph Haydn*, Vol. I and II (Leipzig, 1878 and 1882).

Reichardt, J. F. *Vertraute Briefe geschrieben auf einer Reise nach Wien* (Amsterdam, 1810).

Sandberger, Adolf. "Zur Entstehungsgeschichte von Haydns 'Sieben Worten des Erlösers am Kreuze,'" *Jahrbuch der Musikbibliothek Peters* (1903), pp. 47–59.

Scott, Marion. "Haydn in England," *Musical Quarterly*, XVIII (1932), pp. 260–73.

Seeger, Horst, ed. *Biographische Nachrichten von Joseph Haydn. . . . von Albert Christoph Dies* (Berlin [1959]).

Sondheimer, Robert. *Haydn, A Historical and Psychological Study Based on his Quartets* (London, 1951).

Strunk, Oliver. "Haydn's Divertimenti for Baryton, Viola, and Bass," *Musical Quarterly*, XVIII (1932), pp. 216–51.

———. "Notes on a Haydn Autograph," *Musical Quarterly*, XX (1934), pp. 192–205.

Wallace, Lady. *Letters of Distinguished Musicians* (London, 1867).

INDEX